Campus Diversity

Media, politicians, and the courts portray college campuses as divided over diversity and affirmative action. But what do students and faculty really think? This book uses a novel technique to elicit honest opinions from students and faculty and measure preferences for diversity in undergraduate admissions and faculty recruitment at seven major universities, breaking out attitudes by participants' race, ethnicity, gender, socioeconomic status, and political partisanship. Scholarly excellence is a top priority everywhere, but the authors show that when students consider individual candidates, they favor members of all traditionally underrepresented groups – by race, ethnicity, gender, and socioeconomic background. Moreover, there is little evidence of polarization in the attitudes of different student groups. The book reveals that campus communities are less deeply divided than they are often portrayed to be; although affirmative action remains controversial in the abstract, there is broad support for prioritizing diversity in practice.

John M. Carey is the John Wentworth Professor in the Social Sciences at Dartmouth College and a member of the American Academy of Arts and Sciences.

Katherine Clayton is a political science PhD student at Stanford University and a graduate of Dartmouth College.

Yusaku Horiuchi is Professor of Government and the Mitsui Professor of Japanese Studies at Dartmouth College.

Campus Diversity

The Hidden Consensus

JOHN M. CAREY

Dartmouth College

KATHERINE CLAYTON

Stanford University

YUSAKU HORIUCHI

Dartmouth College

CAMBRIDGE
UNIVERSITY PRESS

CAMBRIDGE
UNIVERSITY PRESS

University Printing House, Cambridge CB2 8BS, United Kingdom

One Liberty Plaza, 20th Floor, New York, NY 10006, USA

477 Williamstown Road, Port Melbourne, VIC 3207, Australia

314–321, 3rd Floor, Plot 3, Splendor Forum, Jasola District Centre, New Delhi – 110025, India

79 Anson Road, #06–04/06, Singapore 079906

Cambridge University Press is part of the University of Cambridge.

It furthers the University's mission by disseminating knowledge in the pursuit of education, learning, and research at the highest international levels of excellence.

www.cambridge.org
Information on this title: www.cambridge.org/9781108477956
DOI: 10.1017/9781108775373

First published 2020

A catalogue record for this publication is available from the British Library.

ISBN 978-1-108-47795-6 Hardback
ISBN 978-1-108-74530-7 Paperback

Dedicated to Lisa, Connor, and Chizuko

Contents

Contents   ix

Figures

Tables

Preface

On the evening of November 11, 2015, close to 200 students gathered at Baker Berry Library on the campus of Dartmouth College. Clad in black and holding homemade posters, they marched to the steps of the iconic Dartmouth Hall chanting, "We shall overcome" and "Black lives matter." One poster summed up the emotions of many students involved in the demonstration: "This is how we REALLY feel."

The week before that march, a #BlackLivesMatter display in the campus student center had been defaced. The display featured seventy-four shirts representing seventy-four unarmed individuals killed by police officers in 2015. Twenty-eight of the shirts were black, representing black individuals who lost their lives. Soon after the display was presented, several of the black shirts were ripped down.

The protesters also wanted to stand in solidarity with students of color at the University of Missouri and Yale University, where racially charged incidents had sparked protests. At Mizzou, a swastika drawn in feces was found in a dormitory bathroom, and reports of racial slurs and an overall climate of bias on campus had inspired a hunger strike by one student and broader demonstrations calling for the university's president and chancellor to step down. At Yale, allegations about a racist fraternity party and a dispute over a faculty member's push-back against university directives on Halloween costumes led to a March of Resilience with over a thousand participants.

In response to these events, the Dartmouth chapter of the National Association for the Advancement of Colored People (NAACP) as well as the Student Assembly sent a campuswide e-mail with an

invitation to wear all black and march as an act of solidarity with the
#BlackLivesMatter movement. At 8:00 pm on the "Blackout Thurs-
day" evening, the protesters began their procession. After gathering in
front of Dartmouth Hall, some students spoke to the crowd about their
personal experiences with racism and exclusion on campus. Then several members of the group moved back toward the library, where the
tone shifted. Some of the protesters allegedly began calling out students
who had chosen not to participate. Viral videos from the evening depict
protesters chanting loudly on quiet floors in the library and directly
asking students who had not joined the march, "Do you think black
lives matter?" In the view of these protesters, failure to participate was,
effectively, an expression of anti-diversity preferences.

* * *

The Dartmouth protest and the events that followed drew national media
attention and revealed sharp divisions in attitudes toward the incident,
and toward diversity more broadly. *Dartmouth Review*, a conservative
publication unaffiliated with Dartmouth College, rebuked the "sign-
wielding, obscenity-shouting protestors" for their "overzealous" protest.
"Their march through the library was an intentional exercise in every
disgraceful behavior they claim to endure themselves, from insults and
physical force, to racial barbs tossed out with disgust," The *Review*
claimed. The *Review*'s article attracted nearly one thousand online comments, most of which slammed the protesters, likening the incident to
everything from terrorism to Nazi Germany.

National conservative outlets including The Daily Caller, The College
Fix, The Blaze, Breitbart, and Fox News picked up the story, echoing
criticism of the protesters for "assaulting" and "terrorizing" Dartmouth
students. Other national outlets, including *USA Today*, *Washington Post*,
and *Chronicle of Higher Education*, as well as the local *Valley News*,
published pieces acknowledging the confusion that arose in the aftermath
of the demonstration.

The main student newspaper on campus, *Dartmouth*, took a different angle, describing the racial tensions on and off Dartmouth's campus
that led to the demonstration of solidarity. According to the president
of Dartmouth's chapter of the NAACP, who was quoted extensively,
the goal of the event was to "show many people really stand for this
issue and how many people care about this issue." Also in support of the
protesters, Dartmouth's Vice Provost of Student Affairs, Inge-Lise Ameer,
called the demonstration a "wonderful, beautiful thing." Reflecting on

critics of the protest, she said, "There's a whole conservative world out there that is not being very nice." Ameer's comments prompted another round of rebuke from conservative students and media outlets, and Ameer ultimately issued an "unequivocal apology" for her remarks.

The controversy continued as the college's administration took an evolving stance, with Dartmouth President Philip J. Hanlon issuing three statements to the broader Dartmouth community about the protests. His initial message to campus affirmed the values of diversity, reminding students, faculty, and staff that "what we must continue to strive for is a diverse community." A second e-mail described the protest as "peaceful" and affirmed that the administration had received no complaints of physical violence. Finally, in a third campuswide message, Hanlon acknowledged reports of abusive behavior that may have occurred during the protest: "I have heard reports of vulgar epithets, personal insults, and intimidating actions used both by students who entered the library and students who were already in the library ... Abusive language aimed at community members – by any group, at any time, in any place – is not acceptable."

The Dartmouth controversy presented a picture of deep divisions among students over the value of diversity on campus. Against that backdrop of apparent polarization, we were initially inspired to write this book.

* * *

While the cascade of campus diversity protests was occurring at colleges and universities around the nation in the fall of 2015, we were all members of the Dartmouth community. Two of us were professors in the government department, and one was a sophomore who had just declared a government major. Our prior research was in areas other than higher education, but we wanted to know whether students were as profoundly divided over diversity as the campus protests, and the coverage of them, suggested.

Building on a preliminary study two of us undertook in the spring of 2015 with other Dartmouth students, we thus decided to embark on an expansive research journey. The goal was to understand student (and some faculty) attitudes on who should be included in campus communities – specifically, on what factors should be prioritized in undergraduate admissions and in the faculty recruitment process. We set ambitious targets, which included not only Dartmouth but also many other colleges and universities, in order to understand whether Dartmouth is a special case or if it reveals a typical display of campus diversity attitudes.

We began by exploring the existing body of knowledge and found case studies, focus group and interview-based research, campus climate polls on diversity, and scholarship based on traditional surveys. But we also appreciated that eliciting honest opinions on a sensitive topic like diversity is notoriously tricky. As the Dartmouth protests underscored, students might be reluctant to offer forthright opinions. Moreover, attitudes toward campus diversity and, in particular, student admissions and faculty recruitment are context-specific and holistic in nature. Even if students express support for diversity in the abstract, it is difficult to parse out whether that priority is greater or less than other relevant considerations in the specific admissions and recruitment contexts we focus on. We wanted to see how students evaluate difficult trade-offs that pit diversity against academic achievement and other salient characteristics.

We conducted a series of survey experiments using a method called conjoint analysis, which is particularly suited to evaluate multidimensional preferences underlying holistic decisions. Our participants chose between hypothetical pairs of applicants for undergraduate admission or faculty candidates for hire at their universities. We partnered with faculty at institutions across the United States and abroad to explore how preferences differ across contexts. To test for the deep divisions across student populations that the campus protests seemed to portray, we also explored whether attitudes differed by students' own demographics and attitudes, such as their race/ethnicity, partisanship, or attitudes toward race and affirmative action. In short, we looked for divergence in every place we thought that it might appear.

Did our surveys reveal the irreconcilable divisions suggested by the campus protests of the fall of 2015? To our great surprise, we found almost no polarization in preferences for diverse campus populations. Rather, students across the board (and faculty) showed support for prioritizing diversity in undergraduate admissions and faculty recruitment. We found a strong, while hidden, consensus in preferences in favor of diversity among college and university campus communities.

* * *

We could not have conducted the research for this book without the collaboration of faculty partners from the universities other than Dartmouth at which we conducted survey experiments. Our partners are Professor Marisa Abrajano at the University of California, San Diego;

Professors Tim Ryan and Layna Mosley at the University of North Carolina at Chapel Hill; Professor Mala Htun at the University of New Mexico; Professor Kevin Carman at the University of Nevada, Reno; Professor John Polga-Hecimovich at the United States Naval Academy (USNA); and Professor Simon Hix at the London School of Economics and Political Science (LSE). These colleagues secured institutional permission and review board approval for the research, offered advice about the design of the experiments and survey instruments, provided data on faculty and student demographics and insight on specific institutional characteristics, and advised on the interpretation of our results. Professor Ryan's contributions to the design of the pooled experiments and the addition of a range of attitudinal questions were particularly critical. Professor Htun's contributions were central to the work reported in Chapter 8. Professor Polga-Hecimovich's and Professor Hix's contributions were equally fundamental to the sections on the Naval Academy and the LSE, respectively, reported in Chapter 9.

We are also grateful for collaboration from colleagues whose home universities ultimately did not approve requests to conduct experiments, or where approval was conditional on our not disclosing the identity of the institution. We appreciate the efforts of Professor Jennifer Hochschild (Harvard), Professor Tali Mendelberg and Dr. Lisa Argyle (Princeton), Professor Jessica Preece (Brigham Young University), Professor Frances Rosenbluth (Yale), Professor Pat Sellers (Davidson), Professor Jeffrey Staton (Emory), and Professor Dawn Teele (University of Pennsylvania). We regret not being able to bring the work we embarked upon with those colleagues to fruition.

At an early stage of work on this project, we had outstanding research assistance from Maddie Brown and Lauren Martin. We are grateful for institutional support from Dartmouth College that allowed for the administration of our survey experiments, and from Dartmouth's Nelson A. Rockefeller Center for Public Policy and the Social Sciences to sponsor and organize a manuscript review workshop. We thank the participants in that workshop – Chris Hardy, Janice McCabe, Bruce Sacerdote, Andrew Samwick, Al Tillery, Natasha Warikoo, and Sean Westwood – for invaluable input. We thank our Dartmouth colleagues Sonu Bedi, Jeff Friedman, Michael Herron, Katy Powers, and Ben Valentino for suggestions on our research design and comments on earlier drafts of the manuscript. We also thank participants at the LSE Political Behavior seminar series, at the Naval Academy, at Harvard University's Universities: Past, Present, and Future seminar series, and at Dartmouth's Institutional

Diversity and Equity seminar series for listening to us present early versions of our research and for providing feedback that improved the final product. Finally, we are grateful to Sara Doskow at Cambridge University Press for thoughtful and essential editorial guidance throughout the process of turning our research into a book.

What We Are Studying, Why, and How

Diversity is hotly contested at colleges and universities. Yet, what campus populations actually think about the issue is not well understood. This book is an effort to understand student (and some faculty) attitudes on who should join campus communities – on what factors should be prioritized in student admissions and in the faculty recruitment process at institutions of higher education.

What do we mean by campus diversity? Our focus is on the race/ ethnicity, gender, and socioeconomic background of undergraduate students, and the race/ethnicity and gender of faculty. These are the most salient attributes of students and faculty in campus diversity controversies. By diversity, we mean the inclusion of students and faculty from racial/ethnic, gender, or socioeconomic groups that have traditionally been marginalized among and excluded from student and faculty populations, and who might continue to be excluded under admissions and recruitment practices that do not take these identity factors into consideration (Bowen and Bok 1998; Espenshade and Radford 2009; Massey et al. 2003; Reardon et al. 2018).

We deploy a new survey experimental method – conjoint analysis – to measure preferences for prioritizing these factors, alongside academic achievement and many others, in decisions about student admissions and faculty recruitment. Across the populations of students and faculty whose attitudes we study, we find broad support for making diversity a priority in undergraduate admissions and in faculty recruitment.

In this chapter, we make the case that the campus diversity is important, as is understanding student attitudes toward it, but that measuring those attitudes is challenging. We argue that we have measured them in a way that improves on standard techniques and sheds new light on student and faculty preferences. We then summarize our key findings with respect to those preferences and provide a map to the rest of the book. But first, we offer a story about campus discourse surrounding diversity and merit that we think illustrates how and why students' sincere attitudes toward these issues can remain hidden.

1.1 IDENTITY VS. MERIT IN THE DARTMOUTH COLLEGE TRIPS PROGRAM

The Dartmouth Outing Club First-Year Trips program was established in 1935 as a way to connect incoming students with the idyllic natural surroundings of the College's New Hampshire campus. Every year, nearly all first-year students spend five days hiking, climbing, canoeing, kayaking, mountain biking, or otherwise enjoying the outdoors before the fall term begins. The Trips program is almost entirely student-run and is headed by a twenty-one-member directorate of students who handle everything from logistics, to risk management, to communicating with parents of incoming freshmen. The director and assistant director of "Trips" are students appointed in consultation with College staff. These two individuals then review student applications and make appointments for the remaining nineteen slots on the directorate.

In the winter of 2018, the director and assistant director, both women, appointed women to fifteen of those slots. A male student whose application was declined then penned an op-ed that was published in the College's main student newspaper, *The Dartmouth*, decrying the gender imbalance as "ludicrous" and contending that "no self-respecting person could believe that one gender, on principle, is four times more likely to write a winning application than the other." The author characterized the actions of the director and assistant director as "prejudice," based on a "pernicious theory that sees race, gender and identity as dictating qualification ... Credentials matter not, but skin tone, womanhood and claims of marginalized status do."

The backlash against this op-ed was swift. More than forty student organizations sent campuswide e-mails in solidarity with the Trips director and assistant director. Several of these e-mails attacked the author of the op-ed, labeling his rhetoric as "hateful," "toxic," "vicious," "privileged," "ignorant," "patriarchal," "white supremacist," "racist," "misogynist," "homophobic," "oppressive," and "endangering lives."

At least ten of the letters condemned *The Dartmouth* for publishing the article to begin with, accusing the newspaper of "giving hate speech a platform" (Magann 2018). A smaller number of student groups and publications sided with the author of the op-ed, publishing their own response pieces and sending out e-mails in solidarity with him (e.g., Jones 2018).

The debate struck a chord with our campus diversity research in progress. We too were concerned with student attitudes toward merit and diversity in competitive selection processes. But the tone of the campus discussion was troubling. The cascade of the public letters "in solidarity" with the Trips directorate suggested to us that to question openly how diversity interests are prioritized and implemented would, itself, not be tolerated by communities on campus. At that point, two of us penned our own op-ed for *The Dartmouth*, entitled "Debating without Deprecating." We discouraged the kind of elevated rhetoric used to characterize the original op-ed and its author, suggesting that "the effect on open discussion of difficult ideas can only be chilling. Anyone who does not hew to established and codified positions will be afraid to express any opinion" (Carey and Horiuchi 2018).

Our article attracted online comments from readers who felt we had failed to appreciate the effects that the *original* op-ed had had on marginalized communities on campus. One held that "[you] talk about how confronting ideas will make us better people, but don't take into account the toll that this has on women … What will discourse do if it's centered on silencing half of the participants? … [Y]ou, as professors, should not be commenting on student affairs unless it is to make sure that marginalized students feel safe and able to learn in their classrooms." Another defended the heated rhetoric we had criticized on grounds that "it would be patronizing to [the original author] if critics were to avoid using certain words that do very accurately describe him; if someone [is] to be misogynistic, ignorant, or, racist, we cannot baby them by tip-toeing around these words."

More telling to us, however, were the differences between the comments posted online and the private messages we received from students via e-mail. One noted that, "I'm sure I'm not the only student who disagreed with the [original] article but also totally supported its publication, but over the past few days it has almost felt like I have to pick a side. Such vitriolic reactions only make the issue more polarized, and immediately shut down any space for open dialogue." Another student wrote, "[High school] taught me that it's important to always take the other side ... just so you could get a better understanding of your own argument and the flaws that may exist there ... because that is the basis of humility as an academic and a person."

In short, the differences between the private messages students sent us and those posted online suggested that the voices *not* heard in such debates may differ systematically from those expressed publicly. In this context, understanding what students think – what they *really* think – is challenging. Our survey experiments allow us to tap into students' views without provoking fear of sharing unpopular opinions. It is therefore particularly noteworthy that we find broad support for prioritizing diversity in admissions and faculty recruitment.

For one other reason, the 2018 Trips controversy was salient to this book's central contribution. In a response op-ed to the original piece, one student wrote, "A majority-female Trips directorate is not evidence of the systematic devaluing of any identity ... Rather, it is an acknowledgement of a nuanced point that escapes the author: that individuals cannot be separated into a set of identities and a set of credentials. 'Identity' and 'merit' are not separable categories as the author claims" (Petroni 2018). We agree that separating identity and merit in any real-world selection process is a conundrum. Real applicants are thoroughly multidimensional and selection processes are holistic. The experimental approach we employ, however, allows us to estimate distinct preferences for demographic diversity and for achievement across a range of endeavors. We find consensual support for both types of priorities.

1.2 CAMPUS DIVERSITY IS A BIG DEAL

Dartmouth College is far from the only place where diversity discourse is paramount. From university communities, to the courts, to journalists, to academics, and beyond, everyone seems to be talking about campus diversity. Much of this debate concerns affirmative action in undergraduate admissions and faculty recruitment. Arguments in favor of diversity considerations tend to rest on one of two pillars. One is that historical exclusions from universities based on race and ethnicity were unjust, and that a positive preference favoring formerly marginalized identity groups would help remedy past injustice (e.g., Valls 1999).

A second argument is more utilitarian, focusing on the benefits of diversity to the whole campus community rather than on righting past wrongs done to particular groups. Proponents of this view claim that cognitive diversity contributes to learning and problem solving – that is, to the core intellectual activities of colleges and universities. Although identity diversity is not the same as cognitive diversity, it nevertheless *contributes* to cognitive diversity by bringing together on campus a broader range of life experiences and perspectives than would otherwise be the case (Page 2017). This utilitarian argument has been at the heart of jurisprudence on campus diversity (*Regents of the University of California* v. *Bakke* 1978). Indeed, for over four decades, the US Supreme Court has regularly confronted litigation concerning one of the core components of campus diversity as we have defined it – whether and how applicants' race and ethnicity should be considered in admissions decisions – and has leaned on the idea that racial diversity brings benefits to the whole university community as a rationale for allowing race to be considered in admissions decisions (*Regents of the University of California* v. *Bakke* 1978; *Gratz* v. *Bollinger* 2003; *Grutter* v. *Bollinger* 2003; *Fisher* v. *University of Texas at Austin et al.* 2013, 2016).

Outside the courts, scholarly debate is fervid over the value of diversity, both to students from underrepresented minority groups and to broader university communities (e.g., Bowen, Chingos, and McPherson 2009; Sander and Taylor 2012). Arguments have evolved alongside changing demographics on college campuses. While women's representation increased among student populations at American colleges and universities in the second half of the twentieth century and surpassed men after the 1980s, imbalances by race, ethnicity, and socioeconomic background remain substantial. There are disputes over whether affirmative action in university admissions designed to mitigate these gaps serves the academic interests of students admitted under such policies (Arcidiacono et al. 2014; Arcidiacono, Aucejo, and Hotz 2016; Arcidiacono, Aucejo, and Spenner 2012; Cortes 2010; Ho 2005; Sander 2004; Stinebrickner and Stinebrickner 2011). Yet long-term studies indicate that the student beneficiaries of affirmative action programs succeed academically and professionally (Bowen and Bok 1998; Charles et al. 2009). What is more, students from groups not targeted by affirmative action may recognize benefits from being educated in a diverse environment (Warikoo 2016).

Others debate the effects of demographic diversity on broader campus culture. Some studies have demonstrated evidence for socialization effects based on racial, ethnic, and socioeconomic diversity, wherein acceptance of people coming from diverse backgrounds and support for redistributive economic policies are associated with the level of diversity on university campuses (Mendelberg, McCabe, and Thal 2017; Sidanius et al. 2008). On the whole, the evidence for socialization effects suggests that increased demographic diversity among students encourages a social climate of greater tolerance (Ahmed 2012; Chang 1999; Chang, Astin, and Kim 2004; Park 2018). Diversity also appears to have important downstream effects on all students' psychological, social, and emotional well-being, with benefits that range from increased intellectual development, to better leadership skills, to higher civic engagement, to vocational success (Gurin 1999; Hu and Kuh 2003; Umbach and Kuh 2006).

Beyond debates about student representation and affirmative action in admissions, discussions about faculty representation permeate campus diversity discourse. Among faculty, racial and ethnic minorities remain vastly underrepresented, and women substantially so, in particular at the senior and tenured ranks. Scholarly research has revealed biases among existing faculty that could obstruct minorities and women in the academic jobs pipeline (Bavishi, Madera, and Hebl 2010; Leslie et al. 2015; Moss-Racusin et al. 2012; Reid 2010; Snyder, de Brey, and Dillow 2016; Turner, González, and Wood 2008; Wu 2017). Moreover, student protests born of frustration over the lack of progress in advancing faculty diversity at many universities have attracted nationwide attention. A number of schools including Yale University (Yale University Office of the President 2015; Yale University 2016), Brown University (Paxson 2016), Dartmouth College (Hanlon et al. 2016; Dartmouth College 2016), and the University of Missouri (Loftin 2016) have recently committed to diversity initiatives aimed at increasing racial and ethnic minority representation among faculty. Yet, there is little evidence that speaks to these programs' effects, and antipathy toward such initiatives and to campus diversity protests more broadly also grabbed headlines (Flier 2019; Lewis 2016; *Wall Street Journal* 2015), revealing a seemingly polarized debate over the issue. It is thus clear that campus diversity has attracted a lot of attention for decades, and increasingly so in recent years.

1.3 KNOWING WHAT STUDENTS THINK IS ESSENTIAL

Should we care what students think about demographic and socioeconomic diversity on campus and, specifically, about how diversity considerations should weigh in decisions about undergraduate admissions and faculty recruitment? After all, students are not the ones making admissions decisions or hiring faculty. And measuring student attitudes is not the same as measuring public opinion overall. Attitudes toward diversity among people who are "in the door" might differ from those among the broader public, applicants who were not admitted, or faculty job candidates who were not selected, including those who perceive their prospects were hurt by policies aimed at fostering diversity. Prominent media commentators argue, for example, that an "embrace of diversity inside higher education does not represent a national consensus" (Lemann 2018).

We maintain that understanding student attitudes matters in its own right. Even if students are not directly involved in admissions or recruitment decisions, they are the largest group of stakeholders at every university. They are the principal subjects of the admissions process and they are the faculty's main constituents. They attend faculty lectures, study readings assigned by faculty, are subject to faculty evaluations of their work, and are guided by faculty mentors. Their peers are other admitted students. They have every reason to care deeply about what factors weigh, and how, in both student admissions and in faculty recruitment.

What is more, although we do not measure opinion beyond the college campus in this study, our results suggest that our participants' attitudes are not simply driven by their position inside the campus gates. For example, if students who were admitted to their top-choice schools bear no grudge against efforts to promote diversity while students denied their top choices are embittered, then the populations at more selective and less selective schools should display starkly different attitudes toward diversity. Yet our experiments revealed few significant differences across schools. And if pro-diversity preferences were a luxury indulged in only by those who fear no loss from affirmative action, then we should see a lack of support for diversity – or even opposition to diversity – among participants who profess opposition to such policies. Solid majorities of our respondents did express opposition to race-conscious admissions and hiring *in the abstract*, yet even these respondents favored minority applicants and faculty candidates relative to whites in our choice experiments. We discuss these results in detail in subsequent chapters, but for now, we emphasize that although our participants are not a representative sample of the broader US population, their attitudes do not appear to be mere products of their institutional status.

Finally, student attitudes toward the value of campus diversity – and, specifically, uncertainty about those attitudes – are prominent in the arguments of diversity critics from both the left and the right. In *The Enigma of Diversity* (2015), Ellen Berrey argues that admissions policies that increase the presence of racial and ethnic minorities on campus foster complacency among whites. She notes that universities advertise not only their diversity but also the *satisfaction of their students with diversity* in promotional materials based on carefully curated interviews and cherry-picked quotations. Yet, as Berrey claims, these arguments and PR materials are rarely based on scientific evidence that probes the students' attitudes systematically (Berrey 2015, pp. 72–73).

From the other side of the ideological spectrum, there is skepticism as to whether broader university communities favor admissions policies to promote diversity at all. A recent Supreme Court decision upheld the University of Texas's consideration of race in admissions in part on grounds that diversity advances "the destruction of stereotypes" and "the promotion of cross-cultural understanding" (*Fisher* v. *University of Texas at Austin et al.* 2016). In his dissent, however, Justice Samuel Alito specifically questioned whether university administrators ought to be the sole judges of whether race-conscious admissions policies serve campus interests:

These are laudable goals, but they are not concrete or precise, and they offer no limiting principle for the use of racial preferences. For instance, how will a court ever be able to determine whether stereotypes have been adequately destroyed? Or whether cross-racial understanding has been adequately achieved? If a university can justify racial discrimination *simply by having a few employees opine that racial preferences are necessary to accomplish these nebulous goals (citing only self-serving statements from UT officials)* [emphasis added], then the narrow tailoring inquiry is meaningless. Courts will be required to defer to the judgment of university administrators, and affirmative-action policies will be completely insulated from judicial review. (*Fisher* v. *University of Texas at Austin et al.* 2016, pp. 15–16)

It remains to be seen whether Justice Alito's skepticism toward race-conscious admissions would be allayed by evidence that campus populations in general, well beyond just a handful of administrators, value diversity. But his argument, like Berrey's, suggests that understanding what students think about campus diversity is of real consequence for policy makers, college administrators, and anyone concerned about the state of higher education. Yet gauging student preferences for diversity is a new area of research that poses significant challenges. We use a new approach to address these challenges.

1.4 HOW WE GAUGE ATTITUDES TOWARD DIVERSITY

Gauging honest attitudes about diversity is difficult for a number of reasons. First of all, diversity is a hot-button issue. Social science has long established that individuals are reluctant to openly express preferences that they suspect could be divisive (Gilens, Sniderman, and Kuklinski 1998; Jiang and Yang 2016; Kuran 1995). As a result, interviews, focus groups, and surveys on sensitive topics can produce biased results. Critics of diversity discourse specifically contend that talking about diversity suppresses the free expression of contentious opinions (MacDonald 2017; McWhorter 2015).

Moreover, even if a researcher could be sure to elicit sincere responses, standard questions about what factors should matter in admissions and faculty recruitment would not capture the essence of those decisions because of the nature of the decisions themselves. Choices among potential new students and faculty members are fundamentally multidimensional, and therefore inescapably holistic. Admissions and recruitment committees choose among candidates who are, themselves, multifaceted bundles of characteristics. Therefore, asking individuals to make choices that prioritize a particular characteristic (such as race/ethnicity) over others could produce an unnecessary "framing" effect by design (Chong and Druckman 2007; Rosen 2017).

Faced with the growing need to understand students' attitudes toward diversity and the challenge of eliciting honest ones, we use a new approach: fully randomized conjoint analysis (hereafter referred to as conjoint analysis). Conjoint analysis has its origins in market research but was recently refined by Hainmueller, Hopkins, and Yamamoto (2014) based on the potential-outcome framework for causal inference (Splawa-Neyman 1990; Rubin 1974, 2005), and has since been applied by many political scientists to measure individuals' multidimensional preferences for policies (Bechtel and Scheve 2013; Horiuchi, Smith, and Yamamoto 2018*a*), politicians (Carlson 2015; Horiuchi, Smith, and Yamamoto 2018*b*; Teele, Kalla, and Rosenbluth 2018), and politicized issues, such as immigration (Hainmueller and Hopkins 2015). This method is particularly suitable to understand opinions on sensitive topics such as discrimination (Caruso, Rahnev, and Banaji 2009), as research shows that it reduces the urge to respond in a "socially desirable" way as compared to alternative survey designs that ask respondents for their preferences directly (Horiuchi, Markovich, and Yamamoto 2019).

The core of our study is a coordinated set of conjoint survey experiments conducted in 2017 and 2018 at four major American universities – the University of California, San Diego; the University of North Carolina at Chapel Hill; the University of Nevada, Reno; and Dartmouth College. In the experiments, participants chose between hypothetical applicants for admission as undergraduate students, or between hypothetical candidates for faculty appointments, at their institutions. Like real applicants and faculty candidates, these hypothetical applicants and candidates were bundles of attributes, all of which could well be salient to their candidacies. Our survey participants, therefore, were confronted with holistic decisions much like those taken by admissions or recruitment committees. We conducted the experiments across these four universities using a consistent format that allows us to pool the results, providing statistical leverage by increasing our sample size, and analytical leverage from the distinct environments and student populations at each institution. We also compare the results to those from related experiments we conducted in 2016 at the University of New Mexico and at the London School of Economics, and in 2018 at the United States Naval Academy.

1.5 THE HIDDEN CONSENSUS ON CAMPUS DIVERSITY

Our results point to strong, broadly shared preferences for prioritizing campus diversity in admissions and faculty recruitment. Specifically, our student participants give preference to admissions applicants and faculty candidates from underrepresented minority racial/ethnic groups, to faculty candidates who are women, and to admissions applicants from disadvantaged economic backgrounds. The estimated preferences for these diversity considerations vary across groups, and are generally stronger among participants from racial/ethnic minority groups (particularly blacks) than among whites, and among women than among men. But notably we find no evidence for *polarization* in preferences across groups on the basis of race/ethnicity. That is, we do not find any set of participants (e.g., nonwhites) favoring student applicants or faculty candidates from a particular racial/ethnic category while another set of participants (e.g., whites) disfavors it. Nor do we find such polarization with respect to men versus women applicants or candidates, or with respect to high-income versus low-income applicants. By contrast, we do find some evidence of polarization with respect to gender nonbinary applicants and candidates, and we elaborate on this in further chapters.

On the whole, however, we find student opinion with regard to preferences for diversity in undergraduate admissions and faculty recruitment to be less polarized than much contemporary media coverage (e.g., Friedersdorf 2015; Heller 2016; Lukainoff and Haidt 2015) suggests. Hence, we characterize our results as reflecting a *hidden consensus on campus diversity* – a consensus because we find more concurrence than divergence in preferences, and hidden because so much public discussion and campus debate on the topic portray college campuses as deeply divided over diversity concerns.

1.6 A MAP OF THE BOOK

The next chapter of this book provides essential background on the demographics of American college campuses and on the debates, policies, and precedents that shape current discussions around diversity. We begin with basic data on the race/ethnicity, gender, and (for students) socioeconomic background of our campus populations. We review long-term trends and the major policy shifts that brought us to the present moment, as well as the unresolved debates that may shape the future trajectory of diversity on campus.

Chapter 3 discusses in more detail the challenges to measuring attitudes toward controversial issues through standard survey methods and describes the advantages of the method we use here, conjoint analysis. It then lays out how we conducted our survey experiments and the populations of individuals who participated. We avoid providing detailed technical explanations as much as possible in this chapter. All the key statistical results are then presented graphically throughout the book.

Chapter 4 presents the preferences toward applicants for undergraduate admissions and candidates for faculty recruitment using a pooled sample of all student participants at the four core institutions in our study. It describes the relative priorities placed on academic and professional achievement and preferences for various racial/ethnic groups, as well as for women and gender nonbinary applicants and candidates. It also shows priorities based on socioeconomic background, parents' educational status, and academic and extracurricular interests, as well as those based on institutional factors, such as varsity athletics recruitment and in-state residential status, for undergraduate admissions applicants.

For faculty candidates, we also examine priorities based on attributes including faculty rank and spouse/partner faculty status, among others.

Chapter 5 then shows how preferences differ across the racial/ethnic groups of our student participants – whites, blacks, Asians, and Hispanics – as well as how preferences differ by participants' gender and by their family income. We narrow the focus in this chapter to the attributes that are most central to debates over campus diversity: race/ethnicity, gender, and class. The results show differing levels of priority across participant groups toward particular attributes of applicants and candidates. For example, participants who are racial minorities on the whole exhibit somewhat stronger preferences for applicants and candidates from minority groups. But the direction of preferences almost never differs across groups (e.g., with one group favoring and another disfavoring a particular attribute), and the differences often are not even statistically discernible. The single exception here is with regard to gender nonbinary applicants and candidates, who are favored by women participants and disfavored by men.

Chapter 6 breaks participants out according to their political beliefs and attitudes, focusing on partisanship, attitudes toward affirmative action, and attitudes toward racial minorities. It shows that, as expected, Democrats, supporters of affirmative action, and those scoring low on a scale of racial resentment all exhibit strong preferences for applicants and candidates from underrepresented minority groups. Yet it also demonstrates that, in our experiments, there is little evidence of disfavor toward such applicants and candidates among Republicans, opponents of affirmative action, or even among participants who scored high on the racial resentment scale items.

Current debates over affirmative action focus on whether applicants of a different race/ethnicity are afforded different rates of return to academic and professional achievement in the admissions and recruitment processes, and whether they should be. For example, pending legal cases claim that Asian student applicants reap lower returns to academic achievement than do whites or other minorities (Mortara et al. 2018). In Chapter 7, we explore whether students' preferences indicate differential rates of return. The results consistently reject the proposition; specifically, undergraduate admissions applicants and faculty candidates for hire are valued more as their academic merits increase, regardless of their race/ethnicity, gender, or socioeconomic backgrounds.

Chapter 8 is based on unique parallel survey experiments we conducted at the University of New Mexico and the University of Nevada,

Reno. At these two schools, we were able to recruit not only students, but also faculty participants, to take the same surveys. We show that pro-diversity preferences are much stronger among faculty than among students at both institutions. The chapter discusses the relative importance of selection versus campus socialization in explaining this divergence.

Chapter 9 reviews evidence from other universities where we conducted experiments similar to those reported in the rest of the book. The London School of Economics and the US Naval Academy each provide a fundamentally different participant population and institutional culture from the other universities we examine. Nevertheless, results from similar survey experiments at those schools corroborate our main findings, with a handful of exceptions that we describe and discuss at the conclusion of the chapter.

Finally, Chapter 10 summarizes the main results of our experiments, and then considers how campus diversity impacts universities. We connect our findings to broader scholarship on effects of campus diversity, and efforts to promote it, on university communities and on their individual members. We also suggest how our results can contribute to current debates over campus diversity as well as those on the near horizon.

Roots of the Current Diversity Debates

Race/ethnicity, gender, and socioeconomic background are central to how we conceptualize campus diversity. We therefore begin this chapter by describing the composition of university populations in the United States according to these demographics over the last few decades.[1]

After describing the campus populations and trends, we then survey landmark controversies and policy responses around campus demographics that shape current diversity debates. We begin with debates over the Jewish quotas at many elite universities in the early twentieth century, and mid-century social assistance programs that sustained, and even amplified, the disparate access to higher education that advantaged whites over nonwhites. We then review prominent judicial decisions that established current practices of affirmative action in admissions, as well as state-level policy responses that often sought to limit or roll back the consideration of race and ethnicity in admissions processes. We also review the evolution of Title IX, which has governed how federal law affects access to educational resources and opportunities by gender.

The last section of the chapter describes the contemporary state of debates over diversity, focusing on the 2015 wave of campus protests around diversity issues, as well as pending legal challenges to the consideration of race and ethnicity in admissions on the grounds that they discriminate against Asian applicants, and finally, arguments that the

---

[1] Although socioeconomic background is salient to undergraduate admissions decisions and to discussions about student diversity, it is generally not central to faculty recruitment, so in that area we focus on race/ethnicity and gender only.

biggest diversity-related challenge on campus today is ideological, not demographic.

2.1 DIVERSITY FACTS AND FIGURES

This section uses data from the *Digest of Education Statistics* (e.g., National Center for Education Statistics 2016), a report from the Teachers Insurance and Annuity Association (Finkelstein, Conley, and Schuster 2016), and other sources to describe the racial/ethnic and gender breakdowns of students and faculty, and the socioeconomic breakdown of students, at US colleges and universities. The periods of our investigation are the last four decades for students and the last three decades for faculty, subject to data availability. We begin with the numbers in terms of race and ethnicity.

Race and Ethnicity

Students

Figure 2.1 shows the relative shares of whites, blacks, Hispanics, Asians and Pacific Islanders, and American Indian and Alaska Natives among undergraduate students at US colleges and universities from 1976 to 2015. Over this four-decade period, the percentage of white students gradually decreased and that of minorities increased correspondingly. In 1976, 83.4 percent of all undergraduates were white. Among the 16.6 percent who were minorities, 10.2 percent were black, 3.8 percent were Hispanic, 1.8 percent were Asian or Pacific Islander,[2] and 0.8 percent were American Indian or Alaska Native. By 2000, the percentage of white students had dropped to 69.8 percent and by 2015 to 56.5 percent, just above the 54.6 percent white share of the college-aged (18–24 years old) population.[3] The largest percent increase over the previous four decades was in Hispanic enrollments, from 3.8 percent to 18.5 percent.

The distribution of students by race/ethnicity is not uniform across all types of schools, however.[4] The most pronounced gap is for white

---

[2] Before 2010, all data on Asian and Pacific Islander students were combined; subsequently, the breakdowns are available for each group.

[3] For the share of college-age population by race/ethnicity, see the National Center for Education Statistics (2016, Table 101.20).

[4] For the relative shares of students enrolled at postsecondary institutions (including undergraduate and postbaccalaureate students) by race/ethnicity and institution types, see the National Center for Education Statistics (2016, Table 306.20).

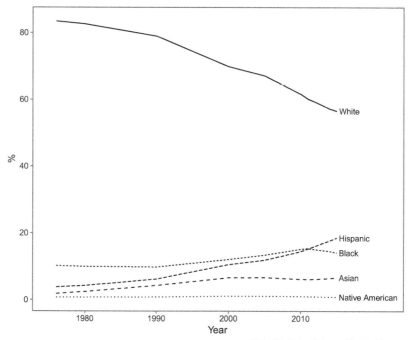

FIGURE 2.1 Demographic composition of undergraduate students over time, by race/ethnicity.
Source: National Center for Education Statistics (2016), Table 306.10.

students, whose share of the population at four-year schools is consistently, and increasingly, higher than its share at two-year schools. The pattern is reversed for black and Hispanic students, who are relatively more concentrated at two-year institutions. At four-year institutions, as of 2015, 61.2 percent of students were white, and 38.8 percent were minorities, whereas at two-year schools, the split was 50.5 percent to 49.5 percent. At the most selective institutions, the increase in enrollments by underrepresented minorities is even more limited. A recent analysis of black and Hispanic representation at top colleges found that whites and Asians are more overrepresented, relative to their shares of the college-aged US population, today than they were in 1980, and blacks and Hispanics are more underrepresented (Ashenkas, Park, and Pearce 2017).

Recognizing that the relative sizes of these demographic groups change over time, Figure 2.2 illustrates the overrepresentation and

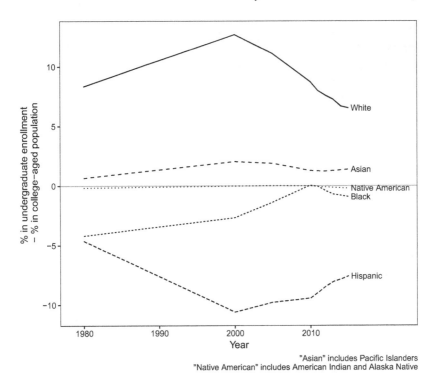

"Asian" includes Pacific Islanders
"Native American" includes American Indian and Alaska Native

FIGURE 2.2 The difference between the share of each group in the college-aged (17–24 years old) population and the share in all undergraduate enrollment. *Source*: National Center for Education Statistics (2016), Table 101.20, Table 306.20.

underrepresentation of various racial/ethnic groups among enrolled students at four-year institutions, relative to shares of the college-aged individuals in the US population.[5] Between 1980 and 2000, white overrepresentation at these universities increased from about 8.3 percent above the population share to 12.7 percent, even while the raw proportion of whites in the college-aged population declined. After 2000, white overrepresentation diminished, although whites remain well above their population share. Enrollments among Asian and Pacific Islander students follow a similar, although more muted, pattern. Among blacks, enrollment gains relative to population share were steady until about 2010, when the gap between students enrolled at four-year schools and

---

5 We focus on four-year institutions because their admissions processes are more likely to be selective than those at two-year institutions, raising the salience of debates over how to balance diversity and other considerations. The relative shares include both undergraduate and postbaccalaureate students.

the college-aged population was erased, although a slight dip followed in the years since. Among Hispanics, by contrast, the enrollment gap widened up to 2000, after which the trend reversed. Nevertheless, at four-year institutions, Hispanics' enrollments still lag behind population shares dramatically.

Faculty

We now turn to racial/ethnic diversity among faculty. Data on the racial and ethnic composition of faculty over time are less comprehensive than the available data on students, but clearly suggest that minority underrepresentation is more pronounced among faculty than among students. Figure 2.3 shows that in 1992, 86.5 percent of full-time faculty were white, 5.2 percent were Asian and Pacific Islander, 5.2 percent were black, 2.6 percent were Hispanic, and 0.5 percent were Native American. By 2015, the percentage of white faculty had declined to

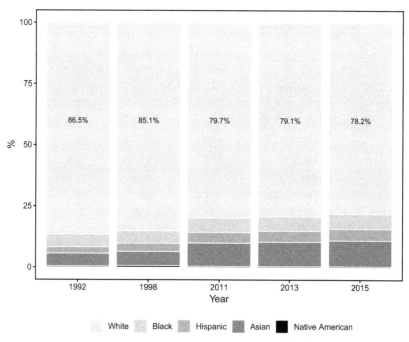

"Asian" includes Pacific Islanders
"Native American" includes American Indian and Alaska Native

FIGURE 2.3 Demographic composition of faculty over time, by race.
Source: National Center for Education Statistics (2016), Table 315.20; Tabs (2002),
Table 5A.

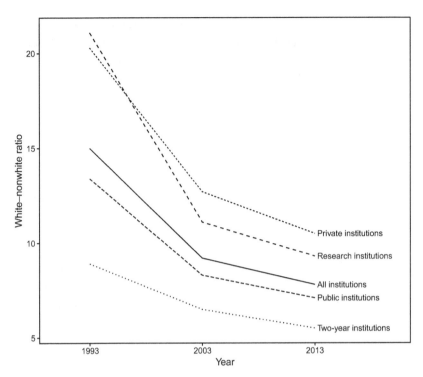

FIGURE 2.4 White/nonwhite ratios over time, by institution type.
Source: Finkelstein, Conley, and Schuster (2016), Table 6.

78.2 percent, while the share of Asians and Pacific Islanders had doubled to 10.5 percent. The proportions of blacks and Hispanics, however,
had edged up only to 6.0 percent and 4.9 percent, respectively, and
Native Americans remained at 0.5 percent. White faculty remain significantly overrepresented relative to their population share, and black and
Hispanic faculty significantly underrepresented (United States Census
Bureau 2011, 2010).

Like students, minority faculty representation is characterized by
imbalances by institution type. Figure 2.4 displays the ratio of white
to nonwhite faculty over time, by type of postsecondary institution. In
1993, among full-time, tenured faculty, the ratio of whites to underrepresented minorities was 15.0 to 1 at all types of institutions. The
ratio dropped to 9.2 to 1 by 2003 and 7.8 to 1 by 2013, representing
measurable gains for faculty from underrepresented minority racial and
ethnic groups, but whites were still substantially overrepresented relative to their population share. The imbalance was most pronounced at

private institutions (10.5 to 1 in 2013) and research institutions (9.3 to 1), and less pronounced at two-year institutions (5.5 to 1) and public institutions (7.1 to 1). There was also a larger gap among tenured faculty than among untenured, non–tenure-track, and part-time faculty (see Finkelstein, Conley, and Schuster 2016).

SUMMARY. Overall, racial and ethnic diversity among undergraduates has increased in the past forty years, although not to the point where racial/ethnic representation on campuses corresponds perfectly to representation in the population. The largest gains for students from underrepresented minority groups have occurred at two-year colleges, including community colleges.

Among faculty, whites remain overrepresented and minorities underrepresented in all faculty positions and at all types of universities, despite increases in representation among minorities in the US population in recent decades. The gaps between shares of the general population and representation on college campuses are broader among faculty than among students.

Gender

STUDENTS. Gender discrepancies in university enrollments have diminished more dramatically than those around race and ethnicity, and have even reversed from their historical imbalance toward men. Historical data on male and female students enrolled at US universities are also more abundant than those on race and ethnicity; the National Center for Education Statistics (NCES) provides data on American men and women among enrolled students at American institutions of higher education from 1869 to the present.[6] In 1869–1870, 21.0 percent of students enrolled in colleges were women. Only 1.3 percent of the 18- to 24-year-old population, however, was enrolled in any institution of higher education at the time.

By the end of the nineteenth century, enrollment had increased slightly, and 35.9 percent of students were women. After 1930, college enrollment saw another significant increase for both men and women. During World War II, women accounted for around half of university enrollments, a figure that dropped to roughly 30 percent after the war, before rising again

---

[6] See Snyder (1993, Table 24) for historical data (specifically, 1869–1991) and National Center for Education Statistics (2016) for more recent data.

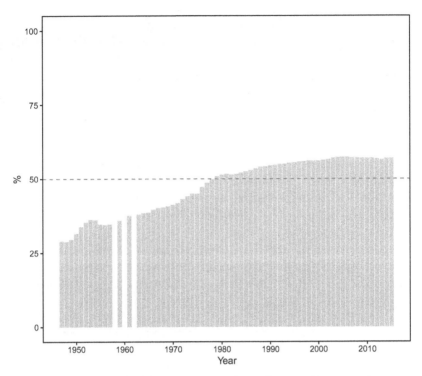

FIGURE 2.5 Percent women among undergraduate students over time.
Source: National Center for Education Statistics (2016), Table 303.10.

in the 1950s and 1960s to 40.7 percent in 1969. Figure 2.5 shows that, by the end of the 1970s, the percentage of women and men attending colleges was nearly equal. By 1980, the share of women among the population of enrolled undergraduates had risen to 51.4 percent and to 57.0 percent by 2015, with the proportion of women expected to continue increasing.

The historical data may overstate levels of gender diversity on campus somewhat, particularly for earlier periods, insofar as many schools were not coeducational until relatively recently. Even after many colleges made the switch to coeducation, it took them years to achieve roughly equal representation by men and women. Yet even accounting for these factors, gender parity among university students is currently well established. Goldin and Katz's (2010, Table 1) analysis of coeducation in colleges from 1835 to the first decade of the twenty-first century uses an insightful metric that captures one aspect of gender diversity in higher education over time. Their "isolation index" computes the degree to which a typical

woman in a given year is educationally segregated from men, where o
equals perfect integration and 1 equals complete gender segregation that
arises in the case of single-sex institutions. In 1897, 56 percent of all
universities and 44 percent of private universities were coeducational,
and the isolation index was 0.44. By 1980, 98 percent of all universities
and 96 percent of private schools were coeducational, and the index was
at 0.05.

FACULTY. Data on gender representation among faculty at colleges
and universities in the United States are more sparse than data for
students. The available figures show a greater disparity between men
and women within top faculty ranks than among all faculty positions.
Figure 2.6 shows women's shares of all faculty and of full professors.
While women's representation among all faculty reached 49.2 percent
by 2013, near parity with the population share for women, we observe
substantial gender differences by appointment type. Despite some gains

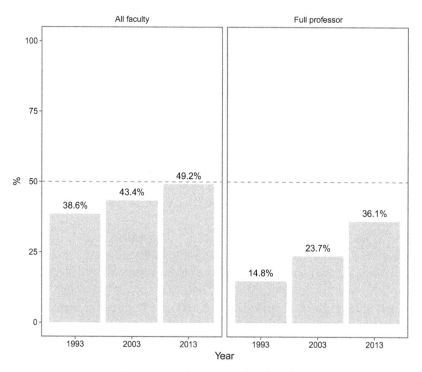

FIGURE 2.6 Percentage of university faculty who are women.
Source: Finkelstein, Conley, and Schuster (2016), Table 2, Table 3.

(women's share among full professors more than doubled from 14.8 percent in 1993 to 36.1 percent in 2013), women clearly continue to trail men at the most senior faculty positions.

SUMMARY. While women were historically underrepresented among enrolled students at American institutions of higher education, they are now overrepresented relative to their population share at colleges and universities. Women faculty, on the other hand, have not yet reached parity with men, particularly within coveted faculty positions.

Income and Class

Socioeconomic background is an important consideration in under-graduate admissions decisions and is a salient aspect of student diversity on campus, but it is generally less relevant to faculty recruitment. In this section, we therefore describe the socioeconomic breakdown of under-graduate students at US colleges and universities only.[7] Thus, Figure 2.7 shows the rate of postsecondary enrollments among the college-aged population, by family income tercile, from 1975 to 2015.[8] In the mid-1970s, about 35 percent of high school graduates from low-income families, 45 percent from middle-income families, and 65 percent from high-income families were enrolled in two-year and four-year colleges. Four decades later, more than 60 percent of low-income and middle-income students, respectively, were attending college, while the number had risen to more than 80 percent among high-income students.

As with race and ethnicity, however, the strongest gains by students from the most underrepresented income groups are at two-year schools and less selective institutions. Reardon, Baker, and Klasik (2012) find that low-income students are underrepresented in four-year colleges, and particularly at the most selective schools. In 2004, for example, 21 percent of students enrolled in four-year colleges came from low-income families, but only 6.3 percent of those at the most highly selective schools were low-income. Notably, the most elite schools were slightly more diverse in terms of income than the second-most highly selective

---

[7] We also note that the available data on university enrollments by socioeconomic class tend to show the percentages of recent high school graduates within each income bracket who are enrolled rather than the percentages of enrolled students from each group, as with race/ethnicity and gender.

[8] The lines overlaid on the dots are based on three-year moving averages.

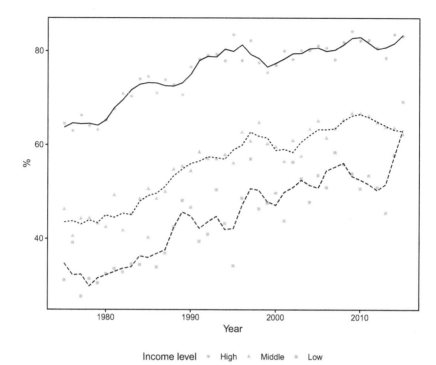

FIGURE 2.7 Demographic composition of undergraduate students over time, by
income level.
Source: National Center for Education Statistics (2016), Table 302.30.

schools, most likely because need-blind admissions policies have been
concentrated in elite schools. Comparing cohorts of students who began
college in 1982, 1992, and 2004, the study concluded that the relationship between income and selective college enrollment has grown stronger
over time, with more students from high-income families, and fewer from
low-income families, enrolling at the most selective institutions.

Recent data corroborate this trend; the *New York Times*' College
Access Index, a measure of economic diversity on college campuses,
shows that many of the most elite institutions have significantly higher
percentages of high-income than low-income students (Leonhardt 2015).
For example, the ratio of students from the top 5 percent of America's
income distribution (with an annual household income above $200,000)
to students in the entire bottom half of the distribution at Dartmouth
College, the University of Pennsylvania, Princeton University, and Yale
University is two to one.

Overall, then, these data suggest that although the percentage of the college-aged population at all income levels attending institutions of higher education has increased over time, the socioeconomic profile of students still varies dramatically by university type. Students from the highest income brackets continue to be significantly overrepresented at top schools. With this section's picture of campus diversity in mind, we now turn to the historical, judicial, and policy origins of diversity debates in the United States.

2.2 HISTORICAL, JUDICIAL, AND POLICY ORIGINS OF CAMPUS DIVERSITY

Current debates over campus diversity have their roots in a long history of controversies, court decisions, and policy responses to issues of minority representation at institutions of higher education. We begin with a discussion of elite universities' attempts to place admissions quotas on Jews in the early twentieth century.

The Rise and Fall of Jewish Quotas

In 1905, Harvard College began evaluating and admitting applicants primarily based on scores on the College Entrance Examination Board test.[9] In just a few years, an institution that had been dominated by white, Protestant graduates from New England boarding schools had increasing numbers of Jewish, Catholic, and public school–educated enrollees who had scored well on the exam. By 1922, Jewish students made up over 20 percent of Harvard's incoming freshman class.

Harvard President A. Lawrence Lowell was a vocal anti-Semite. When his original attempt to establish a quota that would limit Jews to 15 percent of the student body was rejected by the Committee on Admissions, he tried to reduce scholarships available to Jewish students and increase the enrollment of graduates from public schools in the West. These strategies failed as well.

In the fall of 1922, Lowell joined with administrators at other top institutions including Yale and Princeton and decided to rethink the entire admissions process to de-emphasize test scores. The new admissions

---

[9] For statistics referred to in this subsection and further information, see Harvard University Archives (1922*a*, 1922*b*, 1923, 1925, 1928, 1933), Synnott (1974), and Karabel (2005).

procedures required applicants to answer questions about demographics, religion, origin, birthplace, and character; to be interviewed; and to provide letters of reference, photographs, and personal essays. The policies allowed Harvard and other elite universities to admit applicants with lesser academic credentials without explicitly disallowing Jews to join their ranks. By 1933, the percentage of Jews in Harvard's incoming freshman class had dropped to 15 percent.

Sociologist Jerome Karabel argues that the desire of elite schools to exclude certain applicants came down to the aesthetic "image" that these schools wanted to uphold (Karabel 2005, p. 505). In the case of Harvard in the 1920s and 1930s, this image did not include a preponderance of Jews. Contemporary challenges to the consideration of race and ethnicity in admissions point to these exclusionary practices as foreshadowing current treatment of Asian-American applicants (Mortara et al. 2018). Critics charge that the implicit justification for selecting against Jewish applicants a century ago – that they do not contribute the desired characteristics to campus communities – is employed at the expense of Asian-American applicants today (Gladwell 2005; Jacobs 2017). We return to this point later in this chapter, and in Chapters 7 and 10.

Compounding Racial Inequality with the New Deal

Although many discussions of race-based affirmative action start with the Civil Rights Acts of the 1960s and the subsequent implementation of race-conscious policies, key social policy initiatives with racially disparate effects began decades earlier, during the New Deal and after World War II.[10] The Social Security Act of 1935 and the Fair Labor Standards Act of 1938 had substantially different effects on black and white workers in terms of labor protections and income support. The Serviceman's Readjustment Act (the G.I. Bill) of 1944 had similarly disparate effects on accessibility to college/university education (Katznelson 2005). In the former two cases, the economic sectors dominated by black labor – farms and domestic work – were excluded from meaningful protections, leaving black families less positioned to invest in education. Meanwhile, the G.I. Bill's main provisions, guaranteed mortgages and tuition support, proved empty for most black veterans because local practices denied them access to either loans or university admissions. These barriers remained in place for two decades after the passage of

---

[10] For further reading, see Katznelson (2005).

the G.I. Bill. Indeed, the federal government programs that did the most to advance the economic prospects of white Americans in the twentieth century – including, critically, for our purposes, access to higher education – systematically denied benefits to blacks and increased black–white inequality.

Campus Diversity at the Supreme Court: The *Bakke* Case

Although controversies regarding admissions and diversity had been going on for decades, it was not until 1978 that the United States Supreme Court addressed affirmative action policies in university admissions for the first time. Crucially, the landmark case of *Regents of the University of California* v. *Bakke* (1978) established the precedent that diversity on college campuses is a compelling state (and, therefore, university) interest.

Allan Bakke was a thirty-five-year-old white man who had applied to the University of California at Davis School of Medicine twice, and was twice rejected. At that time, the school's admissions policies reserved sixteen slots for "qualified" minorities. Bakke argued that he was rejected on the grounds of race only, because his college GPA and medical school test scores were higher than those of any minorities who were accepted during either application round. The case moved from a California district court to the Supreme Court, where the justices evaluated whether the University of California's policies violated the Equal Protection Clause of the Fourteenth Amendment and the Civil Rights Act of 1964. The *Bakke* case split the Supreme Court. A majority of the nine justices found the medical school's policy of setting aside a fixed number of seats for minority applicants to be discriminatory, and on those grounds found in favor of Bakke. A separate majority, however, also recognized that having a diverse student body "furthers a compelling state interest" provided that "racial or ethnic origin is but a single, though important, element" of the qualifications and characteristics that are considered in the admissions process. In recognizing a compelling state interest in diversity, the *Bakke* decision set the agenda for subsequent jurisprudence on affirmative action. It continues to shape campus discourse by advancing the premise that diversity contributes to a campus culture that benefits the entire community, including white students – a point we return to in the concluding chapter.[11]

---

[11] For related arguments, see Page (2007) and Warikoo (2016).

Affirmative Action Takes a Hit: *Hopwood* v. *Texas*

Opponents of race-conscious admissions scored a partial win in 1996 with the Fifth Federal Circuit Court's decision in *Hopwood* v. *Texas* (1996).[12] Four white students, led by Cheryl J. Hopwood, had applied to and been denied admission by the University of Texas at Austin School of Law. The four had higher LSAT scores and grades than all but nine of the sixty-one black and Hispanic candidates who were admitted during the same application cycle. They filed a federal lawsuit against the university, arguing that they were unfairly rejected because they were white.

In 1994, US District Judge Sam Sparks had ruled that the University of Texas's consideration of race in the college admissions process was permissible. The plaintiffs appealed to the Fifth Circuit, where Justice Jerry Edwin Smith ruled that the law school could no longer consider race when determining which applicants to admit on the grounds that the university had "presented no compelling justification ... that allows it to continue to elevate some races over others, even for the wholesome purpose of correcting perceived racial imbalance in the student body" (*Hopwood* v. *Texas* 1996). The Supreme Court subsequently denied hearing an appeal from the University of Texas. Thus, for the next seven years, the *Hopwood* v. *Texas* decision established that it was not permissible to consider race in college admissions at public universities in Texas, Louisiana, or Mississippi, the three states within the Fifth Circuit Court's jurisdiction.

Refining Race-Conscious Admissions: *Grutter* and *Gratz*

Race-conscious admissions made it to the Supreme Court again in 2003, with two separate cases concerning the University of Michigan's admissions policies – *Grutter* v. *Bollinger* (2003) and *Gratz* v. *Bollinger* (2003). Barbara Grutter was a white applicant who was rejected from the University of Michigan Law School, and Jennifer Gratz along with Patrick Hamacher were white applicants denied admission to the university's undergraduate campus. All three students were residents of Michigan. They filed lawsuits against Lee Bollinger, the president of the University of Michigan and the dean of the law school at the time, arguing that

---

[12] *Johnson* v. *Board of Regents of the University System of Georgia* (2000) also found an affirmative action admissions policy at the University of Georgia to be in violation of the Fourteenth Amendment.

the university violated the Equal Protection Clause of the Fourteenth Amendment and Title VI of the Civil Rights Act of 1964 by giving preference to minority applicants.

Notably, the law school and the undergraduate college differed in their affirmative action policies. The law school simply stated that race was used as a factor in admissions decisions to achieve a diverse student body. The undergraduate office of admissions, however, specifically used a point system that awarded underrepresented minorities an additional twenty points in the consideration process. With this policy in place, nearly every single qualified applicant from certain underrepresented racial and ethnic groups was admitted, whereas the admission of white students with equal or higher academic merit was not guaranteed.

In *Grutter* v. *Bollinger*, the Supreme Court ruled five to four that the law school did not violate the Equal Protection Clause of the Fourteenth Amendment. Even if the highly individualized review process took race into account, the majority reasoned, race was just one of multiple factors considered. According to the law school's policy, no applicant would be automatically rejected or accepted based on his or her race. In *Gratz* v. *Bollinger*, however, decided on the same day, the Supreme Court ruled six to three in favor of the plaintiff. The point system used by the undergraduate admissions office precluded individual consideration, and therefore did not provide sufficient opportunities to consider factors besides race, thus violating the Equal Protection Clause.

These cases helped clarify the extent to which affirmative action policies in college admissions are permissible in the United States. Importantly, the *Grutter* v. *Bollinger* decision abrogated the *Hopwood* v. *Texas* ruling and reestablished the constitutionality of affirmative action in Texas, Louisiana, and Mississippi. The *Gratz* v. *Bollinger* case, however, demonstrated that race can only be considered as one of many factors in a holistic admissions process; racial quotas or point systems are not allowed.

Affirmative Action and Its Compelling Government Interest: *Fisher* v. *Texas*

Affirmative action in admissions reached the Supreme Court again in *Fisher* v. *Texas*, which was first decided in 2013 and heard again in 2016. Abigail Fisher, a white applicant to the University of Texas at Austin, filed a lawsuit against the university after her application for undergraduate admission was rejected. At that time, a Texas state law known as the

Top Ten Percent Rule stipulated that all in-state high school seniors who ranked in the top 10 percent of their graduating class would be automatically admitted, regardless of race. Among applicants who were not in the top 10 percent of their class, however, race was a factor of consideration. Fisher was not in the top 10 percent of her class, and she claimed that the University of Texas violated her right to equal protection under the Fourteenth Amendment.

The district court and the United States Court of Appeals for the Fifth Circuit both decided in favor of the University of Texas and affirmed that the admissions office's policies were not unconstitutional. Fisher then appealed the case to the Supreme Court. The decision was seven to one for Fisher. Although the Court ruled that the Equal Protection Clause of the Fourteenth Amendment *does* permit the consideration of race in college admissions decisions, such policies are permissible only when they are held to a standard of strict judicial scrutiny. Unless a university's affirmative action policy is demonstrated to serve a "compelling government interest," race may not be used as a factor of consideration in college admissions (*Fisher* v. *University of Texas at Austin et al.* 2013). Given that the district court and the Fifth Circuit Court had not held the University of Texas' admissions policy to this standard, their judgments were inaccurate.

After this ruling, Fisher's case was remanded to the lower courts. After scrutiny of the University of Texas' affirmative action policy, both the district court and the appellate court found that the policy served a compelling government interest of promoting diversity in education, and therefore did not violate the Equal Protection Clause of the Fourteenth Amendment. The case returned to the Supreme Court in 2016, and the Justices issued a four-to-three decision for the University of Texas, agreeing that the consideration of race among applicants outside the top 10 percent of their high school class was in the interest of educational diversity.

Fisher v. *Texas* was thus an overall victory for affirmative action in college admissions. But the decision also established that admissions policies considering race are not automatically permissible, that to be permissible they must advance "the educational interests of diversity" (*Fisher* v. *University of Texas at Austin et al.* 2016), and that they must do so in a way distinct from what any alternative race-neutral policy could achieve. The *Fisher* v. *Texas* decision thus further prioritized diversity's benefits to the overall educational mission of the university as the legal basis for race-conscious admissions.

State-Level Legislation on Affirmative Action

BALLOT INITIATIVES. In the wake of the *Bakke* decision that the consideration of race in college admissions is permissible, several states established their own policies on affirmative action. Many of these policies were enacted by ballot initiatives that brought the issue to individual voters. In 1996, for example, California passed Proposition 209, which prohibited the state from "discriminat[ing] against, or grant[ing] preferential treatment to, any individual or group on the basis of race, sex, color, ethnicity, or national origin" in university admissions, public employment, or contracting (California State Legislature 1996). In 1998, Washington State passed Initiative 200, a similar ban on preferential treatment by race, ethnicity, sex, color, or national origin. Michigan's Proposal 2, passed in 2006, banned affirmative action in college admissions and public sector hiring. Nebraska's Measure 424 in 2008, Arizona's Proposition 107 in 2010, and Oklahoma's State Question 759 in 2012 all prohibited affirmative action policies by ballot initiatives. Although racial considerations in admissions, contracting, and/or hiring were not deemed unconstitutional at the federal level, these voter-led, state-level initiatives demonstrate widespread popular opposition to the explicit consideration of race and ethnicity in the admissions process.

PERCENT PLANS. Given the apparent conflict between public opposition to the consideration of race and ethnicity in college admissions and states' and universities' interest in having a diverse student body, some states have used legislation and/or executive orders to establish alternative criteria by which to foster some element of racial and ethnic diversity on college campuses. In 1997, the Texas state legislature passed House Bill 588, the "Top Ten Percent Rule." According to this law, any high school senior in Texas who graduated in the top 10 percent of his or her class would be admitted to at least one of Texas's public universities.[13] Similarly, Florida's Executive Order 99-281, "One Florida," which was enacted in 1999, outlawed racial or gender preferences or quotas

---

[13] In 2009, however, when top 10-percenters accounted for 81 percent of students in the University of Texas at Austin's incoming freshmen class, the percentage of students who could be admitted under the rule in an incoming freshman class was limited to 75 percent. University administrators expressed concerns that without such a cap, they would not be able to accept anyone outside the top 10 percent, which would decrease application rates for out-of-state students, suburban in-state students who were strong

in public university admissions, hiring, and contracting, but established the "Talented Twenty" program, which automatically admitted students who graduated in the top 20 percent of their high school class to at least one of Florida's public universities. Finally, California enacted a percent plan in 1999 that granted automatic admission to University of California schools for California high school seniors graduating in the top 4 percent of their class as part of the Eligibility in Local Context (ELC) program. This standard was raised to 9 percent in 2009 (Flores and Horn 2015).

These percent-based plans were built on several key assumptions. First, residential patterns in the United States, and in public high schools, are highly segregated by both race and socioeconomic class. Second, because school funding is based primarily on local property taxes, schools in poorer communities are underfunded. Thus, students from traditionally disadvantaged racial and ethnic groups tend to be overrepresented in underresourced academic environments that present the greatest obstacles to academic achievement. By basing university admissions on performance relative to academic environment, the logic goes, substantial numbers of applicants from underrepresented minority groups can be admitted without any explicit consideration of race and ethnicity in the admissions process.

POLICY CONSEQUENCES?. What were the effects of state-level legislation banning affirmative action and percent plans on the demographic composition of institutions of higher education? Enrollments of underrepresented minorities dropped at the University of California's more selective campuses after Proposition 209, in Texas after the *Hopwood* decision, and in Washington State after the passage of Initiative 200, whereas the "One Florida" policy had no adverse effects on minority enrollments in that state (Long 2007). But assessing the impacts of affirmative action bans and percent plans is complicated. Although decreases in minority enrollments from the bans appear to be larger than countervailing effects from the percent plans (Cortes 2010; Horn and Flores 2003; Kain, O'Brien, and Jargowsky 2005; Long 2004), the frequent combination of percent plans with affirmative action bans makes the separate effects of each policy hard to tease out.[14] Furthermore, Asians

applicants but who did not fall within the top 10 percent, and prospective football players (Watkins 2015).

[14] Using agent-based models, Reardon et al. (2018) simulate the effect of replacing race-conscious admissions with socioeconomic class-conscious admissions and racially

and whites tend to be overrepresented in the top class ranking percentiles, even at high schools with large populations of underrepresented minority groups, limiting the ability of percent plans to offset the negative effects of affirmative action bans on minority admissions (Horn and Flores 2003; Marin and Lee 2003; Long 2007).

The Evolution of Title IX

Although battles over the consideration of race and ethnicity in college admissions have been most prominent in courts and politically over the past several decades, gender diversity is also essential to diversity debates on campus, particularly with respect to faculty recruitment. At the center of debates about gender and access to higher education is Title IX to the Education Amendments of 1972, signed into law by President Richard Nixon. Title IX states, "No person in the United States shall, on the basis of sex, be excluded from participation in, be denied the benefits of, or be subjected to discrimination under any education program or activity receiving federal financial assistance." Title IX's goal was to establish gender equity in all educational programs that receive federal funding. The law addresses ten key areas, which include access to higher education, career education, education for pregnant and parenting students, athletics, employment, learning environment, math and science, sexual harassment, standardized testing, and technology.

Title IX faced several legal and legislative challenges following its enactment, particularly with regard to the provision of equality in athletics. The current policy is that women and men must be provided equal opportunities to play sports, but that institutions are not required to offer identical sports for women and men. They must, however, offer athletic scholarships to women and men that are proportional to their participation, and offer equal treatment in terms of equipment, scheduling, travel, access to academic resources, coaching, access to facilities, publicity, and recruitment (NCAA N.d.).

In 1999, the interpretation of Title IX broadened with respect to policies that universities must pursue to provide equal access to a learning environment – specifically, regulations about protection from sexual assault. In *Davis* v. *Monroe County Board of Education*, the Supreme Court ruled that a student may file a lawsuit for student-on-student

targeted college recruitment efforts, but are skeptical that the combination can maintain current levels of racial diversity at selective institutions.

sexual harassment under Title IX, and that universities may be liable for monetary damages. These policies are currently coming under fire. In November 2018, Education Secretary Betsy DeVos proposed a series of regulations that would narrow the definition of sexual harassment, tighten requirements to report sexual assault, and relieve colleges of their responsibility to investigate incidents that occurred off campus (Green 2018). These changes would also increase flexibility in legal procedures by allowing schools to choose higher evidentiary standards, establish appeals processes, and allow cross-examinations. Critics argue that these rules will reduce the frequency of Title IX investigations on campus and discourage victims from reporting instances of sexual assault and harassment.

Although the original impetus for the law was to protect women in higher education, it has most recently been applied in cases of alleged discrimination against men. At the University of Minnesota Twin Cities in 2018, university officials changed eligibility requirements for two women-only scholarships after an alumnus complained that they discriminate against men (Whitford 2018*b*). In 2016, the same individual had successfully convinced Michigan State University to close a student lounge that was reserved for women (Jaschik 2016). After receiving Title IX complaints of its own, Tulane University also agreed to review the programs and scholarships associated with its Newcomb College Institute, which grew out of a women's college formerly affiliated with Tulane (Jaschik 2019). Especially since women are no longer underrepresented among student bodies on college campuses, Title IX cases regarding discrimination against men are likely to continue in the near future.

The reach of Title IX is limited as it pertains to faculty gender issues. Although women have increased their representation in fields that were traditionally male-dominated, such as medicine and law, men continue to outnumber women in earning doctoral and professional degrees, particularly in STEM disciplines. Correspondingly, men continue to outnumber women among university faculty, and no provision of Title IX pertains to gender equity in faculty appointments. Moreover, although women who do achieve top-ranked faculty positions should, by law, receive equal pay, several lawsuits in the last several years have specifically addressed issues of compensation discrimination between men and women in higher education (e.g., Flaherty 2018*a*, c). Indeed, with respect to both gender and race, faculty pay gaps are far from resolved, with women faculty of color making 67 cents for every dollar paid to their white male counterparts

(McChesney 2018). Since Title IX was designed to protect students, however, this is an area that falls outside of its protections.

2.3 CONTEMPORARY MOVEMENTS FOR (AND AGAINST) DIVERSITY

Particularly in the past five years, campus diversity debates have expanded beyond courtrooms and university administrations. Movements led by students and interest groups have grabbed headlines both inside and outside of academic circles. We begin this section by reviewing the on-campus diversity protests that began in the fall of 2015 and put diversity issues, once again, in the national spotlight.[15]

The 2015 Campus Protests

UNIVERSITY OF MISSOURI. In October, students launched a high-profile protest in response to a variety of incidents, including graffiti depicting swastikas in dorm bathrooms, that had occurred on campus since the beginning of the school year. Students argued that the university's administrative staff fostered a segregated and unwelcoming environment for minorities (Plaster 2015). On October 10 a coalition of students known as Concerned Student 1950 tried to block the then president of the university, Tim Wolfe, during a homecoming parade. On megaphones, they recited incidents of racism and exclusion that had occurred on campus for decades. Wolfe remained silent during the encounter. In the following weeks, protests spread, including a large student and faculty demonstration, a hunger strike by one student, and the university's football team refusing to play (Pearce 2015). In November, President Wolfe and the university Chancellor, Bowen Loftin, resigned. The university then announced its plan to adopt a series of diversity initiatives, including increased efforts for minority faculty recruitment and retention and the appointment of a chief diversity officer (Pearce 2015).

In a recent paper, University of Missouri law professor Ben Trachtenberg argues that the Mizzou protests can be attributed to a perfect storm of institutional problems and contextual characteristics. Specifically, several top administrators did not get along and could not work together, the administration moved slowly in situations that demanded

---

[15] For more on the wave of protests, see Wong and Green (2016).

dispatch, university leaders did not issue unified statements to the campus community, and the university failed to make use of important information sources that could have helped them address the conflict (Trachtenberg 2018). These characteristics were apparently not unique to Mizzou, however, as the months that followed saw a wave of protests across the nation inspired in part by Missouri student activists.

UNIVERSITY OF CINCINNATI. Students launched a silent campus protest that focused on increasing black representation among students and faculty and improving how the university handles police misconduct. The Irate 8, a student activist group, duct-taped their mouths shut and published a petition outlining a series of demands to address these issues, which received hundreds of signatures (Murphy 2015). Administrators subsequently began discussions with the group and made some of the changes the students demanded, including directing more attention toward increasing the representation of minority students on campus (McCauley 2015). In January 2016, it also announced its plans to pay $4.85 million to the family of a black man killed by a University of Cincinnati police officer and award free tuition to his twelve children (Stolberg 2016).

CLAREMONT MCKENNA COLLEGE. Students acted on a series of demands for a more diverse faculty and additional funding for multicultural events by staging demonstrations on campus. Two students began hunger strikes when the then Dean of Students, Mary Spellman, sent an e-mail to a Hispanic student about increasing support for nonwhite students who "don't fit our CMC mold" (Oh 2015). The protests led to Spellman's resignation on November 12 and an announcement from the president that Claremont McKenna would be instituting a wide range of diversity-related reforms to the leadership, faculty, and on-campus facilities at the college (Watanabe and Gordon 2015).

ITHACA COLLEGE. A student group, the People of Color, organized a Solidarity Walkout during the college's family weekend. They distributed a document entitled "The Case Against Tom Cochon," which accused the then president Cochon of failing to address issues of racism and exclusion on campus (*Ithacan* 2015). In January, Cochon announced that he would be stepping down from his position, after over 75 percent of students and faculty voted that they had no confidence in the way in which he had handled racism on campus (Peralta 2016). The college also announced plans to address the concerns of the student protesters and to establish a new chief diversity officer position.

AMHERST COLLEGE. Students organized a sit-in in solidarity with the University of Missouri students who had launched the initial protests. They wrote a series of demands that included the abandonment of the college's unofficial mascot, Lord Jeff, who is tied to historical mistreatment of Native Americans (Zhang 2015). Many of the students' demands were ultimately not accepted by the college. Over 50 percent of faculty members did vote to find a new mascot, however, and the College officially replaced Lord Jeff in April 2016 (Rosen 2017).

YALE UNIVERSITY. Over one thousand students gathered for a March of Resilience in response to a series of race-related occurrences on campus. First, there were allegations about a fraternity party that was open to "white girls only" (Victor, Wang, and Wang 2015). Another flashpoint was an e-mail written by a lecturer and residential college leader lamenting a previous university memo with guidelines for culturally appropriate Halloween costumes (Hartocollis 2015). In the wake of the protests, administrators promised to meet many of the students' demands, including increasing funding for cultural centers, increasing funds for recruitment to diversify the faculty, and hosting a series of conferences on inclusion (Salovey 2015). Although the university did not agree to fire the faculty member who had written the controversial e-mail, she stepped down from her residential college post.

BROWN UNIVERSITY. The city of Providence saw a wave of protests beginning on November 16 when hundreds of Brown University students and students from Providence College gathered together wearing black and stood in solidarity with the University of Missouri students. A major trigger of the students' discontent was a report of a racially charged incident in which a Dartmouth College student was allegedly "slammed against the wall and then thrown to the ground" in a "heated and physical" encounter while visiting the university for a conference on race, gender, and socioeconomic issues (Harris and Jaffe 2015). The students published a list of demands, and the university subsequently announced plans to spend $100 million on achieving a series of goals outlined in a diversity and inclusion report. These included doubling minority faculty by 2025 and adding staff to student organizations for affinity groups (Stacey 2016).

PRINCETON UNIVERSITY. Students held a thirty-two-hour protest and sit-in in the office of the university's president, Christopher Eisgruber. A specific complaint focused on the university's honoring of the former US President Woodrow Wilson, a former faculty member and Princeton president whose name appears on a number of buildings and programs, but who was a vocal segregationist known for his opposition to admitting black students, and who allegedly admired the Ku Klux Klan (Fisher 2015). In response, Eisgruber agreed to support some of the changes the demonstrators suggested and appointed a special committee to consider the issue of Woodrow Wilson's legacy on campus. The committee ultimately voted to keep the names of the buildings and programs, but also offered a series of recommendations for fostering a more inclusive and diverse campus environment, including instituting programs to encourage more students from underrepresented minority groups to pursue doctoral degrees, commissioning more artwork related to diversity and inclusion on campus, and renaming buildings in recognition of historical individuals who have contributed to the goals of diversity and inclusion (Princeton University Office of Communications 2016).

HARVARD UNIVERSITY. Students and faculty gathered on the campus of Harvard Law School in response to an incident in which black tape was placed over the portraits of black professors. Previously, activists had used the same black tape to cover the seal of the law school, which includes the crest of a "wealthy and ruthless slaveholder" (Lartey 2015). The protestors condemned the "racist and unwelcoming environment" at the law school and pressured the university to respond to a list of demands for greater diversity and inclusion that they had made almost a year before (Graham 2015). In response, the law school decided to abandon the seal and replaced the title of "house master," a faculty position that some argued was associated with slavery, with "faculty dean" (Cunningham, Rodman, and Sabate 2016). Harvard also released a report with a series of proposals for increased diversity and more support for several student groups and multicultural centers (Harvard University Working Group on Diversity and Inclusion 2015).

UCSD, UNR, UNC, UNM, AND DARTMOUTH COLLEGE. Activism for increased campus diversity was not limited to these schools. Some form of protests have occurred on many of the campuses we focus on in this book. In February 2010, well before the 2015 protests, students at the University of California, San Diego declared a "racial state of emergency" and brought a list of diversity-related demands to administrators after a series of racially charged episodes on campus (*San Diego Union Tribune* 2010). The university accepted many of these demands immediately, including a promise to increase funding for recruitment and retention of faculty from underrepresented minority groups, and for safe spaces and tutors for black students.

At the University of Nevada, Reno, in November 2015, black student groups and administrators gathered in the UNR Quad to stand in solidarity with students at the University of Missouri, prompting conversations in the UNR community about diversity and inclusion (Lavergne 2015).

Also in November, students at the University of North Carolina at Chapel Hill disrupted a town hall meeting about racial issues with a list of demands for administrators, including the removal of a Confederate monument from a prominent spot on campus (*News and Observer* 2015). The monument was not taken down, and protests and counterprotests escalated again on UNC's campus in August 2017 after the controversy over the Robert E. Lee statue in Charlottesville, Virginia (CBS News 2017).

University of New Mexico students have protested the university's official seal, which depicts a conquistador and a frontiersman, as offensive to Native American students (Associated Press 2016). UNM students also launched diversity-related protests in 2017 in response to plans for conservative groups that they called exclusive to speak at a UNM campus event (Berrien 2017).

Finally, as we described in the preface, students at Dartmouth College led a protest on November 12, 2015, in conjunction with the national Black Lives Matter movement, in response to vandalism on a Black Lives Matter display in the campus student center (Tang 2015). Dartmouth President Philip J. Hanlon responded to the protests with a campuswide e-mail affirming his commitment to a diverse community on Dartmouth's campus.

THE DEMANDS. Nearly all of the protests that occurred in the fall of 2015 involved the publication of specific demands for diversity and inclusion. These demands were ultimately collected and posted on a website known as TheDemands.org. As of early December 2015, less than two months after the initial protests at the University of Missouri, student groups representing eighty campuses had published lists of demands on the website. The most common demands were to increase faculty diversity, require diversity training for faculty members and students, and fund cultural centers. Other demands included increasing student diversity, requiring diversity classes for students, improving the tracking of race-related offenses on campus, and expanding mental health resources for students. Several of the lists also included deadlines by which students wanted to see the changes underway, and threats to continue or escalate protests in the absence of action.

ON-CAMPUS DIVERSITY INITIATIVES. In response to the 2015 demonstrations and the demands raised by protesters at colleges and universities across the country, many institutions responded with procedural changes to increase the focus on diversity in faculty recruitment. We review some illustrative examples here. These programs are not yet fixtures within American campus culture – data from the Council of Independent Colleges suggest that 30 percent of private colleges and universities do not have programs in place to recruit a diverse faculty (Quintana 2018*b*) – but they represent steps to promote awareness and intentionality around diversity on campus.

At our home institution, Dartmouth College, the Institute for Diversity and Equity (IDE) increased its involvement in the faculty search process by requiring more information on demographics from department chairs, training faculty who are involved in search committees, and working directly with search chairs as they move through the hiring process (Ellis 2018). New software allows IDE to track applicant pools and communicate with search committee chairs about the composition of their lists of potential new hires.

Similarly, in the wake of the diversity protests at Brown University, administrators convened a Young Scholars conference to provide mentoring and guidance for women and nonbinary students in the sciences, created a Presidential Diversity Postdoctoral Fellows Program that provides underrepresented minority PhD students with tenure-track faculty positions, channeled increased funding to faculty mentoring programs, launched networking opportunities for junior faculty of color, and kicked off training programs for faculty involved in the tenure and promotion process about explicit and implicit racial bias (Flaherty 2016*b*).

At the University of Michigan, administrators implemented a program known as STRIDE, which brings together faculty across disciplines who specialize in literature on representation and inclusion to give presentations and lead workshops for other faculty on search committees (Stewart and Valian 2018). The goal of the program is to increase the likelihood that underrepresented minority faculty will be hired, retained, and promoted.

In May 2018, the University of California, Los Angeles announced a new requirement that all candidates for faculty appointments or for promotion must include in their applications an "EDI Statement" describing past, present, and future (planned) contributions to equity, diversity, and inclusion (Waugh 2018). While supporters of this initiative argue that diversity statements will ensure that faculty members play an active role in fostering inclusivity on campus (Mitchell 2018), critics allege that they will backfire, introducing "a political litmus test into faculty hiring and reviews" (Flier 2019).

Other diversity initiatives that universities have piloted in recent years include establishing administrative positions for "inclusive excellence" (Piper 2018), requiring faculty and students to undergo "cultural intelligence" training or racial equity courses (Brown 2018; Dixon Hall 2018), and changing the wording of faculty recruitment ads to attract a more diverse applicant pool (Tugend 2018). Programs like these are increasingly common at colleges and universities across the United States, prompting a new line of inquiry devoted to evaluating the impact of different types of programs (e.g., Leon 2014; Moshiri and Cardon 2019; Stewart and Valian 2018). In the concluding chapter, we describe the effects of these types of diversity initiatives on campus communities.

BEYOND THE 2015 PROTESTS. Despite the progress suggested by an increase in diversity initiatives, on-campus protests for diversity have continued beyond the 2015 demonstrations. In the spring of 2017, for example, students at the Claremont Colleges organized sit-ins, the publication of additional demands, and meetings with administrators about pressing issues of diversity, including having more say over a diverse faculty, curriculum, and housing system (Pappano 2017). Students at Wells College also held a sit-in in the spring of 2018 after a minority visiting assistant professor was not hired for a permanent position (Jaschik 2018a), undergraduates at the College of Wooster arranged a sit-in and created a list of demands after racist posts were made on a campus Facebook page (Jaschik 2018b), and Seton Hall University students who called themselves the "Concerned 44" staged a ten-day sit-in in an administrative building with demands to address institutional racism (Whitford 2018a). Finally, an on-campus group at Reed College known as Reedies Against Racism protested against a required humanities course on the grounds that it did not adequately represent people of color. They issued a set of demands that included changing the curriculum of the course, hiring more minority faculty, and changing the process of investigating racial bias against minority faculty on the tenure track (Flaherty 2018*b*).

The premise that racial and ethnic diversity should be an important factor in college admissions, and in faculty recruitment, underlies many of these diversity-related campus protests. Not all vocal protesters are in favor of increased diversity, however. Critics maintain that admissions and recruitment should be based on academic achievement as reflected in course grades and test scores, and perhaps on extracurricular activities and accomplishments. The most prominent current push-back against the consideration of race and ethnicity in admissions has come from a nonwhite minority group arguing that its members face discrimination in the college admissions process: Asian-Americans.

The Asian Challenge to Affirmative Action

The "bamboo ceiling" critique of current affirmative action policies in undergraduate admissions holds that Asian applicants are held to higher academic standards than others and are directly disadvantaged by consideration given to blacks and Hispanics. Advocates point to an analysis of admissions data from top-tier schools indicating that being Asian carries the equivalent of a 140-point SAT score penalty relative to white applicants, whereas blacks and Hispanics get the equivalent of a 310-point and 130-point SAT score boost, respectively (Espenshade and Radford 2009). Political activist and writer Ron Unz argues that disparities in the number of college-aged Asians in the US population and at top schools show meritocracy in higher education to be a myth (Unz 2012).

Admissions officers at top schools maintain that they do not discriminate against Asian-Americans, that high test scores alone do not satisfy the requirements for admission at top schools, and that holistic admissions processes reward students who are well-rounded (Bugarin 2012). Others point to the fact that relatively fewer Asian-American students are recruited varsity athletes or legacy applicants to explain why white applicants, on the whole, have an advantage over their Asian-American peers (Dhar 2013; Shenk 1991). Some critics suggest that individuals' allegations about discrimination against Asian-Americans are a guise used to advocate for overturning affirmative action policies more broadly and reducing the presence of blacks, Hispanics, and other underrepresented minorities on American college campuses, or that

Asian-American plaintiffs are being manipulated by anti–affirmative-action political actors (Aung 2012; Park 2018). We return to a discussion of the Asian-American legal challenge to race-conscious admissions in Chapter 10 as we take stock of current and imminent debates over campus diversity in light of our own assessments of student attitudes.

Diversity of Ideas

A separate – and emerging – angle of push-back against the priority afforded to racial and ethnic diversity concerns diversity of ideas. The central claim here is that campus cultures have grown increasingly mono-lithic in terms of ideology, and even that a presupposed commitment to demographic diversity contributes to that effect. According to this view, many universities have become liberal bubbles that preclude exposure to a wide range of viewpoints and produce students with a uniform world-view and set of values. John McWhorter, an African-American professor at Columbia University, argues:

The new idea is that even occasionally stubbing your toe on racism renders a university a grievously "unsafe space" and justifies students calling for the ouster of a lecturer who calls for reasoned discussion (Yale) and even of a dean stepping down in shame for an awkwardly worded email (Claremont McKenna). (McWhorter 2015)

Regardless of the impact of increased minority representation at institutions of higher education, McWhorter advocates changes to campus climates to increase viewpoint diversity – including views that challenge identity diversity.[16]

McWhorter is not the only scholar to advance this view. In *The Coddling of the American Mind*, Greg Lukianoff and Jonathan Haidt argue that recent conflicts over diversity and free speech on college campuses have their roots in changes to the ways in which children are raised. "Fearful parenting" and "safetyism," according to the authors, have made it difficult for today's generation of college students to handle ideas they disagree with, making campus climates hostile to free expression with respect to diversity and other contentious issues (Lukainoff and Haidt 2018). Likewise, in their book, *Free Speech on Campus*, Erwin Chemerinsky and Howard Gillman contend that although universities have an obligation to strive for inclusivity, "all ideas and views should

---

[16] For further reading on viewpoint intolerance on college campuses, see Vance (2016) on the intersection of ideology and class and Kipnis (2017) on sexual culture.

be able to be expressed on college campuses, no matter how offensive or how uncomfortable they make people feel" (Chemerinsky and Gillman 2017, p. 19).

Although they do not take a single position on affirmative action, these critiques add another dimension to the campus diversity debate, to which we return in the concluding chapter in light of our experimental results.

Summing Up

We draw a few broad conclusions from this chapter. First, diversity in terms of race/ethnicity, gender, and socioeconomic class on college and university campuses in the United States has been increasing in the past few decades. However, minorities continue to be underrepresented among student and faculty ranks at top schools, women are underrepresented within senior faculty positions, and students from high-income families outnumber those from low- and middle-income families at the most highly ranked institutions. The emergence of controversies about these demographic gaps and other issues of diversity dates back to more than a century ago, and these debates have evolved over time with high-profile court decisions, state and federal legislation, and, most recently, movements led by students and interest groups both for and against affirmative action in admissions and the campus climate for diversity.

Campus diversity debates in the United States are therefore far from resolved. With this context in mind, we now describe the survey experiments we used to explore this issue and gauge what students *actually think* about diversity in undergraduate admissions and faculty recruitment on their campuses.

3

Our Conjoint Experiments

Asking students, or asking anyone, about diversity presents a challenge. Diversity is a hot-button issue, as fraught as any topic on contemporary college campuses. We approach this challenge by deploying a method for conducting survey experiments known as conjoint analysis (or conjoint experiments). This technique is time-tested in marketing research, but it has been adapted and improved more recently by social scientists for identifying the multidimensional preferences underlying individuals' choices. Since selecting undergraduate applicants or recruiting faculty candidates is a "holistic" decision with due consideration to multiple characteristics of applicants and candidates, this method is particularly suitable for our purpose. Conjoint analysis is also an effective way to elicit honest opinions about sensitive issues.

This chapter describes the motivation and rationale behind our approach, as well as the mechanics of how we conducted the conjoint experiments. Once this foundation is set, we proceed in subsequent chapters to present our results. For now, our goal is to establish transparency in our methods. We also make a complete replication package, which includes our deidentified original survey data, all of the computer scripts we wrote to build and analyze the data, and all of our relevant documentation, publicly available at Dataverse: `https://doi.org/10.7910/DVN/KMS5ZY`.

3.1 ESTIMATING PREFERENCES ON DIVERSITY

There is a substantial body of research on the value students place on campus diversity. Some is qualitative, based on case studies, interviews, and focus groups (e.g., Berrey 2015; Warikoo 2016). In quantitative research, the most common approach is to administer surveys and ask students about their support for affirmative action policies to promote diversity, for example (Sax and Arredondo 1999; Smith 1998; Whitla et al. 2003). Increasing concern about divided opinions on campus has also led some universities to administer campus climate surveys, which include questions about diversity and inclusion (e.g., Dartmouth College 2016; Massachusetts Institute of Technology 2010; Napolitano et al. 2014). At the University of California, Los Angeles, for example, an app sends notifications to students' smartphones with survey questions on diversity-related topics (Whitford 2018c). To understand how campus diversity (or any other campus activities, events, or policies) may *change* student attitudes, other researchers have used panel surveys that poll students entering college, then return to the same respondent pool after exposure to campus environments (Bowman 2012; Bowman, Denson, and Park 2016; Denson and Chang 2009; Locks et al. 2008; Park, Denson, and Bowman 2013; Sidanius et al. 2008). Park (2009) deployed this approach to estimate how variation in campus demographics affects changes in student attitudes toward affirmative action in admissions. All these lines of survey research, however, face methodological challenges, which our conjoint experiments can help to address.

ELICITING HONEST OPINIONS. A primary concern with standard approaches is that it is difficult to elicit honest opinions about sensitive topics, such as affirmative action or diversity-related initiatives on campus. For questions about any controversial issue, there is a well-established phenomenon known as "social desirability bias," by which survey participants tend to offer answers they believe are favored by those conducting the research (for reviews, see Krosnick 1999; Krumpal 2013; Nederhof 1985; Richman et al. 1999; Tourangeau and Yan 2007). For example, student participants (and in particular, whites) may be reluctant to express their opposition to affirmative action or other diversity programs, even if they actually oppose them, when campus climate is – or when they *think* campus climate is – in favor of diversity.

This methodological problem would be a particular matter of concern in face-to-face interviews or interviewer-administered surveys (Krumpal 2013). Self-administered online surveys, which have become increasingly common, are known to mitigate socially desirability bias (Kreuter, Presser, and Tourangeau 2008; Kuhn and Vivyan 2018), but survey methodologists have also shown that survey mode itself does not completely solve this problem. A typical example is the misreporting of voter turnout (Holbrook and Krosnick 2010). Self-reported voter turnout rates among survey participants, even when the participants are randomly selected from the population, are substantially higher than the official voter turnout rate. This is in part because voters tend to avoid reporting that they abstained from voting, based on a widespread belief that going to the polls is socially desirable.

Unlike postelection surveys, which usually include a range of questions for multiple purposes, surveys specifically designed to gauge attitudes toward a socially sensitive topic may discourage those who do not want to express their honest opinions from participating altogether, particularly if the invitation to take the survey explicitly states the researchers' objective(s). If they do take the survey, participants may exit when they see questions they do not want to answer, or skip questions they find controversial. These nonresponses would result in a related methodological problem, selection bias. Opinions expressed by a sample of self-selected participants cannot represent the broader opinions of a targeted population, such as the entire community of students on campus. Self-selected, nonrandom samples are problematic in many self-administered online surveys. But if the mechanism of self-selection is directly relevant to the survey's objective, such as measuring students' opinions on diversity, selection bias is aggravated and becomes more difficult to adjust with statistical techniques.

These attitudinal and behavioral reactions to surveys on sensitive topics are increasingly relevant to the current debate over diversity. This is because ideological orientations at universities and colleges are becoming predominantly liberal on many campuses, and views questioning – not necessarily condemning – diversity initiatives could be discouraged by other vocal students (Lee 2017; McWhorter 2015; Quintana 2018a). The controversy over gender diversity that we described in the first chapter is a clear illustration of this point; viewpoints that do not explicitly defend the merits of race-conscious policies on college campuses today can generate severe push-back, and students who hold such attitudes might well be cautious about expressing them.

PREFERENCES UNDERLYING HOLISTIC DECISIONS. A second issue with standard approaches to gauging attitudes toward campus diversity concerns holistic decision-making. Put simply, standard questions used in surveys are typically not suitable for understanding opinions about selecting undergraduate applicants or faculty candidates. Consider, for example, a question asking whether students agree or disagree with their institution's effort to increase the percentage of nonwhite faculty members. Leaving the issues of social desirability bias and selection bias aside, this type of question is problematic because it is about a *particular* individual characteristic – race/ethnicity. All candidates have many other attributes that are relevant in the selection process, such as their research areas, publication records, and teaching credentials. The actual process of granting admission to an undergraduate applicant or giving a job offer to a faculty candidate involves a *holistic* decision, in which applicants and candidates are considered as *multidimensional* individuals with many different and relevant characteristics. Survey questions highlighting just one particular attribute could therefore be misleading.

An analogy is a consumer's choice of an automobile. If the consumer were asked whether she prefers a relatively cheaper or more expensive car, she would most likely choose the cheaper one. But price is only one attribute relevant to a consumer's decision to buy a new car, and preferences with respect to that attribute are inextricably bound up with trade-offs against others. More expensive cars have different features than cheaper ones. Likewise, our primary interest is not whether students absolutely prefer greater diversity on campus. Rather, we seek to determine whether they prioritize it *more* or *less* than other attributes that are relevant to decisions about undergraduate admissions and faculty recruitment, and how those other attributes factor into their preferences.

LIMITATIONS OF OBSERVATIONAL DATA. There are also challenges to inferring priorities for diversity by observing the composition of actual students enrolled or actual faculty members at any institution. This is because such breakdowns are the result of sequential decisions by applicants and universities. In the case of student admissions, for example, there is a pool of *potential* applicants, a subset of which actually submits applications, and a subset of which receives an admissions offer, which might be either accepted or declined. The fact that decisions of both applicants and universities interact to produce campus populations makes it hard to estimate preferences for campus diversity at a given institution based on aggregate data on the student population.

Researchers may have access to individual-level data on actual applicants (e.g., Espenshade and Radford 2009). Multiple regression analysis

using such data to estimate the relevance of various applicant characteristics to the likelihood of admission can be regarded as informative
and scientifically valid, but important obstacles remain. First, some
applicant characteristics are highly correlated, but data for *all* of the relevant characteristics may not be available. In admissions, for example,
applicants' socioeconomic status and race/ethnicity are correlated, but
socioeconomic status is also correlated with legacy status, first-generation
status, status as a recruited varsity athlete, extracurricular activities, and
so on. Complete data on all of these variables are rarely available to
researchers.[1] Second, the observed applicant pool is still the product of
prior decision-making and attrition. If there are few candidates from a
given group with a particular set of attributes, identifying the impacts of
those attributes *separately* for the likelihood of members of that group
receiving an offer will be very difficult. For example, researchers may
be interested in understanding the likelihood that Hispanic women will
receive job offers, but the number of Hispanic women applying for
the jobs may be very small to begin with. In this case, the statistical
power to estimate the relevance of race/ethnicity and gender is inevitably
weak.

OUR APPROACH. To mitigate these problems, we undertook survey
experiments using conjoint analysis, which has been used extensively in
marketing research for many decades as a tool to measure the multidimensional preferences underlying an individual's choices (Agarwal et al.
2015; Green and Srinivasan 1978). Recently, Hainmueller, Hopkins,
and Yamamoto (2014) introduced a new approach of fully randomized
conjoint analysis based on the potential-outcome framework of causal
inference (Splawa-Neyman 1990; Rubin 1974, 2005). Some previous
studies have applied the method of conjoint analysis for campus-related

---

[1] Fundamentally, each individual's race/ethnicity or gender is *causally prior* to many
attributes relevant to admissions. Methodologically, running a regression to estimate the
impact of race/ethnicity or gender on admissions outcomes (or *any* behavioral or attitudinal outcome, for that matter) – after controlling for a range of attributes affected by
race/ethnicity or gender – would introduce the problem of "post-treatment bias" (Rosenbaum 1984; also see Montgomery, Nyhan, and Torres 2018). Even more fundamentally
(and epistemologically), examining the *causal* effect of race/ethnicity or gender of *actual*
individuals is a "fundamentally unidentified question" (Angrist and Pischke 2009). As
Holland (1986, 2003) emphasizes, there is "no causation without manipulation." These
fundamental issues are the basis for our project. We are trying to understand *preferences*
rather than *outcomes* using the profiles of *hypothetical* rather than *actual* applicants and
candidates.

Which applicant do you think should be given priority in undergraduate admissions? Even if you are not entirely sure, please indicate which of the two you would be most likely to choose.

	Applicant 1	Applicant 2
Recruited Varsity Athlete	No	No
State Residence	In-state applicant	In-state applicant
Gender	Man	Woman
High School Type	Public	Parochial
Parents' Education	Parent(s) attended Dartmouth College	Parent(s) attended Dartmouth College
High School Class Rank	60th percentile	80th percentile
SAT Score	2170 (1500 New SAT)	2000 (1410 New SAT)
Annual Family Income in US Dollars	$466,000	$54,000
Extra-Curricular Interest	Outdoor Recreation Club	Outdoor Recreation Club
Race/Ethnicity	Native American	White

If you had to choose between them, which of these two applicants should be given priority to be admitted as an undergraduate student at Dartmouth College?

Applicant 1   Applicant 2

FIGURE 3.1 Screenshot of a conjoint table from the undergraduate admissions experiment

issues (Brown, Swinyard, and Ogle 2003; Sohn and Ju 2010; Wang et al. 2003), but they do not study diversity in undergraduate admissions and faculty recruitment – the subjects of our study.

The core of our studies were survey experiments in which participants chose between pairs of hypothetical applicants for undergraduate admissions, or hypothetical candidates for faculty recruitment, at their universities. Figures 3.1 and 3.2 show screenshots from our admissions

Which candidate do you think should be given priority in faculty recruitment? Even if you are not entirely sure, please indicate which of the two you would be most likely to choose.

	Candidate 1	Candidate 2
Research Record	Excellent	Excellent
Faculty Position Being Considered For	Tenured Professor	Untenured Visiting Instructor
Received Undergraduate Degree From	Columbia University	Dartmouth College
Spouse/Partner is a Current or Potential Faculty Member	Yes	Yes
Gender	Man	Man
Teaching Record	Fair	Good
Race/Ethnicity	White	Black
Department/Program	Biology	Computer Science
Received Ph.D. From	University of Georgia	University of Michigan

If you had to choose between them, which of these two candidates should be given priority to be hired as a new faculty member at Dartmouth College?

Candidate 1	Candidate 2

FIGURE 3.2 Screenshot of a conjoint table from the faculty recruitment experiment

and recruitment experiments, respectively, conducted at the authors' home institution, Dartmouth College – the details of which we describe later in this chapter. Our approach has several important advantages relative to conventional survey questions.

First, our experiments were carefully designed to elicit honest and representative opinions as much as possible. To avoid low response rates caused directly by the objectives of our experiments, our invitations to participate never mentioned diversity or any diversity-related attributes, such as race/ethnicity, gender, or class. They simply asked students (and, in some cases, faculty) to participate in a survey experiment on under-graduate admissions or on faculty recruitment – issues that are important to students and faculty for reasons that encompass far more than diversity concerns. Furthermore, our experiments avoided psychologically priming participants to focus on any particular set of attributes or characteristics when selecting admissions applicants or faculty recruits. Hypothetical individuals presented in the experiments have multiple attributes, only some of which are relevant to diversity. By randomizing the order of the attributes and randomly generating combinations of these attributes,[2] we minimized signaling any particular focus on diversity. Participants could focus on whichever of the attributes included in our experiments they found most salient.

Indeed, for both of these reasons, conjoint experiments are an effective way to mitigate the social desirability bias that plagues traditional survey research on attitudes toward diversity. On the one hand, respondents can rationalize their preferences in terms of a number of non–socially sensitive attributes (e.g., academic or professional achievement) without explicitly violating social norms. Additionally, the conjoint design itself does not single out and signal any specific target of the study (in our case, preferences toward diversity). Horiuchi, Markovich, and Yamamoto (2019) empirically show that the conjoint experimental format reduces social desirability bias in multiple contexts through these mechanisms. Considering that our main interest is, by nature, a socially sensitive topic, these findings give us confidence in our methodological approach.

Second, conjoint analysis is suitable to identify *multidimensional* preferences. Participants were asked to choose which of the two hypothetical individuals presented in the table format should be given priority in undergraduate admissions or faculty recruitment. They were never asked to express their preference for a particular attribute, such as race/ethnicity or gender. In a nutshell, they were asked to make a *holistic* decision, analogous to what admission officers or selection committee members do in the actual processes.

Third, our approach allows us to build estimates incrementally that address important and distinct elements of debates on affirmative action and campus diversity. Our first step establishes whether or not, and by

---

[2] The order of attributes was randomized across individuals, but constant across conjoint tasks for each participant to reduce cognitive strain. See Krosnick and Alwin (1987) and Hainmueller, Hopkins, and Yamamoto (2014) on the merits of randomization to avoid order or priming effects.

how much, an undergraduate applicant or a faculty candidate from an underrepresented group should be given priority over one who is not from such a group when all other relevant attributes (e.g., academic achievement) are held constant. As a next step, by statistically interacting the attributes of hypothetical applicants and candidates with the characteristics of study participants themselves, we can estimate how the marginal effect of shifts in a given attribute differ across groups of participants. Thus, for example, we can estimate whether changing an applicant's race/ethnicity has a different impact on the choices made by white versus black participants, or men versus women, or participants from high-income versus low-income families, or for any other meaningful distinction in our population. These comparisons thus reveal levels of consensus or disagreement on diversity in campus populations. Finally, we can also explore interactions among the attributes of the hypothetical applicants or candidates, which allows us to address how preferences operate when all else is *not* equal. For example, we can assess whether participants react to a jump (or a drop) in SAT scores differently for an Asian applicant versus a white applicant, or for a woman versus a man, and so forth. Subsequent chapters illustrate our results at each of these levels of analysis, but first, we describe in greater detail exactly how we collected our data.

3.2 POPULATIONS AND SAMPLES

Working with faculty colleagues at partner institutions, we conducted survey experiments in 2017 and 2018 on split samples of undergraduate students enrolled at Dartmouth College, the University of California, San Diego (UCSD), the University of North Carolina at Chapel Hill (UNC), and the University of Nevada, Reno (UNR).[3] The dates of the surveys, the number of invitations to complete the surveys that were sent, the number of participants completed, and the response rates for the undergraduate admissions (UA) and faculty recruitment (FR) experiments are shown in Table 3.1.[4]

---

[3] Our faculty partners at these institutions were Marisa Abrajano, Professor of Political Science at UCSD; Timothy Ryan, Associate Professor of Political Science at UNC; Layna Mosely, Professor of Political Science at UNC; and Kevin Carman, Professor of Biology and University Provost at UNR. Each set of survey experiments was approved by the respective institution's IRB.

[4] At UNC, a third of undergraduate students participated in a related survey experiment for different purposes. The figures reported in Table 3.1 exclude these participants. At

TABLE 3.1 *Survey experiments at each institution*

University	Dates	Invitations sent	Completed	Response rate
Dartmouth	1/6/18 – 1/17/18	2,285 (UA) 2,285 (FR)	528 (UA) 528 (FR)	23.1% (UA) 23.1% (FR)
UCSD	1/25/17 – 3/14/17	2,500 (UA) 2,500 (FR)	349 (UA) 307 (FR)	14.0% (UA) 12.3% (FR)
UNC	1/30/17 – 1/12/17	4,184 (UA) 4,185 (FR)	391 (UA) 259 (FR)	9.4% (UA) 6.2% (FR)
UNR	2/15/17 – 3/14/17	8,897 (UA) 8,897 (FR)	705 (UA) 622 (FR)	7.9% (UA) 7.0% (FR)
UNM	12/1/16 – 2/1/17	17,337 (FR)	1,387 (FR)	8.0% (FR)

Note: UA refers to the undergraduate admissions experiment; FR refers to the faculty recruitment experiment. At UNM, we conducted an experiment on faculty recruitment only. These data were not pooled with those from the other four institutions. In Chapter 8, we compare the UNM data with those from UNR in our analysis of student versus faculty preferences.

TABLE 3.2 *Surveys of faculty at UNM and UNR (faculty recruitment)*

University	Dates	Invitations sent	Completed	Response rate
UNR	02/15/17 – 03/14/17	1,086	203	18.7%
UNM	10/11/16 – 10/31/16	3,625	870	24.0%

Note: UNM and UNR were the only institutions at which we administered surveys to faculty.

At a fifth institution, the University of New Mexico (UNM), we surveyed students only on faculty recruitment.[5] Because UNM uses a nonselective process for undergraduate admissions, the rationale behind an admissions experiment did not apply there. Due to certain particularities of UNM, the structure of the attributes included in the conjoint experiment there differed slightly from the other institutions, precluding us from pooling data from UNM into our main analysis.

At UNM and at UNR, we were also able to conduct survey experiments on faculty recruitment with *faculty* participants. This allows

UCSD, 2,500 randomly selected students received an invitation to participate in either of the experiments.

[5] Our faculty partners at UNM were Mala Htun, Professor of Political Science at UNM, and Brittany Ortiz, Deputy Director of Equity and Inclusion, City of Albuquerque.

us to compare student and faculty preferences on that critical element of campus diversity. The results are presented in Chapter 8. The particulars of these experiments are shown in Table 3.2.

Our set of schools is not a representative set of universities and colleges in the United States.[6] Nevertheless, the institutions possess a range of important characteristics. Dartmouth is a small, private, Ivy League institution. The others are large state universities. All of them attract students from across the country, although a large percentage of students at each of the state schools is from the home state. UCSD and UNC are two of the most selective public universities in the country. UNC, UNR, and UNM are the flagship public universities in their respective states.

POPULATIONS. The states themselves, and the corresponding university populations vary substantially, which gives us leverage in understanding how preferences could vary by different groups of students in different demographic contexts. Table 3.3 shows the percentage of the statewide population, and of the student populations, by racial and ethnic groups.[7] In each case, we break down populations according to the five race/ethnicity groups we use in our analysis: Asian, black, Hispanic, non-Hispanic white, and Native American.[8] California is the most demographically diverse, with no group reaching even 40 percent of the state population, about equal proportions of Hispanics and non-Hispanic whites, and an Asian population of about 15 percent. Nevada and New Mexico also have large Hispanic populations. North Carolina has the largest black population at 22 percent, and New Mexico has a relatively large Native American population at 11 percent.[9] New Hampshire, where Dartmouth is located, is overwhelmingly white.

The degree of correlation between the state population and the student population also varies across institutions. Whites are the largest racial or ethnic group at UNC and UNR, and Hispanics are at UNM, roughly in correspondence with their shares of the statewide populations in each case, but Asians are the largest group at UCSD, far above the shares of whites and Hispanics. Blacks and Native Americans are underrepresented

---

[6] We tried to administer our experiments at other institutions, but some administrators demurred to avoid subjecting their students to surveys, and others were reluctant for their university to be identified in reports on the results.

[7] These state demographic data are taken from the US Census, relying on figures as of 2016. University population figures are provided by the institutions.

[8] For the latter category, we combined the census's categories of "American Indian and Alaska Native" and "Native Hawaiian or Pacific Islander."

[9] But recall that our New Mexico data can be incorporated only into some of our analyses.

TABLE 3.3 *State population versus campus student population demographics*

University	Race/ethnicity	(A) State population	(B) Student population	(B) − (A) Difference
Dartmouth	Non-Hispanic white	90.8	50.0	−40.8
	Asian	2.7	15.0	12.3
	Black	1.5	7.0	5.5
	Hispanic	2.9	10.0	7.1
	Native American	0.4	2.0	1.6
	Other	1.7	16.0	14.3
UCSD	Non-Hispanic white	37.7	20.0	−17.7
	Asian	14.8	46.0	31.2
	Black	6.5	2.0	−4.5
	Hispanic	35.0	16.0	−19.0
	Native American	2.2	0.0	−2.2
	Other	3.8	14.0	10.2
UNC	Non-Hispanic white	63.5	61.2	−2.3
	Asian	2.9	13.0	10.1
	Black	22.2	7.8	−14.4
	Hispanic	7.5	7.5	0.0
	Native American	1.7	0.4	−1.3
	Other	2.2	9.9	7.7
UNR	Non-Hispanic white	49.9	57.3	7.4
	Asian	8.7	7.7	−1.0
	Black	9.6	3.3	−6.3
	Hispanic	25.2	19.2	−6.0
	Native American	2.4	0.7	−1.7
	Other	4.2	11.9	7.7
UNM	Non-Hispanic white	38.1	34.0	−4.1
	Asian	1.7	3.7	2.0
	Black	2.5	2.4	−0.1
	Hispanic	44.4	47.2	2.8
	Native American	10.8	5.9	−4.9
	Other	2.5	6.7	4.2

Note: The state demographic data are taken from the US Census, relying on figures as of 2016. "Other" for (A) is "two or more races." The percentage of "Hispanic" for (A) is 100 percent minus the sum of other percentages. University population figures are provided by the institutions.

at each of our public universities relative to their shares of the state population. As a private institution, Dartmouth's student population is tied far less to its home state demographics than those of the other schools in our study.

Gender distributions across states are much more uniform than race/ethnicity distributions. Nationwide, women narrowly outnumber men, 51 percent to 49 percent, and in the states examined here, the splits run between that ratio and fifty-fifty. At three of our universities, women outnumber men among students (whereas at UCSD and Dartmouth, a bare majority are men). By contrast, at both schools where we recruited faculty to our experiments, men outnumber women among the faculty population – 58 percent to 42 percent at UNR and 53 percent to 47 percent at UNM. This overrepresentation of men among faculty is roughly equivalent to the national average of 55 percent (Snyder, de Brey, and Dillow 2016).

SAMPLES. Figure 3.3 compares the demographics of the samples that participated in our survey experiments with the overall populations of students at each university (and faculty at UNR and UNM). The circle dots represent the percentages among all students or faculty members in the population, whereas the triangle dots represent the percentages among our survey respondents (either students or faculty members). When these dots are closer to each other, our sample demographics are more similar to population demographics. By and large, the racial/ethnic breakdown of our participant samples corresponds well to the campus populations. The most notable exceptions pertain to proportions of non-Hispanic whites, who are overrepresented in the samples, and Hispanics, who are underrepresented. The imbalance is most pronounced at UNM, where the Hispanic population is largest. The apparent discrepancy, however, is due at least in part to a difference in how racial/ethnic identity is tallied in the universities' population statistics as compared to our survey.[10] In terms of gender, the imbalance is small, but at all institutions, women are overrepresented and men are underrepresented. Note that we were not able to obtain population statistics on students and faculty who identify their gender as nonbinary. On the whole, our participant samples track their corresponding university populations closely.[11]

[10] According to UNM's official enrollment report, for example, individuals may self-identify as Hispanic or not Hispanic, and also as one or more races, but "anyone who selects Hispanic is reported as Hispanic regardless of any other races selected" (Office of Institutional Analytics 2017). By contrast, our survey instrument asked participants about the racial/ethnic category with which they *most* identify. University population statistics may thus overcount Hispanics relative to our survey responses.
[11] Still, in a related study, we replicated our analyses with poststratified sampling weights via entropy balancing (Hainmueller 2012) to correct for any discrepancies between observable characteristics in the samples and populations (Brown et al. 2017). The

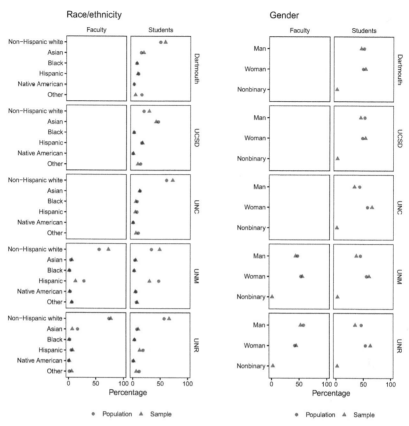

FIGURE 3.3 Comparison of student population versus student sample

3.3 MECHANICS AND SUBSTANCE OF THE CONJOINT EXPERIMENTS

At each institution, the admissions and recruitment experiments were conducted simultaneously to prevent any sequencing or spillover effects, and we divided potential participants randomly into groups receiving invitations to only one of these two experiments. In other words, we administered split-sample survey experiments, in which the participant

substantive results were not affected. In the analyses presented in this book, we do not use the poststratified weights because, having pooled data across four universities, we have no clearly defined populations to serve as references. Furthermore, some scholars question the validity of using weights in survey experiments, and no standard operating procedure exists for how to use weights in this context (Franco et al. 2017).

pools should not differ between the groups systematically. We fielded the experiments in accord with each partner institution's academic calendar to try to minimize the imposition on students (e.g., coincidence with vacation or exam periods). After obtaining approval from their ethics committee, our faculty partners at each participating university sent e-mail invitations to students (and faculty in some cases) at their respective schools.

Each survey experiment contained four parts, the second and third of which warrant the closest attention: first, an introduction to the study and an option allowing each participant to choose whether or not to participate in our survey; second, the conjoint experiment exercises; third, a short conventional survey with direct questions on participants' demographics and attitudes; and fourth, an invitation to write comments on the survey if the participants desired.

In the conjoint experiment, each participant was shown pairs of hypothetical admissions applicants or faculty candidates. Each applicant (or candidate) is a composite profile consisting of a bundle of attributes, which are described in a tabular format, with the applicants' (candidates') characteristics juxtaposed. The heart of the exercise is the participant's choice of which applicant (candidate) should be given priority for admission to (for hire at) the university. The exercise is repeated ten times, with the participants making a separate binary choice on each of ten distinct pairs of hypothetical applicants (hypothetical faculty candidates). This format, with pairs of applicants (candidates) shown side by side in a table (see Figure 3.1 or Figure 3.2) and the participant selecting the more favored of the two, is known as *paired conjoint with forced choice*.

Alternative formats include conjoint experiments that provide narrative descriptions of applicants or candidates, that present just one candidate at a time, or that ask participants to rate pairs of applicants or candidates with a separate up-or-down vote (or with a rating scale) for each one. We elected to conduct our experiments using paired conjoint with forced choice to maximize our external validity – that is, whether our participants' decisions reflect how they would act in the real world (if they were members of admissions or recruitment committees) and whether the way we set up our experiment affects our ability to approximate real-world behavior. Hainmueller, Hangartner, and Yamamoto (2015) show that paired choice formats are reflective of real-world collective decisions. Moreover, the forced choice format we employ best approximates university admissions and faculty recruitment

TABLE 3.4 *Attributes and levels comparison table, 1*

Undergraduate admissions	Faculty recruitment
Demographics	*Demographics*
Race/ethnicity	Race/ethnicity
*White	*White
Asian	Asian
Black	Black
Hispanic	Hispanic
Native American	Native American
Gender	Gender
*Man	*Man
Woman	Woman
Nonbinary	Nonbinary
Socioeconomic class	*Academic credentials*
Family income	PhD
$21,000	*Yale University
*$54,000	Oxford University
$112,000	University of Georgia
$157,000	University of Michigan
$466,000	
Parents' education	Undergraduate degree
*Nonlegacy	*Home institution
First-generation	Rival institution
Legacy	Columbia University
	University of California, Berkeley
	University of Mississippi
High school type	
*Public	
Parochial	
Private	

Note: * indicates the baseline category for each attribute.

choices, for which there are hard ceilings limiting the number of applicants who can be accepted, and in which the acceptance of any applicant generally requires rejection of others.

Attributes and Levels

We refer to each hypothetical applicant or candidate as a profile. Each profile is a bundle of attributes, and one of multiple levels is displayed for each attribute in each profile. What does this mean in practice? Tables 3.4 and 3.5 illustrate the full lists of attributes and levels for each of our

TABLE 3.5 *Attributes and levels comparison table, 2*

Undergraduate admissions	Faculty recruitment
Academic achievement	*Professional achievement*
SAT Score	**Research record**
*25th percentile	*Fair
50th percentile	Good
75th percentile	Excellent
98th percentile or higher	
High school class rank	**Teaching record**
*60th percentile	*Fair
80th percentile	Good
95th percentile	Excellent
99th percentile	
Institutional considerations	*Institutional considerations*
State residence	**Position**
*In-state applicant	*Untenured visiting instructor
Out-of-state applicant	Tenure-track assistant professor
	Tenured professor
Recruited athlete	**Spouse/partner hire**
*No	*No
Yes	Yes
Extracurricular interest	**Department/program**
*Intramural sports	*Economics
Outdoor recreation club	Biology
Performing arts	Computer Science
Student government	Environmental Studies
Student newspaper	English
	Gender Studies
	Journalism
	Political Science
	Psychology

Note: * indicates the baseline category for each attribute.

two experiments. In the tables, the attributes are grouped conceptually.[12] Demographics are at the center of campus diversity debates, and for both

[12] The names of the attributes and levels used in our experiments are abbreviated in these tables and all of the figures in this book. For the original attribute wording, please refer to the screenshots in Figures 3.1 and 3.2. We note that for the attribute on parents' education, the levels did not use the terms "legacy" or "first-generation" but instead specified whether the applicant's parent(s) attended college, attended the home institution, or did not attend college.

admissions applicants and faculty candidates, we included race/ethnicity and gender attributes, each of which was randomly assigned a specific level (so, for example, Hispanic for race/ethnicity) for each profile.

In admissions, an applicant's socioeconomic status is salient information, so in the admissions – but not the faculty recruitment – experiment, we included attributes that reflect wealth and class status, including family income, whether the applicant's parents attended college (and whether they attended the institutions under study), and what kind of high school the applicant attended. We used US census data to assign levels at the 20th, 50th, 80th, 90th, and 99th percentiles of family income nationwide.

Faculty candidates generally have longer academic records than do applicants for admission, so we included information on academic pedigree in faculty candidates' profiles with attributes reflecting the institutions from which they received their doctoral and undergraduate degrees. For the PhD, our levels were an elite private university (Yale), an elite foreign institution (Oxford), an elite public school (University of Michigan), and a slightly less prestigious public institution (University of Georgia). For the undergraduate degree, we decided to test participants' institutional loyalties, assigning the home university as one of the levels at each school (so, for example, participants at UCSD saw faculty candidates who had undergraduate degrees from UCSD, participants at Dartmouth saw candidates from Dartmouth, and so on). To liven up the experience and also take the temperature of participants' passion for their alma maters, we also included a regional rival school. For UCSD, the rival was the University of California, Los Angeles; for UNR, it was the University of Nevada, Las Vegas; for UNC, the rival was Duke University (naturally); and for Dartmouth, the rival was Harvard. In parallel to the graduate degrees, we also included a prestigious private (Columbia), a prestigious public (UC, Berkeley), and a less prestigious public (University of Mississippi).

We also included attributes that reflected directly on academic achievement. In the admissions experiment, these consisted of both standardized test scores and high school class rank. With respect to test scores, in order to maintain comparability across the institutions at which we conducted the experiment, we obtained information from each school that included the combined SAT scores at the 25th and 75th percentiles among enrolled students.[13] For the levels of the SAT score attribute, we then assigned

---

[13] We used combined scores from the "old" SAT exam, which range from 600 to 2400. Beginning in March 2016, the exam changed so that scores could range from 400 to

values at the 25th percentile, the median (or, specifically, the 25th plus the 75th divided by two), the 75th percentile, and as an extraordinarily high value, at the 75th percentile + 1.5 × Interquartile range (IQR). At schools for which the 75th percentile + 1.5 × IQR would exceed the highest possible SAT score (UCSD and UNC), we simply substituted a perfect score (2400) for the high end value.

For faculty candidates, we included attributes that reflected records for both research and teaching. The levels we assigned describe candidates' records in the most general terms: fair, good, and excellent. We did not include "poor" on the grounds that candidates with poor records would likely not be viable at any of these schools. We avoided more specificity within these levels, in part because the markers of accomplishment can vary so much across the various disciplines embraced within universities, and in part because of legitimate disagreements over how to measure achievement. Within the realm of research and scholarship, for example, the relative value of publishing books, refereed journal articles, or conference proceedings varies enormously across fields (and even within fields), as do the salience of external research grants, consulting contracts, gallery exhibitions and public performances, providing expert testimony, and so on. Regarding disagreement over students' conceptions of achievement, student surveys are used at most universities to measure teaching effectiveness, but responses have been shown to be subject to bias by the race/ethnicity (Merritt 2008) and gender (MacNell, Driscoll, and Hunt 2015; Stark, Ottoboni, and Boring 2016) of the instructor, and by the instructor's grading leniency (Griffin 2004). We therefore relied upon each participant's own conception of quality performance in research and teaching.

Finally, the profiles were rounded out by attributes that reflected other characteristics that are often central to admissions and recruitment decisions. In admissions, one of these included whether the applicant was an in-state or out-of-state resident. At the four institutions at which we conducted the admissions experiments, demand for undergraduate slots outstrips supply, and at the three public institutions (UCSD, UNC, and UNR), applicants' state residency status is an important factor. Residency can intersect with political and state budgetary issues insofar as

---

1600. Nearly all student participants in our survey experiments would have taken the SAT before these changes, so we reasoned that they would be most familiar with scores out of 2400. The only exception is the Dartmouth experiments administered in January 2018. Since first-year students (Class of 2021) took the new SAT, we showed both old and new scores in the conjoint tasks – for example, "2000 (1410 New SAT)" for the 25th percentile. At all other institutions, only old SAT scores were presented.

out-of-state students pay higher tuition costs than do in-state students – a consideration that may tempt university administrators facing budget constraints to favor out-of-state applicants, even in tension with their commitment to home state residents (Saul 2016). This is a less relevant factor of consideration at Dartmouth, but to make a fully comparable design and to pool data across institutions, we kept the residency status attribute.

We also included an attribute to indicate whether an applicant was being recruited for varsity intercollegiate athletics. College sports are a source of passion and alumni loyalty at many institutions, but their compatibility with the academic mission of universities is controversial (Oppenheimer 2015; Vedder 2015). We wanted to know whether students regard athletics recruitment favorably or unfavorably. Finally, because extracurricular involvement is an important aspect of applicants' admissions dossiers at most selective universities, we included an attribute that reflected participation in a range of other potential interests prominent on many college campuses, including student newspaper, student government, performing arts, outdoor clubs, and intramural sports.

In the faculty recruitment experiment, we included attributes to reflect both the rank and the academic department or program to which the prospective faculty member would be appointed, as well as whether the candidate's spouse or partner is already on the school's faculty (or being considered for an appointment). All of these are central issues in faculty recruitment and potentially salient to students. The increasing tendency of universities to rely on contingent, non–tenure-track faculty for teaching has been widely noted and frequently decried (American Association of University Professors 1993; Fruscione 2014). While acknowledging that in the real world, faculty candidates of different ranks would not necessarily be pitted against one another for the same faculty slot, this limitation is more salient to faculty and administrators involved in search processes than to students, and we opted to include this attribute to round out the faculty profiles. Likewise, the attribute reflecting academic department allowed participants to express preferences that reflected their intellectual interests or their sense of where their universities ought to be directing resources, despite the limited plausibility of choosing between candidates from two different departments. Finally, partner hires present institutional challenges. Finding or creating a slot for a partner is often critical for attracting potential new faculty members or for the retention of valued faculty. But any such hire comes at the potential cost of crowding out other recruits, and partner hires may entail compromises on quality if a full pool of candidates is not considered. These potential trade-offs are staples of recruitment deliberations among faculty, and we were interested in whether the issue would resonate among our student (and faculty at UNM and UNR) participants.

Figures 3.1 and 3.2 presented earlier illustrate the kind of binary choices our participants confronted. Each figure displays a pair of profiles, consisting of ten attributes in the admissions experiment and nine for the recruitment experiment.[14] Above each conjoint table, the following sentences were inserted: "Which [applicant/candidate] do you think should be given priority in [undergraduate admissions/faculty recruitment]? Even if you are not entirely sure, please indicate which of the two you would be most likely to choose." Below the table, we asked the following question: "If you had to choose between them, which of these two [applicants/candidates] should be given priority to be [admitted as an undergraduate student/hired as a new faculty member] at [home institution]?" Each participant then chose either "Applicant 1" or "Applicant 2" in the admissions experiment, or "Candidate 1" or "Candidate 2" in the recruitment experiment. This exercise was repeated ten times.

On most attributes, the levels that appeared in the conjoint tables were uniformly distributed across possible options. For example, a given applicant was equally likely to be an in-state or out-of-state resident, equally likely to have each possible SAT score, family income level, racial/ethnic identity, or extracurricular interest, and so forth. The only exception was gender, on which we assigned a nonuniform distribution of levels in order to prevent the overall set of choices participants faced from appearing implausible. The gender distribution we employed – 45 percent men, 45 percent women, and 10 percent nonbinary – far overrepresents nonbinary relative to the population shares that identify as such in regular surveys (Cummings 2017). Indeed, the share of our own participants who identified as nonbinary in our studies was never more than 2.2 percent

---

[14] The composite applicants and faculty candidates in our experiments were thoroughly multidimensional and, in that sense, the choices our participants confronted were appropriately holistic. One might be concerned that the number of attributes and levels at play would impose too heavy a cognitive burden for meaningful choices, undermining our ability to estimate participant attitudes (Iyengar 2011). But fully randomized conjoint decision experiments do not require participants to have fully developed preferences with respect to all attributes, and recent research demonstrates that that AMCE estimates are robust to the masking-satisficing trade-off even with far larger numbers of attributes than we used (Bansak et al. 2018).

at any of the universities in this study. We selected the 10 percent figure, however, in order to balance two competing demands. We needed the nonbinary level for gender to appear frequently enough to provide statistical leverage on participants' attitudes toward the option, but we did not want it to appear so frequently – and so implausibly relative to its preponderance in the population – that it would prime participants to focus unduly on that attribute. We reasoned that including a nonbinary applicant (or candidate) in one of ten profiles would provide analytical leverage without sacrificing plausibility.

From the thousands of choices participants made between applicant or candidate pairs, we estimated the Average Marginal Component Effects or AMCEs associated with each level on each attribute (Hainmueller, Hopkins, and Yamamoto 2014).[15] These AMCEs tells us how much a participant would be more (or less) likely to choose an applicant or candidate with a particular characteristic (e.g., black for race/ethnicity), compared with a counterfactual scenario under which that attribute was set at a baseline level (e.g., white), given all possible combinations of attribute-levels. We discuss these effects further in the next chapter.

Questions about Respondents

Respondents who completed the set of conjoint tasks were then presented with a set of conventional survey questions that allow us to break participants out into groups based on their demographic, attitudinal, and other characteristics, and to compare preferences among these groups. Specifically, we asked participants to report their expected year of graduation, their areas of academic interest, their areas of extracurricular interest, their combined SAT score, their high school class rank percentile, their gender identity, their racial/ethnic identity, their political partisanship, whether their parent(s) attended college (and if so, whether they attended the home institution), and their family's household income.

To assess participants' attitudes on affirmative action, and race more generally, we also included a question on whether participants favor any consideration of race in the college admissions (or faculty recruitment) process, as well as a battery of questions widely used to construct an index of "racial resentment" (Kinder and Sanders 1996). These questions

---

[15] We used the R package cjoint developed by Strezhnev et al. (2017).

have long pedigrees in US public opinion research, and we included them to facilitate comparison and benchmarking of our data with that from other studies. We describe the responses to them, and present analyses that break out participants according to their attitudes toward race and affirmative action, in Chapter 6.

4

What Students Think: Results across All Students

This chapter presents the results from the full set of student participants in our undergraduate admissions and faculty recruitment experiments at Dartmouth, UCSD, UNC, and UNR. We seek to illustrate how our survey experiments reflect the preferences of students overall, across the full range of attributes on which they were surveyed. Subsequent chapters will break out participants by different groups of students – men and women, white and black and Hispanic and Asian, high-income and low-income, etc. – and compare their responses. There, we focus on groups of students' preferences with respect to the most contentious dimensions of campus diversity only: race/ethnicity, gender, and (for admissions) socioeconomic class status.

As introduced in the previous chapter, we present the results from our experiments in terms of the average marginal component effects, or AMCEs, associated with each level of each attribute, relative to a baseline level (Hainmueller, Hopkins, and Yamamoto 2014). The AMCEs tell us how much more or less likely a participant is to choose a hypothetical candidate (whether for admission or for recruitment) when a particular attribute level is presented, compared to a baseline category. For example, if the attribute under consideration is gender, the levels are "man," "woman," and "nonbinary." If we use "man" as our baseline, then the AMCE for "woman" tells us how much more (if positive) or less (if negative) likely an admissions applicant is to be chosen if her gender is "woman" rather than "man," holding all other factors equal. Likewise, the AMCE for "nonbinary" tells us how much more or less likely a nonbinary applicant is to be chosen than a man. If the attribute under consideration is race/ethnicity, the levels are "white," "Asian,"

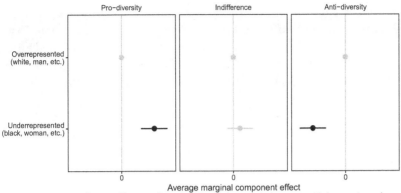

FIGURE 4.1 Hypothetical AMCEs

"black," "Hispanic," and "Native American." If we use "white" as our baseline, the AMCEs for "Asian," "black," "Hispanic," and "Native American" tell us how much more or less likely a faculty candidate from each group is to be chosen relative to a white candidate. Generally, we use the most commonly observed level in the real world as our baseline.

We rely mainly on "airplane" plots to illustrate the results of our statistical analyses graphically, avoiding tables of numerical results. A vertical "zero line" runs through each airplane plot and, for each attribute, represents the baseline against which other levels are compared. AMCE estimates are represented as dots, with a dot to the right side of the zero line indicating a greater likelihood of selection of that particular attribute level, relative to the baseline, and a dot to the left side indicating a lower likelihood. Horizontal lines intersecting the dots (the "wings" of the airplanes) show the 95 percent confidence interval for each estimate. If the wings intersect the zero line, we cannot say with more than 95 percent confidence that the estimated effect is discernible from zero. If the wings are clear of the zero line, our confidence is above 95 percent – a standard threshold in the social sciences.

Figure 4.1 provides an example based on hypothetical data only. If we are considering race/ethnicity, the baseline would be "white." Likewise, if we are considering gender, it would be "man." This comparison category is indicated by a gray dot on the zero line. We are interested in estimating preferences for underrepresented groups relative to our baselines – for example, blacks relative to whites, women relative to men.

In the left panel of this chart, the estimate for our group of interest is positive, and the confidence interval is well clear of the zero line. This indicates that applicants or candidates from the underrepresented group are *more* likely than those from the baseline group to be selected. In the middle panel, the point estimate is slightly positive but the confidence interval spans the zero line, so we cannot infer that there is any difference in preferences for applicants/candidates from the underrepresented group relative to the baseline group. In the right panel, the estimate is negative and statistically significant, indicating that an applicant or candidate from the underrepresented group is *less* likely to be selected than one from the baseline group. In this example, we color the statistically significant estimates black to highlight those results.[1]

4.1 PREFERENCES ON ADMISSIONS

We now turn to the actual results, based on the data we collected in our experiments. Figure 4.2 shows the results from the undergraduate admissions experiments. The first two attributes are essential to demographic diversity considerations: race/ethnicity and gender. Next are the three attributes that reflect the applicant's socioeconomic class background: family income, parents' education, and the type of high school attended. Then come two key reflections of the applicant's academic achievement: their SAT score percentile rank, and their high school class rank. Finally, at the bottom is a cluster of attributes that reflect other institutional considerations often taken into account in admissions: whether the applicant resides in-state or out-of-state, whether the applicant is a recruited varsity athlete or not, and the applicant's extracurricular interests.

The first thing to note from the figure is that, across the full range of participants, applicants from all nonwhite groups are preferred to white applicants. With "white" as the baseline race/ethnicity category, the AMCEs for all nonwhite categories of applicants are positive and statistically significant. Shifting an applicant from white to Asian increases the likelihood that that candidate is selected by 4 percentage points.

---

[1] For most of the comparisons, a positive estimate indicates a preference *for* diversity – that is, in favor of an underrepresented minority group relative to a traditionally advantaged group. The exceptions would be preferences for applicants from above-median-income households (baseline = the median income), or for legacy applicants (baseline = non-legacy, non–first-generation applicants).

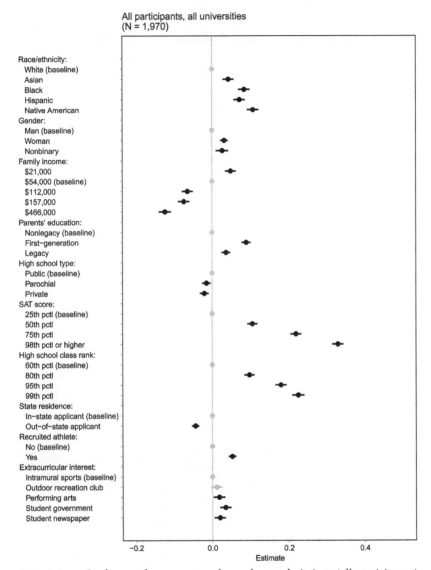

FIGURE 4.2 Student preferences on undergraduate admissions (all participants)

Shifting from white to black increases the likelihood of selection by 8 percentage points, to Hispanic by 7 percentage points, and to Native American by 11 percentage points. These results indicate overall support among our student participants for considering race/ethnicity in university admissions.

The estimates on the gender attribute indicate that women and nonbinary applicants are also preferred to men. This is somewhat surprising insofar as women, at least, outnumber men in the student populations at all the universities surveyed – at UNC, for example, women comprise fully 58 percent of the undergraduate population. Yet the predominance of women in university student populations is a relatively new phenomenon, and there is still reason to regard gender nonbinary applicants as a disadvantaged group (Lannon 2015). At any rate, shifting an applicant's gender status from the baseline of man to woman increases the applicant's likelihood of selection by 3 percentage points, and shifting to gender nonbinary increases it by 3 percentage points, with both estimates reaching statistical significance.

The next three sets of estimates highlight the effects of an applicant's socioeconomic class background. First is family income. We set the baseline at the national median of $54,000. Here, relative to the baseline, an applicant from a household at the 20th percentile family income, $21,000, is 5 percentage points more likely to be chosen. Applicants further up the income scale are progressively less likely to be selected. Moving from the median to $112,000 (80th percentile) drops the likelihood of selection by 6 percentage points, to $157,000 (90th percentile) by 7 percentage points, and all the way to $466,000 (the top 1 percent) by 12 percentage points. Altogether, moving from the lowest to highest income level diminishes the odds of selection by 17 percentage points.

Next is our attribute that characterizes the academic background of an applicant's parents. Here, the baseline level indicates that an applicant's parents attended colleges other than the university at which the survey was being conducted. The alternative levels are (i) neither parent attended college, such that the applicant would be a first-generation college student, or (ii) a parent attended the university at which the survey is conducted, such that the applicant would have legacy status. The former would be an indication of disadvantaged class status and the latter a potential indication of privilege. It is interesting that, relative to the baseline, both alternatives produce measurable *positive* preferences for applicants. Moving from the baseline to first-generation status increases prospects for selection by 9 percentage points. Moving to legacy status produces a smaller, 4-percentage-point bump. Both effects reach statistical significance.

The last attribute reflecting the socioeconomic class of the applicant is high school type. The baseline value is public high school, with the assumption that more socioeconomically disadvantaged applicants are more likely to attend public schools. In this case, the marginal effects of shifting to either a parochial (religious) high school or an unspecified type of private school are negative but small – 1 and 2 percentage points, respectively. On the whole, participants favor applicants from public schools slightly, but high school type appears to have been a less salient marker of social class than income or parents' educational status.

The next two clusters of estimates illustrate preferences with respect to our two primary measures of academic achievement: an applicant's combined SAT score and high school class rank percentile. The sizes of these effects are much larger than those for any other attributes. Shifting an applicant's combined SAT score from the 25th percentile (baseline) among students enrolled at that university to the median SAT score increases the applicant's likelihood of selection by 11 percentage points; moving from the median to the 75th percentile increases likelihood by 22 percentage points; and shifting further to a score that would put the student at the top of the school's distribution increases the likelihood of selection by 33 percentage points.[2]

The effect of high school class rank is also formidable. Moving from our baseline level of the 60th percentile to the 80th percentile increases the chances of selection by 10 percentage points, to the 95th percentile by 18 percentage points, and to the 99th percentile by 22 percentage points. We note the smaller influence of high school class rank on participants' preferences relative to SAT score. In the next chapter, when we break out responses by participants' race/ethnicity and socioeconomic status, we will explore this difference further. For now, however, the central message is that concrete measures of academic achievement, both in standardized testing and in the classroom, are by far the most powerful factors driving preferences for the admission of a hypothetical applicant among our full set of participants.

The last cluster of attributes in Figure 4.2 reflects additional characteristics that flesh out the profile of each applicant in the juxtaposed conjoint tables, and also touch upon considerations salient to admissions at many schools. The first is whether the applicant resides in-state or out-of-state.

---

[2] Recall that we normalized the SAT scores of hypothetical applicants according to the distribution of SAT scores among students enrolled at each university. We defined "top of the distribution" as 75th percentile + 1.5 × Inter-quartile range (IQR). If, for a given institution, that value exceeded the possible range of SAT scores, we assigned the maximum SAT score (2400) to "top of the distribution" applicants.

Our participants disfavor out-of-state applicants by 4 percentage points over in-state applicants.[3]

The next attribute indicates whether the applicant is a recruited varsity athlete. The estimate here shows that, on the whole, varsity status increases an applicant's chances of selection by 5 percentage points. On the whole, student participants do not appear to object to admissions preferences for athletes. Finally, on extracurriculars, relative to a baseline category (intramural sports), all are regarded positively, but the effects are small, ranging from 1 to 3 percentage points. The estimate for outdoor recreation club fails to reach statistical significance.

4.2 PREFERENCES ON FACULTY RECRUITMENT

Figure 4.3 shows the results from the faculty recruitment experiment. As in the admissions figure, the first two attributes are demographic: race/ethnicity and gender. Next are two attributes that reflect professional achievement: research record and teaching record. Below those are two more attributes that reflect on academic credentials: the institutions from which the candidate earned a PhD and an undergraduate degree. At the bottom are clustered a group of attributes that reflect other institutional considerations relevant to recruitment: the faculty rank for which the candidate would be recruited, whether the candidate's spouse or partner is a current or potential faculty member at the institution, and the academic department or program the candidate would join.

The results with regard to race/ethnicity are strikingly consistent with those from the undergraduate admissions experiment. A faculty candidate from every nonwhites category is favored relative to a white candidate. Shifting the candidate's race/ethnicity from white to Asian increases the likelihood of selection by 6 percentage points; from white to black by 10 percentage points; from white to Hispanic by 9 percentage points; and from white to Native American by 11 percentage points. The sizes of the estimates map closely onto those for undergraduate applicants, but are just slightly larger for faculty candidates, perhaps reflecting the fact that nonwhites are underrepresented in the faculty ranks more markedly than among students at all four institutions.

---

[3] Three of the four institutions included in this analysis are state universities, and at each, the preference for out-of-state applicants is negative and significant. At the one private college, Dartmouth, the preference is not discernible from zero. We report the differences across institutions in Section 4.3.

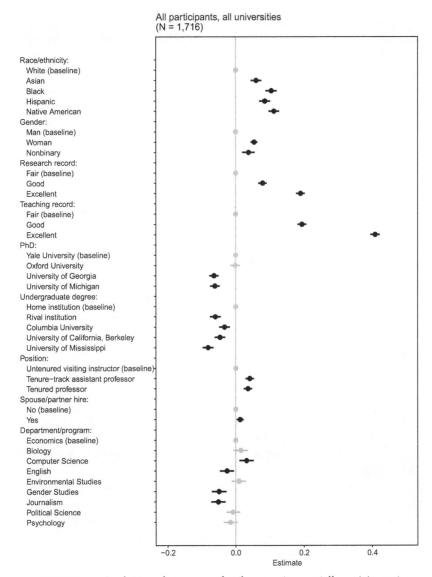

All participants, all universities
(N = 1,716)

FIGURE 4.3 Student preferences on faculty recruitment (all participants)

Preferences with regard to gender also correspond closely to those in the admissions experiment. Shifting a faculty candidate's gender from man to woman yields a 5-percentage-point increase in the candidate's likelihood of selection. Shifting from a man to a gender nonbinary candidate increases the likelihood by 4 percentage points. These effects are statistically discernible. The measurable preference for women is consistent with the preference to remedy their underrepresentation among university faculty. We lack institution-level data to determine whether gender nonbinary persons are also systematically underrepresented among faculty.

Also similar to the admissions experiment, our attributes measuring professional scholarly achievement produce by far the largest impact on likelihood of selection in faculty recruitment. Shifting from a "fair" (baseline) to a "good" research record increases the likelihood of selection by 8 percentage points, and to an "excellent" research record by 19 percentage points. Participants value candidates' teaching records even more, with a jump of 19 percentage points or 41 percentage points for corresponding improvements from fair to good, or from fair to excellent. These results indicate that our student participants' top priorities in faculty recruitment are professional achievement – first, teaching excellence, then research.

The next cluster of attributes reflects on academic credentials – the institutions from which a faculty candidate earned doctoral and undergraduate degrees. For a candidate's PhD, Yale (baseline) and Oxford degrees are statistically indiscernible, whereas relative to Yale, a doctorate from the University of Michigan or the University of Georgia decreases the candidate's likelihood of selection by 6 percentage points. With respect to undergraduate degrees, our participants are institutional loyalists. Their strongest preferences go to alumni from the home institution. By comparison, they disfavor rival school, Columbia, UC Berkeley, and University of Mississippi graduates by 6, 3, 5, and 8 percentage points, respectively.

The last cluster of attributes corresponds to other institutional considerations that frequently enter into recruitment decisions. With respect to faculty rank, students prefer a tenure-track assistant professor or a tenured professor by 4 percentage points each, compared to an untenured visiting instructor. We also included an attribute that distinguished candidates whose spouse or partner is already a member of the home institution's faculty from candidates for which this does not apply (with the latter serving as the baseline category). The move from nonpartner to partner status boosts the likelihood of being selected by just over 1 percentage point – a small but statistically significant effect.

Our final attribute is the faculty candidate's academic department or program. In the interest of statistical leverage, we could not include a level to correspond to every discipline. We selected a set of programs that are common across universities, popular among students, and reflect the range of the arts and sciences, including the humanities (English, journalism), sciences (biology, computer science), social sciences (political science, economics, psychology), and interdisciplinary programs (environmental studies, gender studies). For the purposes of Figure 4.3, we choose as our default category economics, which happens to be the most popular concentration at the authors' home institution. Some of our alternatives (biology, environmental studies, political science, psychology) are statistically indiscernible from economics, whereas computer science is favored by 3 percentage points, and English, gender studies, and journalism are disfavored, by 3, 5, and 5 percentage points, respectively.

4.3   DIFFERENCES ACROSS INSTITUTIONS AND COHORTS

In the chapters that follow, we break out responses by various groups, comparing preferences between, for example, men and women, whites and nonwhites, and Democrats and Republicans. Before going down that path, however, we want to address two comparisons that do not figure into those results – comparisons across institutions and across student cohorts. The analyses in the next few chapters draw on responses from participants across four universities, and across all class years. Pooling the data provides statistical leverage, but if preferences are systematically different at, say, UCSD versus Dartmouth, or among first-year students versus seniors, then pooling the data could obscure as much as it reveals. Indeed, there are reasons that attitudes could differ. The demographic composition of the schools varies, as we saw in Chapter 3. If attitudes are driven by the demographic mix at a given campus, then that effect would be shrouded by pooling the data across schools. Alternatively, if students' attitudes change systematically from exposure to campus culture, we could miss this by pooling across class years. When we test for these effects *in the choices participants made in our conjoint experiments*, however, we find systematic differences neither across universities nor by class cohort.[4]

---

[4] Note the emphasis here on preferences as expressed in the conjoint experiments. We will distinguish below between these and the attitudes expressed in the respondent-level survey questions we asked after the conjoint task. But our primary focus here is on the experiments, as it is throughout the book.

Consider the cross-university comparison first. Figure 4.4 shows the AMCEs from the undergraduate admissions experiments at each of the four universities separately. The most striking pattern is the consistency of attitudes. On race/ethnicity, for example, the estimates are positive and significant for every nonwhite group relative to whites at every university. On gender, at every university, the estimates for women relative to men are positive and significant, and for nonbinary relative to men they are all positive (falling short of significance at UCSD and UNR). On family income, the patterns are virtually identical, with low-income applicants favored and diminishing preferences as family income grows (with two exceptions that are barely insignificant at the 0.05 level). Similarly, first-generation applicants are always strongly favored, and the estimates for legacies are always positive (and significant everywhere except at UCSD). High school type has only weak effects across institutions. SAT scores and high school class rank have the strongest influence on preferences at every school. Varsity athletes are favored everywhere, and to about the same degree. Out-of-state applicants are disfavored as well, except at Dartmouth, the one private school, where state residency does not affect preferences. Even extracurricular interests show similar patterns across schools.

The same consistency of preferences across institutions that we observe in the admissions experiments also characterizes the experiments on faculty recruitment. In the interest of space, we make the corresponding airplane plots available as part of our replication package at Dataverse, but as with admissions, the direction and significance of almost every estimate – and all of those associated with diversity – are the same across all four schools.

Across student year cohorts, the results are even more uniform. This (null) result is, to us, more striking than the similarities across universities because of evidence from other scholarship suggesting that socialization on campus affects student attitudes on diversity-related issues (Mendelberg, McCabe, and Thal 2017; Sidanius et al. 2008). The implication of such findings is that as students spend more time on college campuses or within campus communities, their preferences with regard to diversity change. Yet, when we test to see whether student preferences differ between first-year and second-year students, and so forth, we find virtually no differences. Figure 4.5 shows the AMCE estimates for students in their first, second, third, and fourth years, pooled across institutions. As with the cross-school comparisons, the patterns are virtually identical. And as with the cross-school comparisons, the patterns for

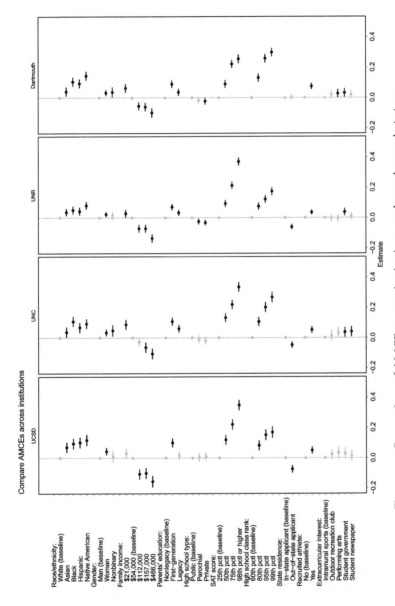

Figure 4.4 Comparison of AMCEs across institutions, undergraduate admissions

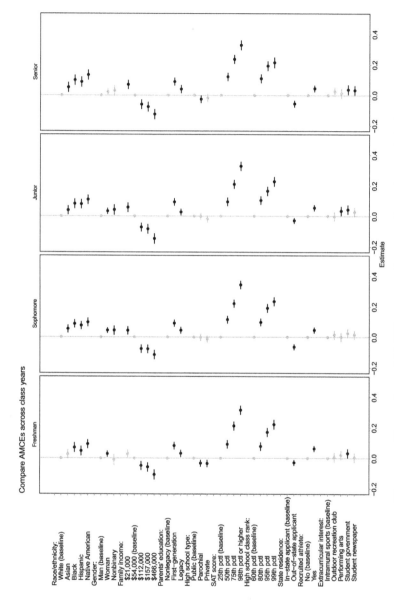

Figure 4.5 Comparison of AMCEs across cohorts, undergraduate admissions

the faculty recruitment experiments (available in our replication package) are precisely the same across cohorts as those from the admissions experiments.

The airplane plots facilitate comparison of the results across groups visually, and they make plain that the direction and scale of preferences are fairly consistent across all cases. We also conducted more fine-grained tests for *any* statistically significant differences in preferences across schools or across cohorts – for example, if the positive preferences for Hispanic applicants are stronger at the University of New Mexico than at Dartmouth, or if the preferences for nonbinary faculty candidates are stronger among fourth-year students than among those in their first year. We report on the results of these tests in the appendix to this chapter, but we note that the number of potential comparisons is vast (comparing every combination of schools and class cohorts with every other with respect to every attribute and level related to diversity). We summarize them here simply by noting that the results are consistent with what a visual assessment of the airplane plots suggests. Preferences in favor of some underrepresented minority groups, relative to baselines, are stronger at some institutions than at others (e.g., preferences for Native American applicants are stronger at Dartmouth than at UNC), but the differences that exist are always variants of overall preferences that run in the same direction. With regard to class year cohorts, preferences are even more consistent, and we cannot reject the null hypothesis that overall there is no difference in attitudes by class cohort.

In short, student preferences as expressed in our conjoint experiments do not differ systematically across the four institutions at the center of our study, nor do they differ across class cohorts. We find this uniformity surprising in light of differences in the composition of the student populations at each school and expectations that socialization on campus could affect student attitudes toward diversity.

To explore these matters further, we look to diversity-related attitudes based on the questions about respondents that we asked at the end of each survey. Here, in contrast to the conjoint experiments, we relied on a question that has long been included in public opinion surveys about whether and how race should factor into university recruitment. Note that we used different terms for the undergraduate admissions and faculty recruitment studies, as indicated below in square brackets.

Some people think that universities should [admit students / hire new faculty] solely on the basis of merit, even if that results in few minority [students being admitted / faculty being selected]. Others think that [an applicant's / a candidate's] racial and ethnic background should be considered to help promote diversity on university campuses, even if that means [admitting some minority students / hiring some minority faculty] who otherwise would not be [admitted / hired]. Which comes closer to your view about evaluating [students for admission into / candidates for new faculty at] a university?

Response options:
- Strongly prefer that colleges and universities [admit students / hire faculty] solely on merit
- Somewhat prefer that colleges and universities [admit students / hire faculty] solely on merit
- Slightly prefer that colleges and universities [admit students / hire faculty] solely on merit
- I don't have a preference one way or the other on this question
- Slightly prefer that colleges and universities consider race
- Somewhat prefer that colleges and universities consider race
- Strongly prefer that colleges and universities consider race

Question wording can affect survey responses about affirmative action (Hoover 2019*b*; Kinder and Sanders 1990; Kopicki 2014; Steeh and Krysan 1996). We acknowledge that this formulation, which directly pits consideration of "merit" against race, is potentially objectionable. However, it is one with a long provenance in US public opinion research (Longoria 2009; Moore 2003), so we deployed it to allow comparability with the existing literature.

Figure 4.6 summarizes the comparisons, showing regression estimates for responses to the affirmative action question, first on the respondent's institution, then on respondent class cohort.[5] In contrast to student preferences expressed through our experiments, responses to this

---

[5] These regressions are based on responses from white students only. Our expectations about attitudes toward affirmative action – and, particularly, about socialization effects – are strongest among whites. That is, opposition to affirmative action is strongest among whites, such that the potential for socialization to have an effect should be greatest. The direction and statistical significance of the estimates presented in the figure, however, are the same if we include responses from all students. Similarity across institutions in the composition of our student participant pools would suggest that student-level factors do not drive these results. As a robustness check, we also ran the same regressions controlling for respondent gender, first-generation student status, family income, SAT score, high school class rank, political partisanship, survey type (either undergraduate admissions or

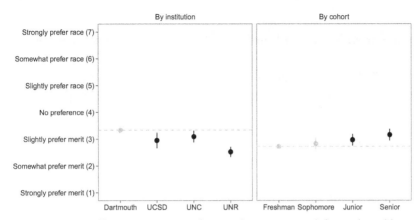

FIGURE 4.6 Affirmative action preferences by institution (left panel) and by cohort (right panel). The estimated regression coefficients show the difference from the baseline (freshman or Dartmouth). The vertical bars show the 95 percent confidence intervals.

question differ across institutions and across class cohorts. The left panel shows that, with Dartmouth as the baseline, respondents at other institutions are less inclined to support the consideration of race in admissions and faculty recruitment decisions. Respondents at UCSD and UNC score 0.4 or 0.2 points lower than those at Dartmouth on the seven-point scale, and respondents at UNR score 0.8 points lower. The right panel shows that each successive class cohort is more inclined than the previous one to support the consideration of race. Relative to the baseline category of first-year students, these effects were statistically significant for junior and senior respondents.[6]

In contrast to our experiments, then, the conventional survey responses show differences across institutions and evidence of a socialization effect, by which students are increasingly supportive of race-conscious admissions and faculty recruitment the more time they have

---

faculty recruitment), and either institution or class cohort (if the main independent variable is class cohort or institution). The substantive effects we estimate across institutions and across cohorts are unaffected.

[6] The questions about respondents asked at the end of each survey also included a series of items that are conventionally used to construct an index of "racial resentment" toward blacks among whites. When we run analogous regressions of the index on university and class cohorts, we find parallel results. Resentment indices are lowest among whites at Dartmouth and highest at UNR, and higher among freshmen and sophomores than among juniors and seniors, indicating that campus socialization affects responses to those survey questions. We discuss the racial resentment index and present results related to it in Chapter 6.

spent in the campus environment. Campus environments, then, appear to shape attitudes toward affirmative action as an abstract concept, yet students' dispositions toward different types of people – the applicants and candidates they encountered in our experiments – are more durable and consistent across these contexts. Existing studies on affirmative action, campus debates, and legal controversies tend to gauge opinions about policies. But the results from our experiments indicate that attitudes toward affirmative action in the abstract do not necessarily line up with choices made with regard to individuals in a holistic selection process. We further explore how these attitudes differ in Chapter 6.

4.4   DISCUSSION

The results presented in this chapter provide an overview of preferences on undergraduate admissions and on faculty recruitment from students across four major universities. The figures tell a rich story about students' priorities and how they compare across a range of attributes salient to admissions and to faculty recruitment decisions. Student priorities are broadly consistent with what one might expect or even hope for – for example, with regard to the powerful effects of high academic achievement and professional quality on students' choices.[7] There are also signs that the survey experiment instruments worked on more subtle levels. For example, responsiveness to the family income attribute in the admissions experiment rises monotonically across income levels. In the faculty recruitment experiment, students' sensitivity to institutional rivalry also suggests that they are attentive to details in the pairs of profiles presented in our conjoint experiments.

We are thus reassured about the effectiveness of our instrument and confident that we have a textured portrait of student preferences. Overall, students' greatest priorities are for scholarly excellence, as reflected in our profiles, in both admissions and faculty recruitment. Critically, however, participants also express strong preferences for key attributes associated with campus diversity. The results show consistent preferences for nonwhites over whites, and slightly more modest, but still measurable preferences for women and nonbinary applicants and candidates over men, other things being equal. They also show strong preferences for admissions applicants from disadvantaged socioeconomic backgrounds.

---

[7] They are also consistent with results from a 2019 survey conducted by the Pew Research Center on what factors should be considered in college admissions decisions (Graf 2019).

On the whole, these results are compatible with principles of affirmative action that would give priority to applicants and candidates from groups that have traditionally been underrepresented in campus populations.

The strong preferences in favor of underrepresented racial and ethnic groups are striking for their contrast with landmark studies in economics that present evidence of employment discrimination *against* the same groups, and the difference here warrants careful consideration. Bertrand and Mullainathan (2004) report on an experiment in which the authors sent thousands of fictitious resumes to help-wanted ads in Chicago and Boston. The resumes differed only in that half carried "white-sounding" names (e.g., Laurie or Matthew) and the other half had "black-sounding" names (e.g., Tamika or Jermaine). The white-sounding applicants received 50 percent more callbacks than did those with black-sounding names. The study generated an avalanche of follow-on research. Some similarly structured resume experiments find no race effects in callbacks (Darolia et al. 2016; Deming et al. 2016). Exploring four decades of census data on children born in California, Fryer and Levitt (2004) find no relationship between having a black-sounding name and life outcomes after controlling for background characteristics. Yet other resume studies do find antiblack bias akin to Bertrand and Mullainathan's result (Gaddis 2015; Nunley et al. 2014; Pager and Quillian 2005), and meta-analyses of the broader genre show that about three-quarters of such audit experiments find evidence for discrimination against blacks (and in some cases, also Hispanics) in hiring (Baert 2018; Bertrand and Duflo 2016; Neumark 2016).

Our results are consistent with the minority of studies that uncover no evidence of discrimination by race/ethnicity in hiring and recruitment. Indeed, the preferences we find run in the opposite direction. Why might this be so? For one thing, the populations in our studies are distinctive – students at major research universities. There is no reason to expect that attitudes and behavior among these rarefied cohorts reflect those of the general population, or even of the population of managers and administrators who oversee hiring and recruitment in the broader economy. Perhaps universities are progressive bastions where the barriers to advancement for racial/ethnic minorities, women (but not gender nonbinary individuals), and those from disadvantaged economic backgrounds are relegated to the past. Another possibility is that our experiments did not fully eliminate social desirability bias. Perhaps despite our efforts not to prime participants, they nevertheless masked discriminatory attitudes or implicit biases in our experiments but would act on them in the context of real admissions or hiring decisions.[8]

Alternatively, it might be that the *positive* results on racial discrimination in many of the audit experiments are driven by would-be employers leveraging additional assumptions about applicants on top of their baseline assumptions about race *precisely because a fuller information set about individual applicants is lacking* in most such studies. Furthermore, with these experiments, which manipulate candidates' names *only,* we cannot assess employers' *holistic* considerations. An important question is, as we emphasized earlier, the *relative* importance of race/ethnicity (or gender) in decision processes. These resume experiments do not provide a suitable way to fully examine this question.

An important exception is a recent ingenious study by Agan and Starr (2018). They submitted online job applications on behalf of fictional applicants who differed with respect to race, criminal record, education, and employment. The key innovation was to field the experiment both before and after the implementation of "ban-the-box" laws in New Jersey and New York City, which prohibit employers from requiring information about criminal convictions in initial job applications. Ban-the-box requirements are intended to reduce the employment disadvantage faced by people with criminal records and are regularly defended as a measure to reduce race gaps in employment (Clarke 2012; Mullin 2013; Southern Coalition for Social Justice 2017).

The results are intriguing. Employers who were informed about applicants' criminal records (those who had included a box to indicate prior convictions on their online applications when doing so was allowed) did favor applicants without records. However, racial differences in callback rates were negligible among employers using the box (Agan and Starr 2018, p. 204). By contrast, after ban-the-box went into effect, callback rates for whites increased whereas rates for blacks decreased. That is, when employers lacked individualized information, they appeared to be generalizing based on a stereotype that black applicants would be more likely than whites to have criminal records (Agan and Starr 2018, p. 195). Noting that the absence of racial difference in callback rates among employers using the box stands in contrast to prior audit studies that do find racial differences, Agan and Starr conjecture that "a

---

[8] Although, given Horiuchi, Markovich, and Yamamoto's (2019) findings on the effectiveness of conjoint experiments in mitigating social desirability bias, we find this unlikely.

substantial share of the racial discrimination observed in other studies might be driven by employers who lack criminal record information and make negative assumptions about black applicants' criminality" (Agan and Starr 2018, p. 208). If this is the case, then an explanation for the difference between our results and those of many prior audit studies is that the holistic choice exercises provided by our conjoint experiments allow participants to weigh a fuller range of characteristics, and that doing so mitigates the disadvantages faced by members of underrepresented minority groups.

The results from this chapter are of general interest, but are not (yet) sufficient to address our main question. Above all, we want to explore whether university communities are divided on issues of campus diversity, and whether different subgroups of students have distinctive – even polarized – preferences with respect to these matters. To do that, we focus in the next chapter on group differences. We will rely on a similar method for presenting our results, using variants of the now-familiar airplane plots. But as we pull responses apart by groups, we will also narrow our focus to the attributes included in our survey that pertain most directly to matters of campus diversity: race/ethnicity, gender, and socioeconomic status.

Appendices

Here, we present more detailed analyses of cross-institutional and cross-cohort differences using data from the admissions and recruitment experiments at the four core institutions in our study.

4.A DIFFERENCES ACROSS INSTITUTIONS

In order to determine whether student attitudes differ systematically across institutions, we first calculate the AMCEs for each institution, and then measure the differences in all of the AMCEs for each pair of institutions. Thus, with regard to race/ethnicity, for example, we first estimate, for each institution, participants' likelihood of selecting an Asian versus a white applicant (baseline). We then take the difference in the AMCEs for the same attribute level (e.g., Asian for race/ethnicity) between Dartmouth participants and UNC participants, between UCSD participants and UNR participants, and so on.

Figure 4.7 shows the statistically significant differences between pairs of institutions on preferences for undergraduate admissions. The top-left panel summarizes differences across schools on preferences related to race/ethnicity, the top-right panel on gender, the bottom-left on family income, and the bottom-right on parents' education. In each case where a characteristic is listed, participants from the school identified in the table *row* show stronger preferences for applicants with the listed characteristic (relative to the baseline level for that attribute) than do participants from the school identified in the *column*. Of 72 interactive coefficients, we find statistically significant differences on 16. This is more than we would expect to find purely by chance if there were no

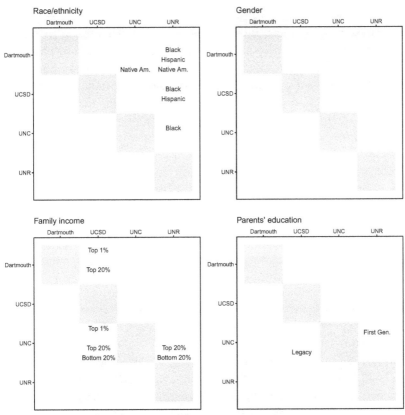

FIGURE 4.7 Statistically significant differences across institutions
(undergraduate admissions)

systematic differences in preferences across schools, but as the amount of blank space in the table indicates, in most areas we find no measurable differences across institutions in diversity preferences.

What do the differences we find tell us about preferences at these schools? The top rows of each panel in Figure 4.7 show the measurable difference between Dartmouth and each other university. Starting with race/ethnicity, Dartmouth student participants exhibit stronger preferences for admitting Native American applicants than do participants at UNC, and they show stronger preferences for black, Hispanic, and Native American applicants than do participants at UNR.[9] By

---

[9] Note that participants at all institutions demonstrate positive preferences toward applicants from all nonwhite groups relative to whites. This table shows that those positive

contrast, there are no statistically significant differences between Dartmouth participants and those at UCSD on preferences with regard to applicant race/ethnicity. Nor are there any measurable differences between Dartmouth participants and those from any other school with regard to applicant gender. On family income, Dartmouth participants are measurably more favorable toward applicants from the top 1 percent and top 20 percent income brackets than are participants at UCSD.[10] Dartmouth's relative preference for applicants from the top income brackets may follow from the income representation on campus. The median family income among Dartmouth students is $200,400. As many as 69 percent of students come from the top income quintile, and fully 21 percent come from the top 1 percent, the highest share of students among the Ivy League and other elite institutions, and more students than are drawn from the bottom 60 percent of family incomes in the United States (The New York Times 2017). In sum, comparing Dartmouth to the other three institutions, we can say that Dartmouth student participants show stronger pro-diversity preferences on race/ethnicity than participants at UNC (for Native Americans) and UNR (for blacks and Hispanics), but also weaker preferences for socioeconomic diversity than participants at UCSD.

The rightmost column of the top-left panel also indicates that, relative to UNR, students at each of the other schools exhibit stronger preferences in favor of at least some underrepresented minority racial/ethnic group. UCSD participants show stronger preferences for black and Hispanic applicants than do UNR participants, and UNC participants show stronger preferences for blacks. Note that UNR participants are, on net, more favorable toward applicants from each of these groups than toward whites, but the strength of these preferences is measurably less than at other institutions for some race/ethnicity categories.

Finally, UNC participants demonstrate some difference from participants at both UCSD and UNR with regard to applicants' socioeconomic status, although these effects are idiosyncratic in direction and do not reveal any clear pattern. UNC participants are more favorable toward

---

preferences are stronger among Dartmouth participants relative to participants at paired schools for the specific groups listed.

[10] Here again, both Dartmouth and UCSD participants, as well as those from every other institution, *disfavor* applicants from the top income brackets relative to the baseline category of median US household income.

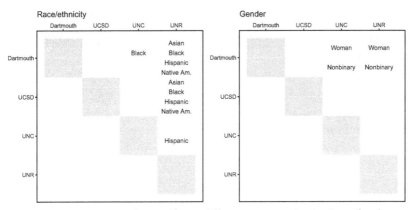

FIGURE 4.8 Statistically significant differences across institutions (faculty recruitment)

applicants at the highest (99th percentile) and the upper middle (80th percentile) income brackets *but also* toward those from the lower (20th percentile) bracket (relative to applicants at the median income) than are participants at UCSD. UNC participants are also more favorable toward applicants at the 80th, but also at the 20th income percentiles than participants at UNR. The bottom-right panel shows that UNC participants are more favorable toward legacy applicants than participants at UCSD, but also toward first-generation applicants than participants at UNR.

Figure 4.8 shows the differences between pairs of institutions with respect to race/ethnicity and gender from the faculty recruitment experiment. On race/ethnicity, Dartmouth participants show stronger preferences for black candidates than participants at UNC and stronger preferences for every nonwhite group than participants at UNR. Similarly, UCSD participants favor candidates from all of the nonwhite categories more than UNR participants do. The preferences of participants at UNC, compared to UNR, are stronger with regard to Hispanic faculty candidates. On gender, the differences between Dartmouth and both UNC and UNR are significant for women and nonbinary candidates relative to men.

On the whole, then, we see some measurable differences across institutions on preferences for diversity. But we find statistically indistinguishable preferences far more frequently, and even when preferences with respect to a given characteristic differ, they never run in opposite directions across different universities.

4.B DIFFERENCES ACROSS COHORTS

In addition to differences across institutions, we are also interested in potential differences across cohorts of students. As we discussed earlier, the existing literature suggests that there is good reason to believe that students' preferences with respect to diversity might change over the course of their time in college. If this were the case, then pooling responses from first-year students and seniors could mask key information about how preferences evolve over time. To determine whether this occurred among our participants, we conducted statistical tests similar to those described above for cross-institutional differences, but rather than grouping participants by university, we grouped them by their class year – first-years, sophomores, juniors, and seniors – estimating differences between each pairing of years for each attribute level related to diversity. We do not show the full tables here because the differences by class year are so few, and so idiosyncratic, that we conclude they indicate no systematic effects.

To illustrate the nonsystematic nature of the effects we estimated, for the undergraduate admissions experiments, the top panel of Figure 4.9 plots the p-values for the estimated differences in AMCEs between pairs of class years (y-axis) against a hypothetical uniform distribution (x-axis) of p-values – one that would be obtained if the differences between class-year pairings were entirely random. Note that the figures include p-values for the estimates of all attribute levels, including attributes related to diversity and other attributes. If the actual distribution of p-values approximates the uniform distribution, the dots on the so-called "QQ plot" should be along the 45-degree line.

The results suggest that the distribution of observed p-values is indeed close to the uniform distribution. With regard to the estimates of diversity-related attribute-levels, only 3 of 72 values fall below the 0.05 cutoff.

The bottom panel of Figure 4.9 plots the same statistics for the class-year pairings using data from the faculty recruitment experiments. Although the "curve" deviates slightly away from the 45-degree line, it is still fairly close. More importantly, with regard to the diversity-related estimates, 5 of 36 values fall below the 0.05 cut-off. There are slightly more pronounced differences across class-year pairings in preferences for faculty recruitment. Yet, if these effects were systematic – that is, if immersion in campus culture steadily pushed preferences in a particular direction over time – then one would expect that the differences

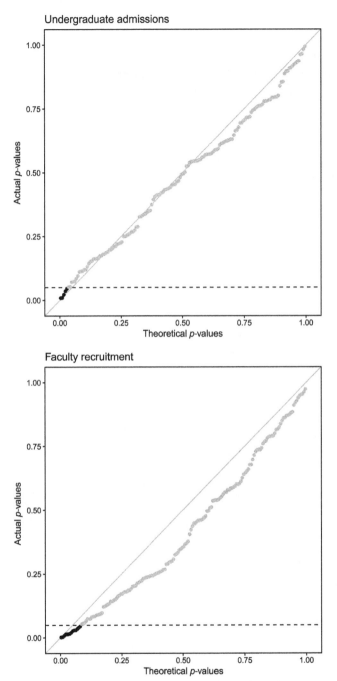

FIGURE 4.9 QQ-plot showing the distribution of actual *p*-values, as compared to the theoretical (uniform) distribution, for all estimated differences in AMCEs between all pairs of class years for undergraduate admissions (top panel) and faculty recruitment experiments (bottom panel)

between seniors and first-year students would be the most pronounced and consistent of those between any pairing. They are not. Of the six potential relationships on which seniors and first-years might have different preferences (four race/ethnicity categories, and two on gender), they are statistically discernible on only one.

In short, our experiments do not reveal systematic differences in student preferences for diversity across class years on either undergraduate admissions or faculty recruitment.

5

How Attitudes Differ across Groups

Many of the most hot-button issues in American politics show race-based divisions (Horowitz and Livingston 2016; Pew Research Center 2016; Tuch and Weitzer 1997). Campus diversity is regularly portrayed as one of these deeply divisive issues across demographic groups. Media accounts of campus politics often focus on protests and controversies over university policies on race, ethnicity, and gender. Such events are regularly tied to movements like #Black Lives Matter, feature students of color speaking out to university administrations, or are organized by identity-based affinity groups (Arditi 2015; Fisher 2015; Hartocollis 2018; Naskidashvili 2015). On the other side of the spectrum, coverage of "anti-diversity" perspectives is most often linked to men, whites, and/or conservative groups or individuals (Bever 2016; Quintana 2018*a*). Moreover, high-profile court cases related to campus diversity tend to focus on zero-sum conflicts in which individual plaintiffs claim to have been denied rightful access to a coveted position because of their membership in one demographic group rather than another (*Regents of the University of California v. Bakke* 1978; *Gratz* v. *Bollinger* 2003; *Grutter* v. *Bollinger* 2003; *Fisher* v. *University of Texas at Austin et al.* 2013, 2016; Students for Fair Admissions 2017). But the positions that drive *visible* public debate among vocal players do not necessarily represent the opinion of entire campus populations.

This chapter and the next chapter break out our experimental results by many of the key divisions that appear to mark campus controversies and other vexing political issues. We first examine how student preferences map onto demographic divisions. We build on the basic method established in the previous chapter, but we break participants out into distinctive groups for comparison. Compared with Chapter 4, there are two key differences in how we present the results here. First, rather than showing the estimates for preferences on every attribute-level included in our experiments, we present just those related to the attributes most central to campus diversity debates: race/ethnicity, gender, and socioeconomic class background. Note that the estimates we present are based on conjoint experiments with all the attributes listed in Table 3.4 or Table 3.5. When there are noteworthy preference differences across groups with respect to attributes not directly relevant to campus diversity debates, we describe them in the text, but in the interest of economy and simplicity, we do not present all the estimates in our figures.

A second difference concerns our figures. Unlike the figures in Chapter 4, which include a single panel, this chapter's figures include three panels – the first showing AMCE estimates for one group, a second showing AMCEs for a comparison group, and a third panel that shows the difference between the AMCEs for the two groups. Before presenting the experimental results and comparisons using these figures, we describe how we interpret the three-panel charts in terms of two concepts that are key to our analysis: consensus and polarization.

5.1 CONSENSUS AND POLARIZATION

The subtitle of this book refers to a hidden consensus on campus diversity. We call it "hidden" because public discourse about diversity on campus tends to reflect conflict, not consensus. In this section, we spell out what we mean by "consensus," specifically as it relates to the results of our experiments on undergraduate admissions and faculty recruitment.

Figure 5.1 shows a generic example based on hypothetical results. As with the figures in the previous chapter, dots ("airplane bodies") represent point estimates, while bars ("wings") represent confidence intervals. If the wings do not touch the vertical line at 0, the estimates are statistically significant. Each row of panels in the figure shows a comparison between two participant groups (say, between men and women) with respect to their preferences on one attribute. The attribute has two levels – the overrepresented level (say, white, if the attribute is race/ethnicity), which serves as our baseline, and an underrepresented level (say, black), the preferences for which we estimate relative to that

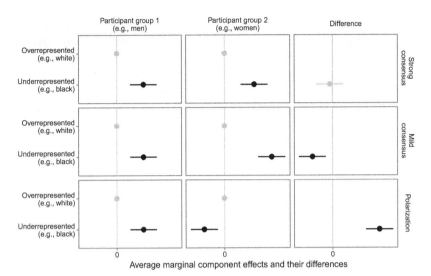

FIGURE 5.1 Hypothetical comparisons of AMCEs

baseline. The leftmost panels in each row show preferences among members of one group (men, in this example) for an overrepresented (white) applicant versus an underrepresented (black) applicant. The middle panels show preferences among members of another group (women) for the same set of applicants. The rightmost panels show the estimated *differences* between the preferences among the first group (men) minus the preferences among the second group (women).

In our hypothetical example, the first group's preference for the underrepresented group is positive and statistically significant in each case; men always exhibit a positive preference for black applicants. In the first row, the second group (women) also show a positive preference. In this case, the positive preference among women is slightly stronger than that among men, so the point estimate of the difference between the estimates (the first group minus the second group) leans just to the left of the zero line. The estimated *difference* in preferences between men and women, however, is not statistically significant, so we color that "airplane" gray rather than black. When preferences for both groups run in the same direction, are both statistically distinguishable from zero, and are statistically indiscernible from each other, we characterize that as *strong consensus*. In this hypothetical example, men's and women's pro-diversity preferences are strongly in line with each other.

The second row of Figure 5.1 shows a variant in which the preferences for an underrepresented group run in the same direction among participants in both groups, but the estimated preferences among members of one group (women) are sufficiently stronger than those in another group (men) such that the estimated difference in their preferences, shown in the right-hand panel, is statistically significant (and thus colored black). We characterize this as *mild consensus* because although the scale of the preferences differs between groups, the preferences share both direction and statistical significance. Here, men's and women's pro-diversity preferences are still in line with each other, but to a lesser degree than in the previous hypothetical example.

In the bottom row of panels, one group's preferences are positive and significant while those of another group are negative and significant – that is, women *dis*favor applicants/candidates from the underrepresented group relative to those from the overrepresented group. The preferences are opposite in direction, and each is statistically distinguishable from zero. These hypothetical results are also statistically distinguishable from each other. We characterize this configuration as *polarization*. In this example, men's and women's attitudes do not line up; while men are pro-diversity, women are anti-diversity.

Finally, when one or both groups' preferences are indiscernible from zero, we classify the configuration as *no consensus* (and no polarization either, for that matter). There are many variants of this type, which includes a kind of "consensus" case, in which estimates in the three panels are all statistically insignificant; namely, there are neither pro- nor anti-diversity preferences for both groups, and there is no statistically discernible difference between them. We do not, however, broaden our definition of consensus based on these results, as our focus is whether there is any consensus *for or against diversity*.[1]

---

[1] A recent paper by Leeper, Hobolt, and Tilley (2018) emphasizes that comparing AMCEs across subgroups of participants in conjoint experiments does not necessarily reflect cross-group differences in the *overall likelihood* of selecting applicants with specific characteristics (say, blacks rather than whites). (Also see Clayton, Ferwerda, and Horiuchi (2019), who make the same argument and take a novel approach to examine multidimensional preferences between subgroups of study participants based on conjoint analysis.) Rather, the comparison of AMCEs shows the *marginal difference* in the likelihood of choosing a particular applicant that results from a shift from the baseline level of an attribute to a given level (say, from white to black, to keep with our example). If the attribute has more than two levels (as race/ethnicity does), then the *difference* in AMCEs between groups depends on which level is selected as the baseline. Leeper, Hobolt, and Tilley (2018) focus on the *overall likelihood* within each subgroup of selecting a given

The rest of this chapter describes preference differences across participants by their own race/ethnicity, by gender, and by socioeconomic background, using the real data from our experiments. As the book's subtitle indicates, we find a great deal of consensus, and almost no polarization, in these comparisons.

5.2 DIFFERENCES BY RACE/ETHNICITY

Because race is central to campus diversity discourse, we start with a comparison of preferences between all white and all nonwhite participants. Figure 5.2 shows this breakdown for the admissions experiments. With respect to the race/ethnicity of the applicant, both whites and nonwhites show measurable preferences in favor of applicants from all nonwhite groups relative to white applicants, but the preferences among nonwhites tend to be more pronounced. Specifically, among white participants, shifting from a white applicant to various nonwhite categories increases the likelihood of selection by 2 percentage points for an Asian applicant, 7 percentage points for a black applicant, 5 percentage points for a Hispanic applicant, and 9 percentage points for a Native American applicant, whereas among nonwhites, the range runs from 7 percentage points for an Asian candidate to 13 percentage points for a Native American candidate.

The right-hand panel shows the preference *differences* between white and nonwhite participants. (Hereafter, when we present similar figures comparing two sets of AMCEs, the differences that are statistically significant at the 0.05 level are highlighted in black, while nonsignificant differences are shown in gray.) The differences

outcome, and they recommend characterizing differences in AMCEs across subgroups as "causal effects" rather than as descriptions of subgroup "preferences." We take Leeper, Hobolt, and Tilley's (2018) point, and throughout this chapter and the next we regularly describe differences across subgroups in terms of how the effect of a shift in a given attribute – for example, of shifting from a white to a black applicant, or from a man to a woman, or from an applicant from a low-income to one from a high-income family – differs (or does not differ) between groups. The cross-group comparisons we present reflect these *marginal* effects. But we also frequently refer to these comparisons as describing subgroup *preferences* because we regard the marginal impact of shifting, say, from a white to a black applicant as reflecting something important about preferences within a given group. We should also note that the comparison of AMCEs between subgroups, which Leeper, Hobolt, and Tilley (2018) criticize generally, is a valid approach as long as the selection of baselines is justifiable. In our case, each baseline (e.g., white, man) is an overrepresented group for the corresponding attribute.

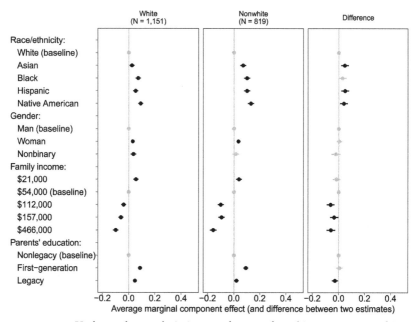

FIGURE 5.2 Undergraduate admissions preferences for whites versus nonwhites

are all statistically distinguishable at the 0.05 level for each of the
nonwhite categories, except for black. That is, the expressed preferences among whites and nonwhites in favor of black applicants are
positive and statistically indistinguishable, indicating strong consensus.
For Asian, Hispanic, and Native American applicants, both whites and
nonwhites express positive preferences, and those preferences are measurably stronger among nonwhites than among whites, indicating mild
consensus.

   With respect to the gender and socioeconomic class attributes, the differences between whites and nonwhites are negligible. On gender, both
groups show preferences for women over men, and for nonbinary applicants over men (although the latter preference falls short of statistical
significance among nonwhite participants) with no statistically significant
preference differences across the white/nonwhite divide. On socioeconomic class attributes as well, there are strong and clear preferences
in both groups for applicants from lower-income families and for first-
generation applicants. The statistical differences within these clusters are
that nonwhites disfavor high-income applicants (those at the 80th, 90th,
and 99th family income percentiles) more strongly than do whites, so
consensus on these items is mild.

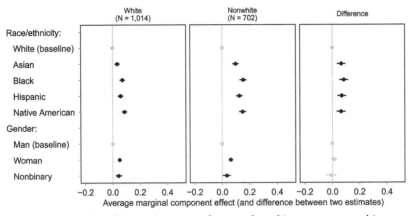

FIGURE 5.3 Faculty recruitment preferences for whites versus nonwhites

Figure 5.3 compares faculty recruitment preferences for whites and nonwhites, and shows a similar story to that for admissions. White participants show measurable preferences for candidates from all nonwhite groups, but among nonwhite participants, such preferences are stronger. In this case, the differences between white and nonwhite preferences are statistically distinguishable (so consensus is mild) with respect to every nonwhite group, with likelihood-of-selection gaps ranging from 7 to 9 percentage points. Also similar to admissions, there is no discernible difference in preferences with respect to gender; both groups exhibit moderate, statistically significant, and equivalent preferences for women and gender nonbinary candidates over men – so we classify consensus there as strong.

Next, we further break out the race/ethnicity of our participant groups to make more precise comparisons. In particular, preferences might differ systematically across participants from various nonwhite groups, and we have sufficient numbers of responses from black, Hispanic, and Asian students to get statistical leverage and provide more granularity. Figure 5.4 breaks out white versus black participants from the admissions experiment. The estimates for white participants, in the left panel, are the same as in Figure 5.2. The estimates for black participants in the middle panel also show pro-diversity attitudes.[2] But there are a couple of notable differences between whites and blacks. First, the expressed preference for

---

[2] The confidence intervals ("wings") are wider primarily because of the smaller number of observations.

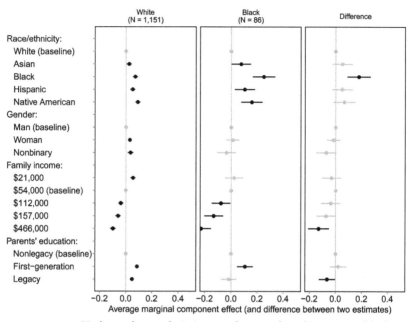

FIGURE 5.4 Undergraduate admissions preferences for whites versus blacks

black applicants among black participants, relative to the baseline (white
applicants), is more than three times as large as the preference for black
applicants among white participants. A white participant is 7 percentage points more likely to select a black applicant than a white applicant,
whereas a black participant is 25 percentage points more likely to select
a black applicant than a white applicant. Second, black participants also
disfavor applicants at the 99th income percentile, relative to the national
median, more strongly than do whites. And black participants are, on the
whole, indifferent toward legacy applicants whereas white participants
favored legacies. With respect to all other attributes including the other
three racial/ethnic categories, gender, family income throughout most of
the distribution, and first-generation status, the groups' preferences are
statistically indistinguishable.

This pattern is replicated in the responses to the faculty recruitment
experiment, shown in Figure 5.5. Here again, white participants lean
toward candidates from all nonwhite groups, but black participants lean
more heavily in that direction – with the exception of Asian candidates. The strongest preference by far among black participants is in
favor of black faculty candidates. Shifting a candidate from white to

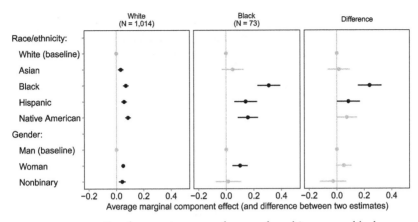

FIGURE 5.5 Faculty recruitment preferences for whites versus blacks

black increases the likelihood of selection by 31 percentage points for a black participant, whereas the corresponding increase among white participants is 7 percentage points. Black participants also express stronger preferences in favor of Hispanic and Native American candidates than do whites, but the differences in the latter case fall just short of statistical significance. With respect to candidate gender, white and black participants do not differ in their preferences.

We conduct analogous comparisons between white participants and Hispanic participants. In the interest of space, we only describe the results here.[3] The white–Hispanic comparison on admissions runs parallel to the white–black comparison. Hispanic participants' preference for Hispanic applicants is pronounced – 14 percentage points – and statistically distinguishable from that among whites, which is 5 percentage points. With regard to other race/ethnicity groups, Hispanics' preferences are indistinguishable from those of whites. Similarly, with regard to applicants' gender, there are no measurable differences. On family income, Hispanics, like blacks, have measurably stronger preferences *against* applicants from households above the national median. With respect to parents' education, however, Hispanic students' preferences are not discernible from those of whites.

In the recruitment experiment, Hispanics also favor Hispanic candidates more strongly than whites do, at 18 percentage points relative to 6 percentage points, but stronger Hispanic preferences are also discernible

---

[3] All of the additional results reported are included in our replication package.

with respect to black (18 to 7 percentage points) and Native American (17 to 8 percentage points) candidates. On gender, the expressed preferences of Hispanic and white participants are, effectively, the same in both experiments.

The fourth racial/ethnic group for which we have sufficient responses to make a comparison is Asians. Although they are a nonwhite minority, Asians also have the highest average scores on traditional indicators of academic achievement, such as SAT score and high school GPA (Jaschik 2015). Thus, *prima facie*, it is not clear whether we should expect admissions preferences among Asian students to conform with those from other minority groups. Further obscuring our predictions, existing studies do not clearly tell whether Asians are more pro-diversity. Some studies find lower support for affirmative action programs among Asians than among other minorities (Baynes 2012; Sax and Arredondo 1999), whereas others report Asian support for affirmative action on par with that of blacks and Hispanics (Bell, Harrison, and McLaughlin 1997; Fukurai and Lum 1997; Kravitz, Bludau, and Klineberg 2008; Oh et al. 2010).

We compare Asian preferences on admissions with those of whites in Figure 5.6 and with non-Asian minorities in Figure 5.7. Our results confirm the idea that Asian preferences align closely with those of other groups. In comparison with whites, Asian participants' preferences are statistically indistinguishable with respect to every attribute estimate but one (legacy status). Most notably, they express stronger favorable preferences toward Asian applicants, with a 10-percentage-point increase in likelihood of selection relative to a white applicant, as compared to a 2-percentage-point increase among whites.[4] In contrast to non-Asian minority participants, Asians' preferences are significantly different on three estimates. Asians are more favorable toward Asian applicants and toward gender nonbinary applicants, and they disfavor applicants in the top income category slightly less than do other nonwhite participants.

With respect to faculty recruitment, we again only describe the results. The differences between Asian and white preferences are more pronounced on faculty recruitment than on admissions. Asian participants favor Asian faculty candidates by 15 percentage points (compared to 3 percentage points among whites). They also favor black candidates

---

[4] They also impose a slightly larger penalty than do whites on applicants from the 80th percentile of household income relative to the median income (but not on applicants in the 90th or 99th percentiles).

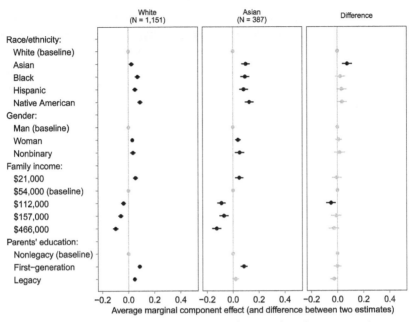

FIGURE 5.6 Undergraduate admissions preferences for whites versus Asians

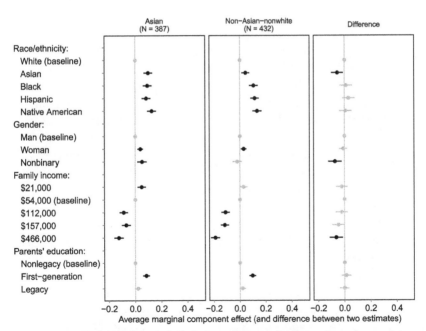

FIGURE 5.7 Undergraduate admissions preferences for Asians versus non-Asian minorities

(by 14 compared to 7 percentage points among whites), Hispanic candidates (11 compared to 6 percentage points), and Native American candidates (14 to 8 percentage points). All the differences are statistically significant. In comparison with non-Asian minority participants, the differences are less consistent. Asian participants' preferences for Asian candidates are much stronger (15 to 6 percentage points), but preferences with regard to other race/ethnicity categories are similar and statistically insignificant. On gender, Asian participants have measurably positive preferences toward gender nonbinary candidates (7 percentage points) whereas non-Asian minorities neither favor nor disfavor nonbinary candidates.

The results from our experiments are consistent with previous research suggesting that Asian preferences on campus diversity fall in between those of whites and non-Asian minorities, but are closer to the views of other minorities than they are to those of whites (Fukurai and Lum 1997; Kravitz, Bludau, and Klineberg 2008; Oh et al. 2010).

5.3   DIFFERENCES BY GENDER

We also break out our experimental responses by gender. Because only about 2 percent of the participants in our experiments identified as gender nonbinary, we have statistical leverage to compare only those from men versus women. Figures 5.8 and 5.9 show the differences on the admissions and faculty recruitment experiments, respectively.

Women exhibit stronger preferences in favor of women than do men. On admissions, the difference is moderate (4 versus 1 percentage points), but women are not underrepresented among students. On faculty recruitment, pro-woman preferences are stronger among both women (7 percentage points) and men (3 percentage points), and the difference between the groups' preferences is significant, indicating mild consensus.

Preference differences are also pronounced with regard to gender nonbinary applicants and candidates, whom women consistently favor whereas men actively *dis*favor (marginally on admissions, significantly on faculty recruitment). Indeed, it is with respect to recruiting gender nonbinary faculty where we see one of our only examples of *polarization* in preferences. The overall pattern is also consistent with a substantial body of research indicating that men are, on the whole, more hostile than are women toward gender nonconformity (Blashill and Powlishta

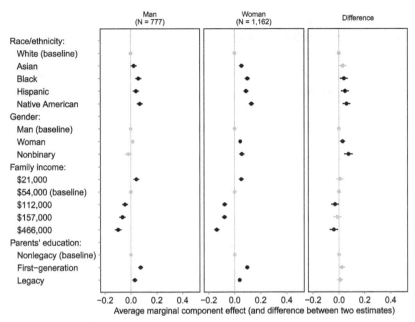

FIGURE 5.8 Undergraduate admissions preferences for women versus men

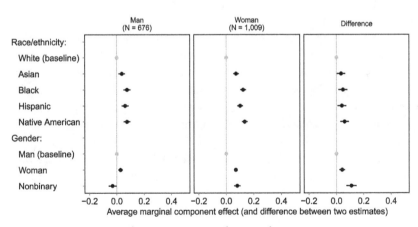

FIGURE 5.9 Faculty recruitment preferences for women versus men

2009; Glick, Wilkerson, and Cuffe 2015; Glotfelter and Anderson 2017; Herek 2002).

With regard to race/ethnicity, women also lean more in favor of under-represented minority groups than men in every instance. Although the gaps are generally modest (between 3 and 6 percentage points), they are statistically significant for almost all race/ethnicity categories across both the admissions and recruitment experiments (with the exception of the difference in preferences for Asian applicants in the admissions experiment). In the admissions experiment, preference differences by gender on applicants' socioeconomic status are also modest. Women disfavor some higher-income applicants more than men do, but are indistinguishable from men with regard to first-generation or legacy status.

5.4 DIFFERENCES BY SOCIOECONOMIC CLASS

We can also distinguish participants in our experiments by socioeconomic class. After they completed the experiments, we asked participants to estimate their families' annual household incomes, and also whether their parents went to college. In this section, we contrast participants from households below the national median with those above the median, and participants for whom neither parent attended college with those who had at least one parent who did.[5]

Figures 5.10 and 5.11 compare the estimated preferences of below-median versus above-median income participants on admissions and faculty recruitment, respectively. The consistency of preferences with respect to demographics and the contrast with respect to socioeconomic status are both remarkable. On race/ethnicity and gender, preferences are nearly identical. Indeed, in the admissions experiments, the point estimates are almost exactly the same. The same is true on faculty recruitment, with one exception – less-affluent students favor Asian and Native American candidates a bit more strongly than do more affluent students. In the admissions experiments, the differences between the estimates for each level of the parents' education attribute are also insignificant between two groups, while the estimates for each group are all statistically significant in favor of diversity.

---

[5] We also cut the data different ways, comparing below-median income participants with those whose families earn an annual income of $200,000 or more), and comparing legacy students with nonlegacy (but non–first-generation) students (see our replication package for the exact estimates). The comparison between below-median-income students and students from families with the highest incomes is virtually identical to that of below-median and above-median students. Legacy students are slightly more favorable toward nonbinary applicants, and they are also slightly more favorable toward applicants from the top 1 percent for family income. The differences between legacy and nonlegacy students, however, are just barely significant. One other notable result is that legacy students prefer legacy applicants more than nonlegacy students, although both groups favor legacy applicants. This in-group effect is similar to the result we find for other subgroups.

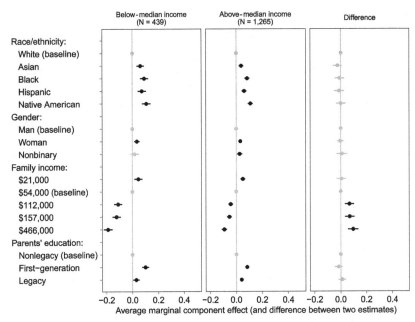

FIGURE 5.10 Undergraduate admissions preferences for below-median income versus above-median income

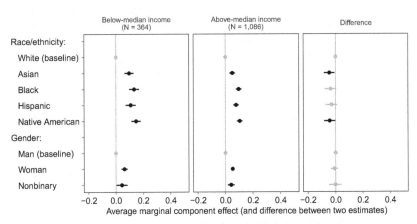

FIGURE 5.11 Faculty recruitment preferences for below-median income versus above-median income

The big divergence, however, is in the admissions experiment, which included an attribute for the applicant's family income. Participants from all income levels favor applicants from lower-income families, but participants from lower-income families weigh economic disadvantage more heavily than do those from wealthier families. Shifting from an applicant with a family income in the top 1 percent (99th percentile) nationally to an applicant in the bottom 20th percentile increases the likelihood of selection by 14 percentage points (−9 percentage points to 5 percentage points) among participants from above-median families, whereas the increase is 23 percentage points (−19 percentage points to 5 percentage points) among participants from below-median families. The differences in AMCEs are significant at each of the three above-the-median income levels (the 99th, 90th, and 80th percentiles).

The figures comparing estimates from first-generation participants and others are similar (results included in our replication package).[6] On admissions, there are no differences with respect to race/ethnicity or gender except one: they are not as strongly in favor of Native American applicants (8 to 12 percentage points). With respect to family income, first-generation participants more strongly disfavor applicants from the top two family income categories than do others. Furthermore, as expected, first-generation participants more strongly favor first-generation applicants (11 to 8 percentage points). On faculty recruitment, first-generation participants exhibit stronger preferences for black (14 to 9 percentage points), Hispanic (11 to 8 percentage points), and Native American candidates (14 to 10 percentage points). On all other attributes and levels, there are no measurable differences between first-generation participants and others.

5.5 DISCUSSION

Comparisons across groups of participants in our experiments reveal several notable patterns. First, across racial/ethnic groups, preferences in favor of minority applicants and candidates tend to be stronger among nonwhite participants than among whites. The direction of these differences is consistent, although the differences do not always reach statistical significance, because white participants also exhibit positive preferences for all nonwhite groups. This means that there exists at least mild, but in some cases strong, consensus. On race/ethnicity, we find no cases of polarization across participant groups in which, for example,

---

[6] We use whether or not a participant came from a family of college graduates as a measure of social class. As Putnam (2015) shows, this measurement of class predicts a range of outcomes and life circumstances.

some racial/ethnic group disfavors a particular category while another group favors that category.

Second, among nonwhite participants, the strongest preferences are toward in-group applicants and candidates. This is where we regularly see statistically significant differences in preference between whites and other racial/ethnic groups. So, for example, the preferences among black participants for black applicants and candidates are far stronger than those of whites. The same is true for preferences among Hispanic participants for Hispanics, and among Asians for Asians.

Third, the preference differences across racial/ethnic groups are more pronounced on faculty recruitment than on undergraduate admissions. The driving factor here appears to be preferences among nonwhite participants. That is, white participants exhibit about the same level of preference for nonwhite faculty candidates as for nonwhite undergraduate applicants (ranging from 2 to 9 percentage points), whereas preferences among nonwhite participants for nonwhite faculty candidates are more pronounced (in the 10- to 15-percentage-point range) than for nonwhite undergraduate applicants (in the 7- to 13-percentage-point range). These amplified preferences among nonwhite participants for nonwhite faculty candidates are consistent with the fact that minorities are far more dramatically underrepresented among faculty than among students at the schools where we conducted our experiments and at universities across the nation.

Next, preferences with respect to Asians warrant particular attention, from two angles. We are interested in preferences *toward* Asian applicants and candidates across all participants in our experiments (explored in Chapter 4), and also in preference differences *between* Asians and other participants. As for the former, relative to the white baseline, Asian applicants and candidates are favored, but the scale of that preference (measured as the increase in likelihood of selection for an Asian applicant relative to a white applicant, other things equal) tends to be smaller than the analogous preferences favoring blacks, Hispanics, and Native Americans.[7] The moderate preferences for Asians among our student participants contrast with results from studies suggesting that, in actual undergraduate admissions decisions, Asian applicants are *dis*favored relative to applicants from all other racial/ethnic groups, once academic

---

7 The results using all participants are presented in Figures 4.2 and 4.3. The results focusing on subgroups, which are presented in this chapter, show similar patterns.

achievement is accounted for (Espenshade, Chung, and Walling 2004; Mortara et al. 2018; Students for Fair Admissions 2014).

With respect to the preferences of Asian participants themselves, our experiments revealed few and small differences from other groups. Asian preferences for nonwhite applicants and candidates tend to be slightly stronger than those of white participants and slightly weaker than those of non-Asian and nonwhite participants (i.e., blacks, Hispanics, and Native Americans). But across all groups, congruence in preferences is at least as striking as dissonance, and the preferences of our Asian student participants are squarely in the mainstream. This overall pattern of preference similarities is distinctive to our conjoint experiments in which participants chose between pairs of specific individual applicants and candidates. Standard surveys asking about support for affirmative action more generally suggest larger cross-group differences. We come back to this topic in the next chapter.

Some of the patterns visible across race/ethnicity are replicated when we break out our participants by gender. Women are moderately more favorable toward women applicants and candidates than are men (who also favor women applicants and candidates, if less markedly). This gap is more pronounced on faculty recruitment than on admissions, which is consistent with the underrepresentation of women among faculty but not among students.

Importantly, women are also measurably more favorable than are men toward gender nonbinary applicants and candidates. This is the one area where we observe polarization of preferences, with men disfavoring nonbinary faculty candidates (by 3 percentage points), whereas women are 8 percentage points more likely to select a nonbinary candidate than a man, other things equal.

When we break participants out by socioeconomic class, we find few preference differences with respect to race/ethnicity or gender, but we do find differences with respect to class-related attributes of candidates and applicants. Here again, preferences run in the same direction across class divides. Students from poorer families and first-generation students favor applicants from disadvantaged backgrounds more heavily than do students from wealthier households and those with university-educated parents. But participants from advantaged and disadvantaged backgrounds alike tend to favor applicants from disadvantaged backgrounds in the admissions experiments. But we should also note that participants from advantaged and disadvantaged backgrounds both *prefer* legacy applicants – those with strong advantages – compared to baseline (nonlegacy, non–first-generation) applicants. The differences between the subgroups of participants are statistically indistinguishable, which is one example of an "anti-diversity" consensus.

All these cross-group comparisons demonstrate measurable in-group affect among groups that have been historically marginalized in higher education: racial/ethnic minorities, women, and the less affluent. On each of these dimensions, participants from marginalized groups identify with applicants and candidates most like themselves, and favor them. There is also some evidence of support *across* marginalized groups. Hispanic participants favor black and Asian applicants slightly more than white participants do; Asians favor blacks and Hispanics more than whites do. Women favor all nonwhite groups more than men do. But these effects are smaller than in-group affect effects and often not statistically significant.

In sharp contrast, we observe almost no in-group affect among traditionally favored groups, including whites, men, and the affluent.[8] To the contrary, whites favor all nonwhite groups, men favor women, and the wealthy favor the economically disadvantaged. They tend to do so to somewhat less pronounced degrees than do the comparison groups we examine here, but the preferences expressed among overrepresented groups *for* underderrepresented groups tend to be statistically significant.

5.6 SUMMARIZING THE HIDDEN CONSENSUS

We can summarize our comparisons across groups of participants with reference to the classification system for consensus and polarization we outlined at the beginning of the chapter. We compare preferences across the following participant groups defined by racial/ethnic identification, gender identification, and socioeconomic class status:

- Whites versus all nonwhites
- Whites versus blacks
- Whites versus Hispanics
- Whites versus Asians
- Asians versus non-Asian nonwhites
- Men versus women
- Family income below versus above the national median

[8] The exception is that men favor men over gender nonbinary faculty candidates.

- First-generation college students versus those with at least one college-educated parent

We classify each cross-group comparison as either strongly or mildly consensual, nonconsensual, or polarized on a range of preferences related to campus diversity – specifically, on preferences for:

- Asian, black, Hispanic, and Native American applicants/candidates, relative to whites
- Women and gender nonbinary applicants/candidates, relative to men
- Applicants from the 20th, 80th, 90th, and 99th family income percentile, relative to the national median
- First-generation and legacy applicants, relative to those whose parents attended another university

Figure 5.12 illustrates the patterns of cross-group consensus and polarization in preferences from the undergraduate admissions and faculty recruitment experiments. Each column represents a cross-group comparison – white participants versus all nonwhite participants, white versus black, white versus Asian, and so on. Each row represents how preferences align with respect to a specific attribute. Squares with plain, solid, and gray coloring indicate pro-diversity consensus (lighter for mild consensus, darker for strong consensus) between groups with respect to a given characteristic. White squares indicate nonconsensus. Squares with a heavy border and marked with a capital "A" indicate *anti*-diversity consensus (again, lighter fill indicates mild consensus and darker fill, strong consensus). Finally, a black square marked with a "P" indicates preference polarization.

The first, and predominant, point about the figure is that the tiles are overwhelmingly plain-bordered and solid-colored, indicating pro-diversity consensus. The top panel summarizes results from the admissions experiments, and the bottom panel from the faculty recruitment experiments. Across almost every paired group, on almost every diversity-related attribute, and across both sets of experiments, we find pro-diversity consensus in preferences. With respect to every underrepresented minority race/ethnicity (relative to whites), we find preference consensus shared across nearly every group.[9] Similarly, with respect to

---

[9] The preference among black participants for Asian faculty candidates is not significant, in part due to the small number of black participants ($N = 73$), producing a single "nonconsensus" square.

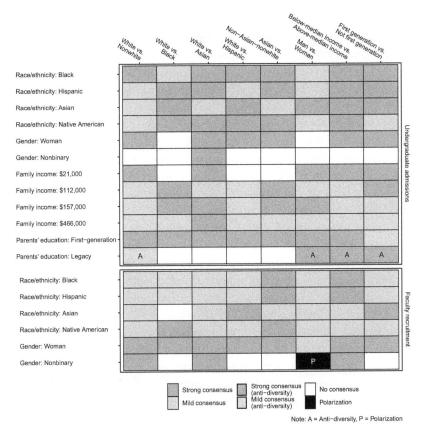

FIGURE 5.12 All comparisons in Chapter 5

family income in the admissions experiments, preferences in favor of applicants from lower family income brackets relative to higher ones, and especially strong preferences in favor of first-generation applicants, are nearly universally shared. Note also that preferences in favor of women, relative to men, are widely shared across groups, even in undergraduate admissions, despite the fact that women now outnumber men among students. Where women *are* dramatically underrepresented, among the faculty, the preference consensus in their favor is universal.

The rare exceptions to consensus are worth noting. The most prominent is with respect to gender nonbinary undergraduate applicants and faculty candidates. In the admissions experiments, we find cross-group consensus with respect to nonbinary applicants only once. Both whites and Asians demonstrate statistically significant preferences in favor of nonbinary applicants over men. In the faculty recruitment experiments, we find similar consensus across whites and all nonwhites, whites and Asians, and low- and high-income participants. Yet across most comparisons in both experiments, there is always at least one group whose preferences with respect to nonbinary applicants or candidates are not discernible from zero, and in many instances the estimates are negative, indicating *dis*favor toward nonbinary applicants or candidates relative to men. And we find our *only* evidence of preference polarization in comparing men versus women in the faculty recruitment experiment. Men have measurably negative preferences against nonbinary candidates whereas women are measurably positive. Nonconformity with the gender binary thus stands apart from other traditionally disadvantaged identities as one on which campus attitudes have not converged – at least, not yet.

Finally, the other attribute on which we do not find a pro-diversity consensus is legacy status among applicants in the admissions experiments. We classify pro-legacy preferences as anti-diversity, given the historical predominance of whites, high-income, and (going further back) men among college students, and of whites and men among faculty, as described in Chapter 2. We find measurable pro-legacy preferences among at least one group in each pairing, and sometimes in both. That is, pro-legacy preferences predominate among our participants, sometimes broadly enough to yield anti-diversity consensus with regard to this one attribute.

These exceptions aside, the key point from Figure 5.12, and from this chapter as a whole, is the overwhelming evidence of consensus across groups in favor of undergraduate applicants and faculty candidates from groups that have been traditionally underrepresented and whose recruitment would diversify campus communities. These preferences are shared across groups defined by their race/ethnicity, gender identification, and socioeconomic status. They are stronger among members of underrepresented minority groups than among those from advantaged groups in some cases, but the dominant message here is that campus consensus with respect to the value of diversity is strong and broadly shared. In Chapter 6, we examine the extent to which these preferences differ if we break our participants out not by race/ethnicity, gender, and socioeconomic background, but by political beliefs.

6

How Preferences Differ by Political Beliefs

The group differences explored so far tend toward core elements of identity: race/ethnicity, gender, and class status. There are serious debates over the extent to which even these characteristics are immutable (Ely 1995; Torche 2015; Tuvel 2017), and we merely note here that they are different from political beliefs and policy preferences. Yet political beliefs are also at the heart of the debates over campus diversity, and particularly over how race, gender, and class ought to factor into decisions on admissions and faculty recruitment. Students' academic achievement factors in as well; debates about merit in university admissions have long been tied to standardized test scores. Because our studies included questions on participants' partisanship and SAT score, as well as on attitudes toward affirmative action, and a short battery of questions designed to elicit a more general measure of racial animus,[1] we can also explore the contours of these divisions.

This chapter presents comparisons of responses by different types of participants, analogous to those in the previous chapter, but the participants are broken out according to political beliefs and other characteristics expressed in the survey. We start with the central division that dominates all others in American politics: partisanship.

---

[1] These (nonexperimental) questions about respondents themselves and their attitudes were asked after the conjoint tasks in both the undergraduate admissions and faculty recruitment experiments at each of the core institutions – Dartmouth, UCSD, UNC, and UNR. See Chapter 3 for our survey designs.

6.1 PARTISANSHIP

Our studies included a query about participants' partisanship.[2] Unlike in the previous chapter, where we observed few strong differences in preferences among most racial/ethnic, gender, and class groups, Figure 6.1 shows stark differences between Democrats and Republicans on preferences for undergraduate admissions applicants.

Democrats, in the leftmost panel, favor applicants from all nonwhite groups, women and gender nonbinary applicants, and first-generation applicants and those from families with lower incomes. Republicans are different in important ways on each of these attributes. First, Republican

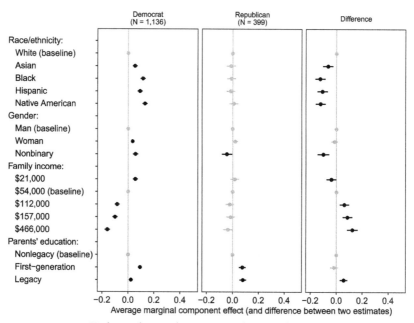

FIGURE 6.1 Undergraduate admissions preferences for Democrats versus Republicans

[2] The question we asked was: "Generally speaking, do you think of yourself as a Democrat, a Republican, an independent, or what?" The response options included "Strong Democrat," "Democrat," "Independent, lean Democrat," "Independent," "Independent, lean Republican," "Republican," "Strong Republican," "Other," and "Don't know." For purposes of this analysis, leaners are grouped with their corresponding parties. We exclude "Other" and "Don't know" responses, which constitute 11 percent of all participants.

participants as a group show no measurable preference with respect to any racial/ethnic category – they are indifferent to an applicant's race/ethnicity. In this regard, their preferences are statistically different from those of Democrats for every nonwhite group. Second, on gender, Republicans lean slightly toward women over men, and on that count they are not discernible from Democrats; but they also disfavor gender nonbinary applicants significantly, in contrast to Democrats, who favor them. On socioeconomic class, whereas Democrats distinctly favor less-wealthy over more-wealthy applicants, Republican preferences are unaffected by family income brackets, yielding cross-party differences that are all statistically discernible. Finally, participants from both parties favor first-generation applicants almost equally, but Republicans also indicate a more pronounced preference for legacy applicants than do Democrats.

Figure 6.2 shows similar partisan differences with respect to faculty recruitment. Again, Democrats express strong preferences for candidates from every nonwhite group relative to whites, and for both women and nonbinary candidates relative to men. Republicans, by contrast, are indifferent on average with respect to race/ethnicity and with regard to women rather than men, but as in the admissions experiment, they actively disfavor gender nonbinary candidates relative to men. The differences in preferences by party are significant for every racial/ethnic and gender category.

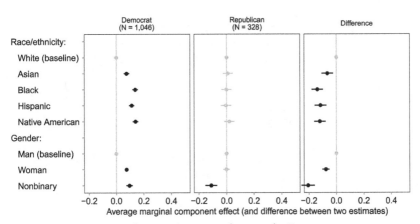

FIGURE 6.2 Faculty recruitment preferences for Democrats versus Republicans

6.2 AFFIRMATIVE ACTION AND ACADEMIC ACHIEVEMENT

Attitudes toward Affirmative Action

Our studies also asked directly about whether and how race should factor into admissions and recruitment. We first discussed responses to our survey question on race-conscious admissions (and faculty recruitment) in Chapter 4, but we present the question and response options again here for easy reference.

Question:
Some people think that universities should [admit students / hire new faculty] solely on the basis of merit, even if that results in few minority [students being admitted / faculty being selected]. Others think that [an applicant's / a candidate's] racial and ethnic background should be considered to help promote diversity on university campuses, even if that means [admitting some minority students / hiring some minority faculty] who otherwise would not be [admitted / hired]. Which comes closer to your view about evaluating [students for admission into / candidates for new faculty at] a university?

Response options:
- Strongly prefer that colleges and universities [admit students / hire faculty] solely on merit
- Somewhat prefer that colleges and universities [admit students / hire faculty] solely on merit
- Slightly prefer that colleges and universities [admit students / hire faculty] solely on merit
- I don't have a preference one way or the other on this question
- Slightly prefer that colleges and universities consider race
- Somewhat prefer that colleges and universities consider race
- Strongly prefer that colleges and universities consider race

Preferences about race-conscious admissions (and hiring), as measured by standard surveys, are notoriously sensitive to how the question is framed (Hoover 2019*b*; Kinder and Sanders 1990; Kopicki 2014; Steeh and Krysan 1996). Recent survey data from Gallup show a solid majority of Americans favoring "affirmative action programs for racial minorities" (Norman 2019) at the same time that data from Pew show a solid majority holding that "race or ethnicity should not be a factor in college admissions decisions" (Graf 2019). We are aware that our measure, which asks respondents to compare "merit" and race on a unidimensional space, is controversial, but as we noted in Chapter 4, it has been widely used in the existing literature.

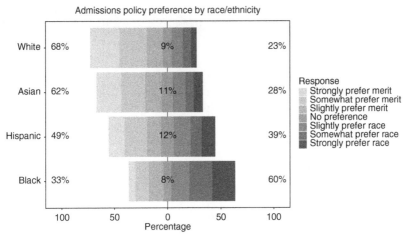

FIGURE 6.3 Distribution of admission policy preferences by race/ethnicity

The responses, broken out by our main racial/ethnic groups, are illustrated in Figure 6.3. The differences across groups are striking. The modal response among both whites and Asians is strong preference for merit only, and 68 percent and 61 percent of whites and Asians prefer, at least slightly, for decisions to be made purely on grounds of merit, whereas only 23 percent and 28 percent of each group prefer any consideration of race. Hispanics also are inclined toward merit only, with 49 percent leaning in that direction whereas 39 percent favor some consideration of race. Among black participants, by contrast, 60 percent favor the consideration of race, whereas 33 percent lean against.

Figure 6.4 returns to our conventional airplane plot format, contrasting those who object to the consideration of race in student admissions with those who welcome it on the admissions experiment.[3] The corresponding results from the faculty recruitment are shown in Figure 6.5. As expected, those open to the consideration of race (middle panel) exhibit strong preferences for nonwhites relative to whites. Note, however, that even those participants who object to any consideration of race show statistically discernible preferences in *favor* of applicants from underrepresented minority racial/ethnic groups relative to white applicants. This result is remarkably consistent, applying to almost all nonwhite groups

---

[3] We exclude participants who chose "I don't have a preference one way or the other on this question."

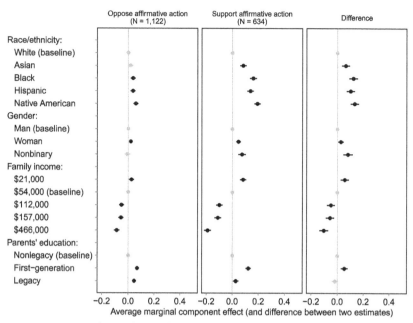

FIGURE 6.4 Undergraduate admissions preferences for those opposed to any consideration of race versus those open to considering race

in *both* the undergraduate admissions and faculty recruitment experiments, with the exception of Asians in the admissions experiment, for whom preferences are statistically insignificant. Recall that neither our experiment recruitment materials nor the conjoint exercises themselves ever mentioned campus diversity, nor did they prime participants in any way to consider race relative to other applicant attributes. And participants completed the experiment *before* confronting the survey question about affirmative action, so the question could not have impacted their responses to the conjoint task. Nevertheless, in the series of paired comparisons, even those who oppose on principle the consideration of race in admissions or recruitment favor nonwhite admissions applicants and faculty candidates over whites.

On other attributes, the comparison between these groups resembles that between Democrats and Republicans. Those inclined to consider race also lean more heavily toward women and gender nonbinary applicants or candidates, with the difference particularly large on faculty recruitment (13 and 19 percentage points, respectively), where women are underrepresented relative to their population share. On the admissions experiment, where applicants' socioeconomic background is

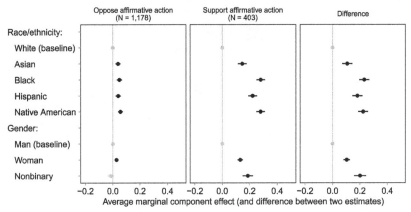

FIGURE 6.5 Faculty recruitment preferences for those opposed to any consideration of race versus those open to considering race

a salient attribute, family income is weighed more heavily by those also open to considering race. That is, both groups favor applicants from poorer families, but supporters of affirmative action favor applicants from economically disadvantaged backgrounds even more strongly than do opponents. Conversely, opponents of affirmative action weigh high SAT scores more heavily, showing greater preferences for applicants scoring high on this measure of academic merit. In parallel fashion, in the faculty recruitment experiment, affirmative action opponents weigh both teaching and research excellence more heavily than do those who favor the consideration of race.[4]

The results, when we break out responses by support for or opposition to the consideration of race, run parallel to those obtained when we compare Democrats and Republicans. Given the salience of the partisan divide on affirmative action nationally, it is worth considering the degree to which responses to the affirmative action question map onto partisanship. Among our participants, the two are correlated at 0.33, indicating that they are related but far from interchangeable. Figure 6.6 breaks down responses to the affirmative action question by partisanship. Republicans, including leaners, almost uniformly oppose any consideration of race in admissions or recruitment, but so do solid majorities of Independents, Democratic leaners, and Democrats. Only among those who identify as strong Democrats (14.0 percent of all participants) do

---

[4] These results are not shown in Figures 6.4 and 6.5 but are included in our replication package.

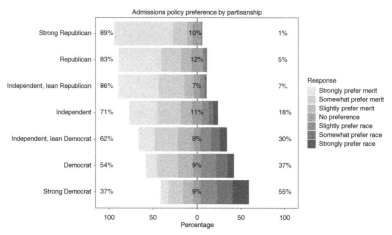

FIGURE 6.6 Distribution of admission policy preferences by partisanship

we see a majority that declares itself in favor of considering race in admissions and recruitment.

SAT Score

To probe even further the potential tension between academic achievement and other considerations in admissions decisions, we break participants out by their self-reported SAT scores. We note that SAT scores are a controversial element of college admissions dossiers, subject to criticism for bias on racial, ethnic, and socioeconomic class grounds (Burton and Ramist 2001; Freedle 2003; Geiser and Santelices 2007; Geiser 2015; Jencks and Phillips 2011; Samson 2009; Santelices and Wilson 2015; Zwick 2013). Yet the "similar-to-me" effect that is well documented in assessments of prospective job candidates suggests that students who scored high on the SAT may be particularly inclined to regard SAT performance as a valid and perspicacious marker of merit (Rand and Wexley 1975; Sears and Rowe 2003). If this is the case, then those who self-report near the top of the SAT distribution may be inclined to weight SAT performance heavily and, correspondingly, to discount other factors in their admissions preferences.

To test this proposition, we compare participants whose SAT scores are high versus low for their respective institutions on the admissions and recruitment experiments. Specifically, our studies identified the SAT quartile ranges for each institution and asked participants to identify the range within which their combined SAT scores fell. The results (included in our replication package) suggest that the differences between participants with high and low SAT scores are minimal. On faculty recruitment, none of the estimates differ. On admissions, participants with low SAT scores favor black applicants slightly more than do those with high SAT scores, and disfavor those in the top household income level slightly more. Otherwise, preferences are indistinguishable across SAT score groups.

6.3 RACIAL RESENTMENT

So far, we have examined how partisanship, support for affirmative action in principle, and self-reported SAT score map onto the choices students undertook in our experiments. But we also want to estimate how racial resentment (if any) shapes preferences toward undergraduate applicants and faculty candidates. To this end, our studies included a battery of four questions intended to measure levels of racial resentment.[5] These questions have been used in political science research for decades (e.g., Kam and Burge 2018; Kinder and Sanders 1996; Kinder and Dale-Riddle 2012; Tesler and Sears 2010). The components of this battery are:

- Irish, Italians, Jewish, and many other minorities overcame prejudice and worked their way up. Blacks should do the same without any special favors.
- Generations of slavery and discrimination have created conditions that make it difficult for blacks to work their way out of the lower class.
- Over the past few years, blacks have gotten less than they deserve.
- It's really a matter of some people not trying hard enough; if blacks would only try harder they could be just as well off as whites.

Responses were measured with a standard five-point agree–disagree scale with the response options: "Agree strongly," "Agree somewhat," "Neither agree nor disagree," "Disagree somewhat," and "Disagree strongly."

Consistent with longstanding practice in US public opinion research (e.g., Kam and Burge 2018), we convert the responses on these four

---

[5] We also included a question on income redistribution that was omitted from our analyses.

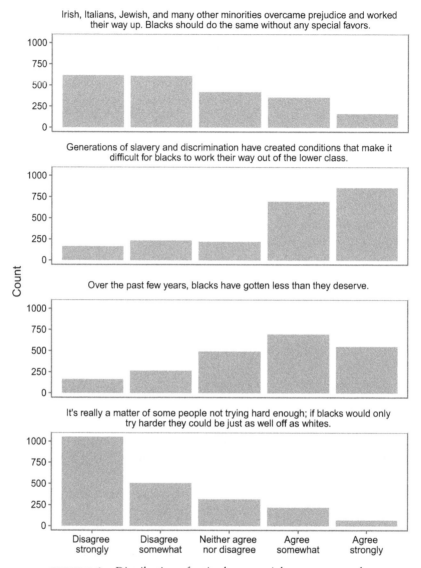

FIGURE 6.7 Distribution of attitudes on racial resentment scale

statements into a single index, which we refer to as the racial resentment index. The index is simply an average response across the four items, with the second and third items reverse coded, such that a higher value indicates a greater level of racial animus.

The racial resentment index is traditionally used to detect animus among whites toward blacks specifically.[6] In this section, we therefore limit our analysis to white student participants in our conjoint experiments. In particular, we want to determine whether and how high levels of racial resentment among whites affect preferences toward hypothetical applicants and candidates from underrepresented minority groups.

Figure 6.7 shows the distribution of responses among white participants for each of the statements in the index. In every case, far more of our participants disagree than agree with the "more resentful" responses, so responses on the overall index are skewed heavily toward low resentment in our sample. To establish a conservative test of the effects of high versus low resentment, therefore, we separate participants who scored above the midpoint (3) on the index from those who scored the midpoint or below the midpoint. The numbers of participants in each group are thus unbalanced, but those in the high-resentment group exhibited substantial racial animus on the survey.

Figures 6.8 and 6.9 contrast responses from high- versus low-racial-resentment participants, first on the admissions experiment, then on faculty recruitment. The results mirror those from the pro- versus antiaffirmative action comparison presented above. Low-racial-resentment (white) participants exhibit strong preferences in favor of all nonwhite applicants and candidates, for women and gender nonbinary applicants and candidates, and for lower-income and first-generation applicants (as well as a slight preference for legacies). High-racial-resentment (white) participants as a group exhibit no measurable preferences for or against any racial/ethnic group, relative to whites, in either set of experiments. Their preferences with respect to socioeconomic class in the admissions experiments are all statistically insignificant, compared to the baseline of the median income. Relative to low-racial-resentment participants, they are less favorable toward applicants from the lowest quintile and less favorable toward those from the top 1 percent.

With regard to gender, high-racial-resentment participants are marginally less favorable than low-resentment participants toward women, and discernibly so on the faculty recruitment experiment. But

---

[6] Some scholars have questioned whether the index could appeal, at least in part, to color-blind principles of individualism (Feldman and Huddy 2005; Huddy and Feldman 2009; Sniderman and Piazza 1993), but recent research confirms that "negative traits ascribed to black Americans are deeply embedded in what goes through people's minds" as they respond to the items (Kam and Burge 2018, p. 319).

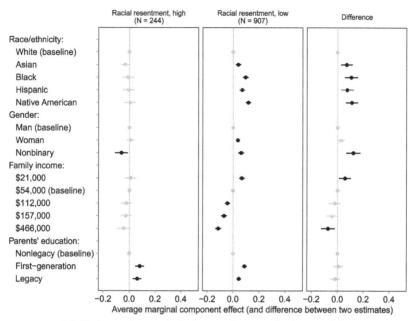

FIGURE 6.8 Undergraduate admissions preferences for low-racial-resentment versus high-racial-resentment participants

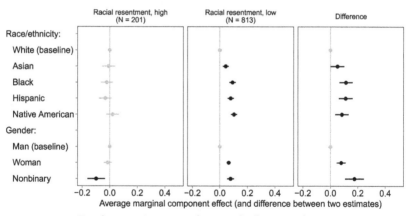

FIGURE 6.9 Faculty recruitment preferences for low-racial-resentment versus high-racial-resentment participants

the biggest difference across groups is with respect to gender nonbinary applicants and candidates. Here again, as with the partisan breakout, we see polarization, with low-resentment participants favoring gender nonbinary applicants and candidates and high-resentment participants disfavoring them.

6.4 DISCUSSION

Figure 6.10 summarizes the cross-group comparisons presented in this chapter. Relative to the analogous figure presented in Chapter 5, we see less consensus and a bit more polarization. But it is remarkable that we find substantial consensus even when we compare preferences across the partisan divide, across participants who took adversarial positions with regard to affirmative action, by SAT scores, and across participants who expressed racial animus versus those who did not.

As in Chapter 5, the only area in which we find outright preference polarization across groups is with regard to gender nonbinary identity. Republicans and high-racial-resentment participants *dis*favor nonbinary

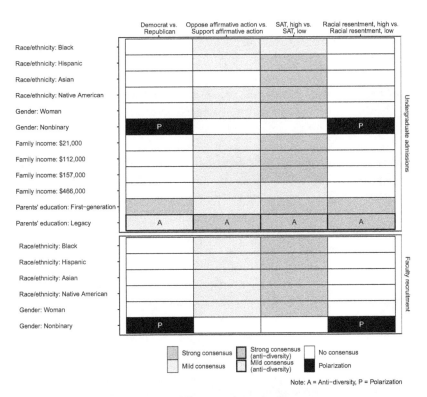

FIGURE 6.10 All comparisons in Chapter 6

undergraduate applicants and faculty candidates whereas Democrats and low-racial-resentment participants favor them, accounting for four black tiles marked with "P". We note that gender nonconformity is a relatively new concept in the mainstream of American political discourse, and that even among our highly cosmopolitan survey population, opinions toward those outside the gender binary may be highly fluid.[7]

On diversity-related characteristics other than nonbinary identity, preference divisions across the partisan divide are larger and more consistent than those across racial/ethnic, gender, or socioeconomic divides. Democrats and Republicans differ consistently with respect to their preferences for all nonwhite groups in both experiments, and with respect to the weight of economic disadvantage in likelihood of selection. So whereas we find mostly consensus across groups broken down by their racial/ethnic identity, gender identity, and socioeconomic class, we find mostly nonconsensus across parties and across levels of racial resentment. That said, there is one prominent exception, which is strong consensus in favor of first-generation college applicants in the admissions experiments. Preference in admissions for first-generation students appears to be a point of universal agreement.

Next, when we break participants out by their support for affirmative action, we find mild consensus on almost every attribute and level included in our experiments. In each instance, those who openly favor affirmative action express stronger pro-diversity preferences than do those who express opposition to considering race, so the consensus across these groups is mild. Yet on all these items – notably including preferences toward every underrepresented minority racial/ethnic group (except Asians in the admissions experiments) and toward women – even those who profess opposition to affirmative action in principle demonstrate pro-diversity preferences in our conjoint experiments. Figure 6.10 also illustrates the consistent pattern of strong preference consensus across attributes and levels among participants who had high versus low SAT scores for their institutions.

What might explain the apparent disjuncture between, on the one hand, opposing a *policy* of race-conscious admissions and faculty recruitment, and on the other hand, taking race/ethnicity (and gender) into consideration when considering individual applicants? We suspect it

---

[7] Recent research, for example, provides the first support for the contact hypothesis with respect to transgender individuals. That is, interpersonal contact with transgender individuals increases tolerance and support for transgender rights (Tadlock et al. 2017).

is critical that our experiments asked participants to choose between (hypothetical) people in a specific context rather than among policies in the abstract. The undergraduate applicants and faculty candidates in our experiments were sufficiently multidimensional that our participants could construct narratives to flesh out the partial information we provided on each. They may have credited applicants and candidates from traditionally marginalized groups with having swum against stronger currents – *in ways not necessarily accounted for by the attributes presented in our conjoint experiments* – than those from traditionally advantaged groups in order to reach their achievements.

Our experiments did not allow us to observe this cognitive process, but it might have looked something like what Princeton University Assistant Professor of Classics Dan-el Padilla Peralta describes when making the case that his merit as a scholar is inextricably tied to his race. After a particularly heated exchange over race and merit with an independent scholar at a classics conference, Padilla wrote, "My merit and my blackness are fused to each other. It is impossible to think of my scholarship, my achievements, without thinking about my blackness" (Pettit 2019). Padilla suggests that scholars from underrepresented minority groups are often not sufficiently credited for the obstacles they confront, arguing that academic gatekeepers too often "overlook the fact that scholars of color have had to overcome extraordinary structural barriers to even field a competitive application" (Pettit 2019).[8] Our results suggest that, in the context of our experiments, most participants – even those who oppose race-conscious admissions and faculty recruitment as policy – take some such considerations into account when making holistic choices about individual applicants. As a result, the experiments reveal preferences that are less polarized than those drawn from a survey question about a policy.

We close this chapter by highlighting a nonfinding. Specifically, we find no evidence of active discrimination against any racial/ethnic group nor against women, even when we break out our participants in ways that reveal racial animus. Those who professed opposition to the

---

[8] Research by Norton, Darley, and Vandello (2004) and Norton et al. (2006) suggests an alternative process by which subjects like ours – undergraduates participating in college admissions experiments – *begin* with a preference for applicants from traditionally underrepresented groups and then "recruit" evidence for that conclusion, selectively weighting applicants' attributes to assemble a narrative that supports a predetermined preference. We cannot disentangle the degree to which our participants constructed narratives that drove their choices, or to which established preferences drove their narratives.

consideration of race in admissions and recruitment decisions – and even the subset of whites whose responses to statements about the legacy of African American slavery and comparisons with other racial/ethnic groups indicate substantial racial resentment – display no tendency to favor white applicants or candidates over underrepresented minorities. We note that our participant pool, consisting of students at major universities, is far from representative of the broader US population. Yet the absence of evidence for preferences *against* those nonwhite groups is noteworthy.

7

What about When All Else Is Not Equal?

Previous chapters showed that, overall, our participants demonstrate preferences for candidates from underrepresented minority groups when all other candidate attributes are held equal. The main question in this chapter is how such preferences operate when other important attributes are *not* constant. The "all else equal" preferences we have described so far are derived from the Average Marginal Component Effects (AMCEs) estimated from our fully randomized conjoint survey experiments. Recalling our discussion from Chapter 3, an AMCE tells us how much more or less likely it is that participants choose a hypothetical candidate with a particular characteristic – for example, a black candidate over a white candidate, or a woman rather than a man – when all other characteristics included in the experiment are the same.

Yet all else is seldom equal, and decisions about admissions and recruitment regularly present trade-offs. If our student participants are 8 percentage points more likely to select a black applicant over a white applicant, other attributes held constant, for example, how does that likelihood shift if the black applicant's SAT scores are in the 80th percentile while the white applicant's are in the 90th, instead of assuming that both applicants' SAT scores are the same? In short, we are interested in this chapter in how our participants regard the trade-offs between demographic and other attributes.

7.1 RATES OF RETURN TO SCHOLARLY ACHIEVEMENT

For all groups of participants across both the admissions and faculty recruitment experiments, the attributes that move the needle most on preferences are those reflecting academic and scholarly achievement – SAT score and high school class rank for undergraduate applicants, and teaching and research performance for faculty candidates. When we think about trade-offs between demographic and other attributes, we are particularly interested in whether the "rates of return" to achievement vary with different demographic characteristics – for example, for black versus Asian applicants in undergraduate admissions, or women versus gender nonbinary candidates for faculty slots.

To examine such relationships, we estimate the Average Component Interaction Effects (ACIEs). In contrast to the AMCEs presented in Chapters 4 through 6, ACIEs reflect the effects of one attribute (e.g., race/ethnicity) on responses at varying levels of another attribute (e.g., SAT score). If the effects of the first attribute vary depending on the value of the second, ACIEs tell us the magnitude of the interaction between the two variables (Hainmueller, Hopkins, and Yamamoto 2014).

To visualize the intuition behind an ACIE, consider Figure 7.1, which uses hypothetical results to illustrate two potential relationships between two key attributes of interest in college admissions: race/ethnicity and SAT score. On the *x*-axis of each graph is SAT score – lower scores are on the left, and higher scores are on the right. On the *y*-axis is the probability of being selected for admission. In each panel, we graph separate lines illustrating the hypothetical likelihood of admission for applicants from four racial/ethnic groups – black, Hispanic, white, and Asian – conditional on SAT score. In both panels and for each group, the higher the

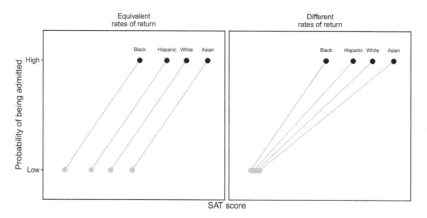

FIGURE 7.1 Hypothetical ACIEs

SAT score, the greater the likelihood of admission. So far, everything is consistent with what we know about actual admissions outcomes.[1]

In the left panel, although black applicants have a higher likelihood of admission than Hispanics (and Hispanics than whites, and so on) at every SAT level, the lines illustrating the SAT-to-admissions relationship for each group run parallel, with equivalent slopes. We can therefore say that the *rate of return to SAT achievement is equivalent* for each group. In the right panel, by contrast, the slopes for each group differ. At low SAT levels, applicants from no group are likely to be admitted, but as SAT scores rise, the likelihood of admission for black applicants rises the most quickly whereas that for Asians rises most slowly. In this hypothetical case, the *rate of return to SAT achievement differs across groups*.

When an ACIE indicates that the rate of return to one attribute (like SAT score) is equivalent across levels of another attribute (like race/ethnicity), as in the left panel, then preferences with respect to race/ethnicity are not contingent on holding SAT scores equal. When an ACIE indicates that the rate of return differs across groups, however, we should explore which groups receive larger (and smaller) returns for shifts on specific attributes, and we should also consider why. In prominent lawsuits currently being brought against Harvard and other universities, for example, plaintiffs allege that Asian applicants receive a lower rate of return for high SAT scores than do other applicants (Mortara et al. 2018).

Given the number of attributes and levels included in our conjoint experiments, the potential number of interaction effects is extremely large. As in Chapters 5 and 6, therefore, we focus on those attributes that are central, and controversial, in debates over campus diversity – particularly those that have to do with interactions among demographics, scholarly achievement, and, in the case of admissions, with socioeconomic class. We use the estimated ACIEs to calculate the likelihood of selection for combinations of undergraduate applicants' or faculty candidates' attribute-levels. For undergraduate admissions, for example, we estimate the marginal effects of shifts in SAT score, and high school class rank, by an applicant's race/ethnicity, gender, family income, and

---

[1] Both graphs are also consistent with Espenshade and Radford's (2009) results, which demonstrate that, for each SAT score level, black applicants are more likely to be admitted than Hispanics, who are in turn more likely than whites, who are in turn more likely than Asians.

parents' education. For faculty recruitment, we estimate the marginal effects of shifts in teaching record and research record by a candidate's race/ethnicity and gender.

We can then plot on the y-axis the likelihood of selection for applicants or candidates from various groups (e.g., by race/ethnicity) as an attribute of interest (e.g., SAT score) rises along the x-axis. As in our hypothetical example shown in Figure 7.1, each attribute-level of interest (e.g., white versus Asian versus black versus Hispanic versus Native American) is plotted as a separate line. If there is no interaction effect between the attribute plotted along the x-axis and the attribute represented by distinct lines in the graph, the slopes are similar and the distance between the lines does not differ across the range of the x-axis. By contrast, in a graph comparing, for example, undergraduate applicants across racial/ethnic groups, if our experiment participants penalize underrepresented minority applicants less than white applicants for low SAT scores, then the line for minority applicants should be flatter at the low end of the SAT scale. Alternatively, if they reward Asian applicants less for high SAT scores, then the line for Asians should be flatter at the high end.

7.2 RATES OF RETURN DO NOT DIFFER ACROSS GROUPS

Starting with real data from our admissions experiment, Figure 7.2 shows the estimated marginal effects of increasing SAT scores for applicants from each racial/ethnic group included in the experiments. More specifically, it shows twelve estimated conditional effects, of three levels of SAT scores (50th, 75th, and 98th percentiles, relative to the baseline level of the 25th percentile), across four racial/ethnic categories (Asian, black, Hispanic, and Native American, relative to the baseline category, white).[2] The marginal effects are all relative to the baselines for these two attributes, the 25th percentile for SAT score and white for race/ethnicity. The value of the y-axis for the baseline combination is, by design, zero.

---

[2] Recall that the SAT score levels in our conjoint experiments were calculated for each institution, relative to the distribution of scores among enrolled students. The top level was calculated as the 75th percentile + 1.5 × the interquartile range (or the maximum score, if 75th + 1.5 × IQR would exceed the maximum). Depending on the shape of the distribution of scores at each institution, that top level represents at least a 98th percentile ranking.

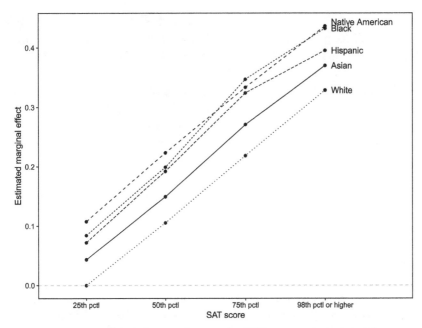

FIGURE 7.2 Admissions preferences by SAT score and race/ethnicity

The lines then connect the estimates for each group at successive SAT levels.[3] Applicants from every racial/ethnic category are rewarded for increasing SAT scores, but the rates at which they are rewarded are statistically indistinguishable across most groups. The figure also shows that for the same level for SAT score, Native American and black applicants are more likely to be selected relative to Hispanics, Asians, or whites. Notably, among our student participants, Asian applicants receive the same boost in likelihood of being selected as their SAT scores rise as do white applicants; these lines are parallel, like the left panel in Figure 7.1.

The results from Figure 7.2 allow us to build on existing debates about trade-offs across attributes. Consider, for example, the seminal work by Espenshade and Radford (2009) on the trade-off in college admissions between race/ethnicity and SAT scores, which draws on actual admissions records from almost a quarter of a million applicants across eight

---

[3] It would be impractical to include confidence intervals around these estimates because they would obscure the lines and any pattern in the results. We will show which of these interaction effects are statistically significant in Figure 7.4 in the appendix to this chapter.

highly selective universities. Espenshade and Radford's raw data suggest that increments in SAT scores raise the likelihood of admission for black applicants at greater rates than for whites, Hispanics, or Asians (see Espenshade and Radford's Figure 3.6, p. 82). Drawing on data on race/ethnicity and test scores, but also on gender, high school grades, socioeconomic status, athletic status, legacy status, and a range of other information about applicants, the authors then estimate the SAT point differential at which applicants from different race/ethnicity categories would be equally likely to be admitted (see Table 3.5, p. 92). Yet their models do not include estimates of the interaction effects of race/ethnicity on SAT score, or of race/ethnicity on high school grades.[4] We consider this to be an important limitation of their analysis.[5] Without modeling the interactions of the attributes, it is difficult to properly assess how the impacts of an additional *increase* in SAT score on the probability of being selected would vary across different racial/ethnic groups. ACIEs are the estimates of this quantity of interest.

Figure 7.2 is just one example of these ACIEs. We can estimate ACIEs to test for interaction effects between numerous other combinations of key attributes in our experiments. As with the combination of race/ethnicity and SAT score, our analyses produce null results across almost every interaction effect we test. There are a handful of exceptions. Figure 7.3, for example, shows the estimates for the marginal effects of SAT score by family income. The higher point estimates for applicants from the median ($54,000) or the bottom 20th percentile for family income ($21,000), compared to richer applicants, for any SAT level are consistent with our findings in Chapter 5. The lines illustrating marginal effects are mainly parallel, but the marginal effects of selecting applicants from the top 20th percentile for family income ($112,000) "sink" when SAT score is at the 50th percentile or the 75th percentile. These are examples of statistically significant interaction effects in which the lines are not parallel.

It is important to bear in mind, however, the large number of potential interaction effects for which we estimate ACIEs. Conventions for determining statistical significance suggest that around 5 percent of estimates will surpass standard benchmarks even in the absence of systematic relationships. And this is precisely what we find. We estimate numerous interaction effects between our attributes reflecting academic and

---

[4] Interestingly, they do estimate the interaction effect of race and socioeconomic status.
[5] We discuss some of the other limitations of using observational data in Chapter 3.

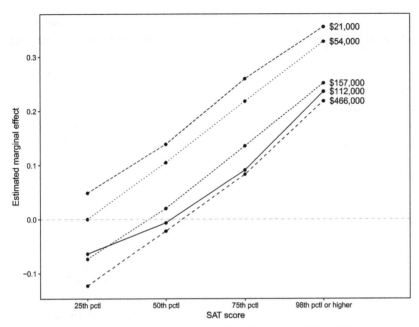

FIGURE 7.3 Admissions preferences by SAT score and family income

scholarly achievement, and those reflecting race/ethnicity, gender, and socioeconomic status, using the full sample of participants. The motivation with all these models is to determine whether the "rate of return to achievement" differs across race/ethnicity, across gender, or across socioeconomic status. We find no evidence that it does. The incidence of statistically significant ACIEs in both the undergraduate admissions experiments and the faculty recruitment experiments are exactly what one would expect if there are no systematic patterns in the data. Figure 7.4 in the appendix to this chapter presents an illustration of these estimates graphically.

7.3   WHAT EQUIVALENT RATES OF RETURN TELL US ABOUT PREFERENCES

The core of our analysis in previous chapters estimates how much more or less likely it is that participants in our experiments select an undergraduate applicant or a faculty candidate if that applicant/candidate has a particular level for a particular attribute, relative to the baseline level, when other attributes are the same. We estimate, for example, how much being a legacy applicant rather than one whose parents attended some other college affects likelihood of selection in our admissions experiment; or the effect of being from a household at the 20th income percentile rather than the median; or of being Native American rather than white – in each case, all else equal.

But the question remained as to what happens if all else is *not* held equal when our participants evaluate undergraduate applicants and faculty candidates. What if the rate of return they award to some attributes varies, conditional on others? In particular, we are interested in whether the rates of return for our core attributes reflecting academic and professional achievement differ across race/ethnicity, gender, and (in the admissions experiments) class status.

Our results demonstrate that the rates of return are equivalent. In concrete terms, this means that the degree by which a participant in our experiments is more likely to select an Hispanic applicant rather than a white one does not depend on whether the applicant's SAT score (or high school class rank) is high or low. Similarly, the degree to which a participant is more likely to select a woman than a man for a faculty appointment does not depend on whether the candidate's teaching or research record is strong or weak.

Note that we are *not* saying here that applicants' and candidates' scholarly achievements do not matter to participants. The results here do not mean that a black applicant with lower academic performance in high school is necessarily more likely to be selected than a white applicant with higher performance, or that an applicant from a poor family who has low SAT scores is more likely to be selected than one from a rich family with higher scores, or that a woman faculty candidate with fair teaching is more likely to be selected than a man with good teaching. In each of these cases, the participants in our experiments value both attributes, and the choices they made in our experiments indicate that they make trade-offs across the attributes they value. How much high school class rank, SAT score, teaching record, or research record they are willing to trade off in order to recruit applicants or faculty candidates from underrepresented minority groups varies across experiments and across participant groups. What the null results from this chapter show is that those trade-offs do not vary with what part of the "achievement scale" the applicants or candidates are on. The magnitudes of preferences for underrepresented minority racial/ethnic groups, for women and gender nonbinary individuals, and for socioeconomically disadvantaged applicants are equivalent across the range of achievements.

Appendices

7.A ILLUSTRATING THE NULL RESULTS

Figure 7.4 illustrates the coefficients for all the interaction effects we estimate using the full sample of participants. To recall, for admissions we rely on SAT scores and high school class rank as indicators of academic achievement. For faculty recruitment, we rely on teaching quality and research quality for professional achievement. We interact each of these with race/ethnicity and gender for both sets of experiments. For the admissions experiments, we also interact our measures of academic achievement with indicators of class status: family income and parents' education. The black markers indicate estimates that are statistically significant at the 0.05 level whereas gray markers indicate estimates that fall short of significance. Note that all estimates are relative to omitted, baseline categories. These are the lowest values for all our measures of achievement. For race/ethnicity, the baseline is white; for gender, man; for family income, the national median; and for parents' education, it is neither first-generation nor legacy status – that is, at least one parent attended college at a different university.

The figure indicates that we find no such evidence. For the admissions experiments, we estimate 72 interactions and 5 of them are significant at the 0.05 level – nearly what one would expect if there are no systematic patterns in the data. For the faculty recruitment experiments, we estimate 24 interactions and only one produces a p-value below 0.05. Again, there is no evidence of any systematic pattern.

The overall lack of patterns can be also presented with QQ plots, which we used in the appendix to Chapter 4. Figure 7.5 plots p-values

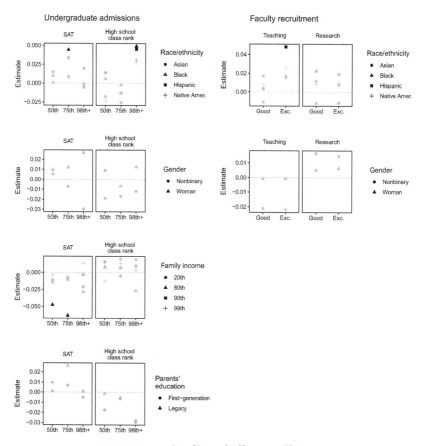

FIGURE 7.4 Conditional effects coefficients

of the estimated 72 (admissions) or 24 (recruitment) interaction effects on the *y*-axis. These dots are equally spaced on the *x*-axis. If the *p*-values are uniformly distributed, these dots should be close to the 45-degree line. The figure shows that the dots are indeed close to the 45-degree line.

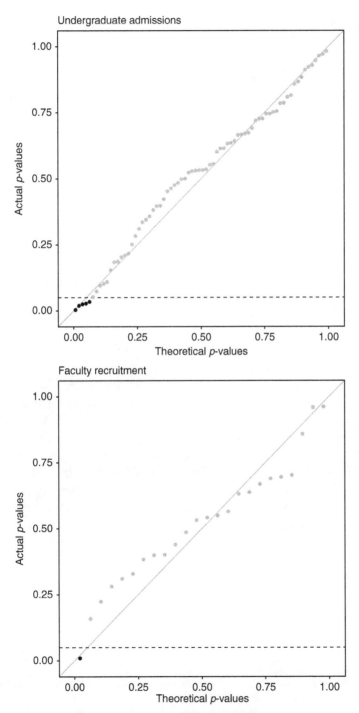

FIGURE 7.5 QQ-plot showing the distribution of *p*-values of ACIEs

8

How Student Attitudes Differ from Faculty Attitudes

The preceding chapters examine preferences among students with regard to admissions and faculty recruitment. This chapter shifts the focus, comparing preferences on faculty recruitment between students and faculty.[1] At two universities, the University of Nevada, Reno, and the University of New Mexico, we were able to recruit faculty as well as students to participate in our conjoint experiments. We limited the experiments with faculty participants to faculty recruitment only. This was necessary for two reasons. Faculty are fewer in number than students, so splitting faculty samples between two different experiments was not viable. Furthermore, at UNM, undergraduate admissions is not selective, so the choices at the heart of the admissions experiment would not have made sense in UNM's context. Our goal was to compare student and faculty preferences on what characteristics ought to drive the recruitment of new faculty. In particular, we explore whether students and faculty share the same views with respect to demographic diversity in faculty recruitment, and the relative weight they place on race/ethnicity and gender versus other characteristics among candidates for faculty positions.

Why are we interested in faculty preferences, and specifically, in how they compare to those of students? First, although students comprise the

[1] The research and writing for this chapter was conducted in collaboration with Mala Htun, Professor of Political Science at the University of New Mexico. An earlier version of this chapter was published as: Carey, John, M., Kevin Carman, Katherine Clayton, Yusaku Horiuchi, Mala N. Htun, and Brittany Ortiz. 2019. "Who Wants to Hire a More Diverse Faculty? A Conjoint Analysis of Faculty and Student Preferences for Gender and Racial/Ethnic Diversity." *Politics, Groups and Identities*, forthcoming.

largest population at almost every university, faculty are directly involved in the recruitment of other faculty, so their preferences are well developed and directly salient to how recruitment operates. The degree to which preferences line up, or differ, between faculty and their main constituency, therefore, can tell us a lot about prospects for future faculty recruitment to satisfy student preferences going forward.

Moreover, we are interested in the degree to which the faculty preferences revealed through our experiments line up with the current composition of faculty, and with the expressed policies of universities over the past several decades. Since the civil rights movement of the 1950s and 1960s, major public and private institutions in the United States have attempted to promote diversity in education, in employment, and in positions of leadership. Universities introduced affirmative action in admissions and hiring, corporations created equal opportunity programs, and the federal government gave preferential treatment to women-owned or minority-owned contractors (Bowen and Bok 1998; Dobbin 2009; Skrentny 2002). As a result of these programs, diversity values and discourse permeate major institutions, which have more women and minorities today than in the mid-twentieth century. Some observers criticize what they regard as an excessive preoccupation with diversity among highly educated cosmopolitans (Lilla 2017). Others counter that women and minorities continue to be underrepresented, particularly at higher levels of institutional leadership (Finkelstein, Conley, and Schuster 2016). The ongoing debate over how much universities ought to value diversity within their ranks, and how much they do so in practice, drives our curiosity to assess the preferences for diversity in faculty recruitment among faculty themselves.

Although some prior studies explore students' views toward diversity and affirmative action (Park 2009; Park, Denson, and Bowman 2013; Rankin and Reason 2005; Sax and Arredondo 1999; Smith 1998; Terenzini et al. 1996; Worthington et al. 2008), examinations of faculty attitudes toward affirmative action are less common (Park and Denson 2009). Furthermore, to our knowledge, ours is the first direct comparison of student and faculty attitudes toward diversity using a common instrument.

To preview our results, preferences for racial/ethnic and gender diversity in faculty hiring are stronger among faculty participants than among student participants in our experiments. Indeed, the differences *between* faculty and students tend to be larger and more consistent than differences *within* faculty or students across racial/ethnic, gender, or socioeconomic class divisions. We propose two interpretations for the student versus faculty differences – first, as symptoms of the pronounced liberalism of university faculty, and second, as a reflection of the greater demographic diversity among contingent faculty and graduate students, with whom students most frequently interact, than among professors on the tenure track.

8.1 THE NEW MEXICO AND NEVADA STUDIES

In Chapter 3, we presented state and university demographic statistics for each of the universities in our study. Recall that the demographic compositions of New Mexico and Nevada differ. In New Mexico, the Hispanic and Native American shares of the population are much larger, whereas white, black, and Asian shares are relatively greater in Nevada. At both universities, the racial/ethnic composition of the student body bears a close resemblance to the composition of the state (Table 3.3), but the deviations are greater among faculty (Table 8.1). In particular, non-Hispanic whites are overrepresented among faculty at both UNM and UNR. Relative to state population shares, Hispanics and Native Americans are substantially underrepresented among faculty at UNM, and Hispanics and blacks are underrepresented among faculty at UNR. On gender, at both universities, women outnumber men among students – 56 percent to 44 percent at UNM and 53 percent to 47 percent at UNR – whereas men outnumber women among faculty – 53 percent to 47 percent at UNM and 58 percent to 42 percent at UNR.[2] Thus, at both institutions, the underrepresentation of minority groups is more pronounced among faculty than among students, and women are underrepresented among faculty while they are overrepresented among students.

There are some minor differences between the UNM and UNR faculty recruitment experiments, driven by institution-specific characteristics and interests. The UNR instrument is as described in Chapter 2 (allowing the UNR results to be pooled with those from Dartmouth, USCD, and UNC in our broader analyses). The UNM instrument includes an attribute for heritage (New Mexican, US citizen, or Non-US citizen) and one for community engagement and service record ("Fair," "Good," or "Excellent").

[2] The statistics (included in our replication package) are based on the figures provided by the institutions.

TABLE 8.1 *State population versus campus faculty population demographics*

University	Race/ethnicity	(A) State population	(B) Faculty population	(B) − (A) Difference
UNM	Non-Hispanic white	38.1	56.0	17.9
	Asian	1.7	4.0	2.3
	Black	2.5	2.0	−0.5
	Hispanic	44.4	28.0	−16.4
	Native American	10.8	3.0	−7.8
	Other	2.5	6.0	3.5
UNR	Non-Hispanic white	49.9	74.0	24.1
	Asian	8.7	16.6	7.9
	Black	9.6	2.3	−7.3
	Hispanic	25.2	5.1	−20.1
	Native American	2.4	0.4	−2.0
	Other	4.2	1.6	−2.6

Note: The state demographic data are taken from the US Census, relying on figures as of 2016. "Other" for (A) is "two or more races." The percentage of "Hispanic" for (A) is 100 percent minus the sum of other percentages. University population figures are provided by the institutions.

UNR's attributes for where a candidate received her or his undergraduate degree, for faculty rank, and for department or program, are not included in the UNM survey.[3]

These minor differences in the structures of the conjoint tables preclude us from pooling the data from UNM and UNR, because AMCEs are only defined given a particular set of attributes and levels included in the analysis. Therefore, we cannot determine whether, for example, the AMCE for a black faculty candidate, relative to a white candidate, among UNM student participants is statistically discernible from that among students at UNR. We can, however, test whether preferences across groups (e.g., white students versus nonwhite students) and between students and faculty are discernible *within each university*. We first show and compare the overall results at UNM and UNR. We then drill down to the within-institution comparisons across different groups of participants by race/ethnicity and gender, as well as comparisons between students and faculty.

[3] The questions on student participants' demographics and attitudes are consistent across institutions, as described in Chapter 2. Faculty participants were asked their gender identity, race/ethnicity, the school or department to which they belonged, and their faculty position or rank.

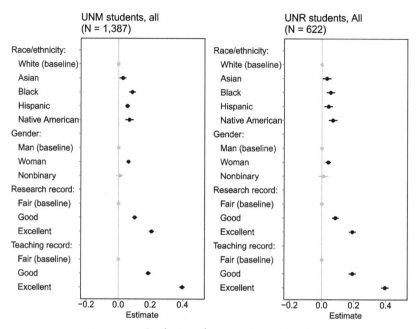

FIGURE 8.1 Student preferences at UNM and UNR

8.2 COMPARING PREFERENCES BETWEEN AND WITHIN INSTITUTIONS

Figures 8.1 and 8.2 show the results for student participants and faculty participants, respectively, at UNM and UNR, focusing on key attributes of faculty candidates.[4] Consistent with previous results, and now including UNM, Figure 8.1 shows that at both universities, students exhibit moderate positive preferences for faculty diversity. Specifically, students prefer a woman or a minority faculty candidate to a man or a white one, but the magnitudes of these differences are less than 10 percentage points. Their preference for a gender nonbinary faculty candidate is not significantly different from their preference for a candidate who is a man. Students' strongest preferences are for candidates with strong teaching records. In particular, at both institutions, students value excellent teaching over all other attributes.

---

[4] Estimates for preferences across the full set of attributes and levels at each institution will be included in our replication package.

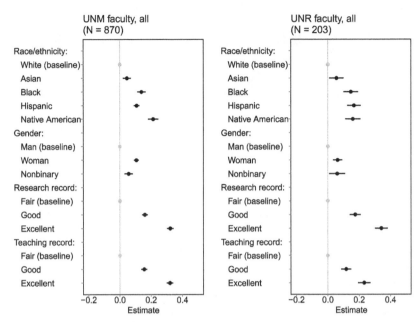

FIGURE 8.2 Faculty preferences at UNM and UNR

By contrast, faculty at both universities register stronger preferences for faculty diversity. Figure 8.2 shows that faculty at both institutions are between 11 and 21 percentage points more likely to select a Native American, a Hispanic, or a black candidate than a white one. Their preferences for an Asian candidate are weaker but still statistically significant. On gender, UNM faculty are more than 11 percentage points more likely to select a woman candidate than a man, and 6 percentage points more likely to select a gender nonbinary candidate. At UNR these preferences are slightly smaller, but they are still positive and statistically significant. Faculty also value strong scholarly records, with the relative weight of their preferences for excellence in research and teaching nearly equivalent at UNM and a slightly heavier weight for research excellence at UNR, in contrast to students who weigh teaching more heavily.

Next, we turn to comparisons across groups of participants within each institution. As in earlier chapters, to simplify presentation, subsequent figures focus on the AMCEs for the attributes reflecting diversity on race/ethnicity and gender only. Figure 8.3 contrasts the preferences of white and nonwhite students at UNM and UNR. The AMCE estimates for candidates from every traditionally underrepresented category

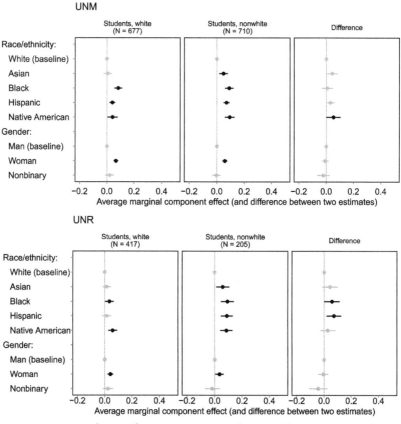

FIGURE 8.3 Student preferences at UNM and UNR, white versus nonwhite

are positive for both white and nonwhite students, although they fall short of statistical significance for whites in some instances, particularly at UNR. Nonwhite students at UNM are slightly more favorable toward Native American candidates than are white students, and nonwhite UNR students are more favorable than whites toward black and Hispanic candidates.

Given that Hispanics are the largest nonwhite group at both universities, we also estimate the preferences of Hispanic students relative to whites (results included in our replication package). Hispanic students at both universities demonstrate stronger preferences than whites for Hispanic faculty candidates, but no measurably different preferences with respect to any other attributes.

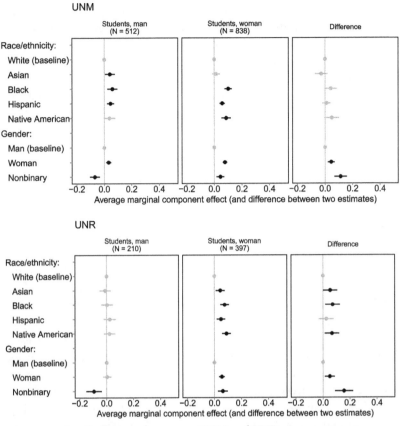

FIGURE 8.4 Student preferences at UNM and UNR, man versus woman

Figure 8.4 breaks out student preferences by gender, and again we see some differences across groups. With respect to the race/ethnicity of faculty candidates, there are no measurable differences in preferences between men and women students at UNM; both groups tend to favor candidates from underrepresented minority groups, particularly blacks and Hispanics. (The effect of Native American is barely insignificant among men students at UNM.) At UNR, by contrast, men are, on average, indifferent to race/ethnicity, neither favoring nor disfavoring candidates from any nonwhite category relative to whites, whereas women favor candidates from all nonwhite categories. The differences between men's and women's preferences at UNR are statistically discernible for Asian, black, and Native American candidates.

On gender, men at UNM favor women candidates slightly, whereas at UNR, men are indifferent between men and women. Women participants at both universities, by contrast, prefer a woman candidate, and the differences between men's and women's preferences are statistically significant at both institutions.

As in earlier analyses, it is with respect to gender nonbinary candidates that we observe our only instances of *polarization* in preferences across participant groups; that is, a statistically discernible negative preference among one group and a positive preference among another. At both UNM and UNR, men are at least 7 percentage points *less* likely to select a nonbinary candidate than a man, whereas women are at least 4 percentage points *more* likely to select a nonbinary candidate relative to a man.

When we break our student participants out by social class, we find few significant differences in preferences (results included in our replication package). First, we compare the preferences of first-generation college students with those of students with at least one parent who is a college graduate. Differences between these groups of students are all insignificant at both schools.

To further probe whether socioeconomic class affects preferences for diversity, we also compare the preferences for racial/ethnic or gender diversity of students from families with incomes below $50,000 per year with those from families above $50,000 per year, or with those from families above $150,000 per year for another comparison. Here again, we find scarce differences between students from low-income and high-income families – only that lower-income students at UNR have stronger preferences than the highest-income (above $150,000 per year) students for Asian faculty candidates. On the whole, across both specifications of social class, and across both the UNM and UNR samples, it appears that class has little systematic impact on whether students are supportive of racial/ethnic or gender diversity in the faculty recruitment process.

Turning now to faculty participants, we find consistent preferences – among whites and nonwhites, among men and women – for candidates from traditionally underrepresented minority groups in most instances (results included in our replication package). That said, preferences for Asian candidates are not significantly different from the preferences for white candidates among faculty at UNM who are men, among nonwhite faculty at UNR, and among both men and women faculty at UNR.

Across groups of faculty, we find only a handful of statistically discernible differences, all of which are matters of degree, with preferences running in the same direction in all cases. At UNM, nonwhite faculty express stronger preferences for Hispanic candidates than do white faculty, and women express stronger preferences than men for candidates who are black, Native American, and women. At UNR, there are no statistically discernible differences between white and nonwhite faculty, whereas women have stronger preferences than men for women candidates and for black candidates. Overall, then, across faculty groups, consensus (sometimes mild, more often strong) dominates.[5]

The student versus faculty comparisons at both institutions reveal more pronounced and consistent preference differences. Figure 8.5 shows the comparisons at UNM and UNR, respectively. At both institutions, faculty members' preferences for black, Hispanic, and Native American candidates are larger than students' (also favorable) preferences for the same groups. Among faculty, shifting a candidate from white to black, Hispanic, or Native American increases the probability that that candidate is selected by about 11–21 percentage points. Among students, the analogous shifts in likelihood of selection are all below 10 percentage points. It is also worth noting that at both institutions, both students and faculty have weak (but positive and significant) preferences for Asian candidates relative to whites, and the differences between students and faculty on this count are insignificant. This may be in part due to the fact that aside from non-Hispanic whites, Asian faculty are the only group that is overrepresented as compared to the state population (Table 8.1). This overrepresentation is particularly large at UNR, where 16 percent of faculty are Asian. The (over) presence of Asian faculty on campus is likely noticeable to both students and faculty at these institutions.

There are also significant differences between student and faculty preferences regarding gender. UNM faculty are more favorable toward women and gender nonbinary candidates than are UNM students, who favor women moderately and are indifferent, on average, to nonbinary candidates. At UNR, student and faculty preferences with regard to women and nonbinary candidates are not statistically distinguishable.

---

[5] In the interest of space, we do not present comparisons across groups of faculty here, but these are shown and discussed at greater length in Carey et al. (2018). The full results are also included in our replication package.

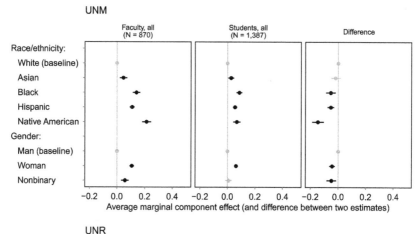

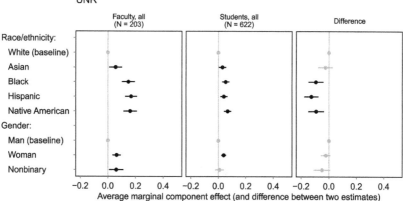

FIGURE 8.5 Preferences between student and faculty participants

Finally, note that although these figures show AMCEs for demographic characteristics only, at both institutions, there are clear differences between student and faculty priority for teaching and research, with students prioritizing teaching excellence more than faculty, and faculty prizing research excellence more than students.[6]

In sum, at both UNM and UNR, we find that nonwhite students express moderately greater preferences for a racially/ethnically diverse faculty than do white students, and students who are women express moderately greater preferences for faculty who are women and substantially stronger preferences for nonbinary faculty, than do students

---

[6] The full results showing these attributes are available in our replication package.

who are men. Carey et al. (2018) also report some differences between subgroups among faculty. Most importantly, however, differences in preferences *between* faculty and students in the aggregate are greater than differences *among* subgroups of faculty and students defined by race/ethnicity, gender, and class. Students show preferences for minority faculty and for women and gender nonbinary candidates, but faculty preferences for these groups are often significantly and substantially larger and more consistent across categories.

8.3 INTERPRETING STUDENT AND FACULTY VIEWS

Much of the scholarly literature on representation and diversity maintains that women and minorities have shared interests in seeing members of their group in prominent positions. Their interests in greater presence in power derive, not necessarily from a common identity or policy position, but from the shared experience of decades, or even centuries, of exclusion and discrimination (Baldez 2002; Htun 2016; Young and Allen 2011). These perspectives imply that group membership would correspond to preferences for diversity in faculty hiring, affirmative action in admissions, and possibly also to other policies such as quotas in politics.

Our results, by contrast, show that membership in a social group defined by race/ethnicity or gender is not the strongest or most consistent predictor of preferences for diversity in faculty hiring. Our findings in this chapter are more consistent with intersectional approaches that challenge the simple association between social identities and policy preferences by calling attention to heterogeneity within social groups. According to some intersectional perspectives, women and minority groups are not single categories, but collections of categories bisected by other salient social differences (Hancock 2016; Htun and Ossa 2013; Weldon 2008, 2011). Women who employ nannies and maids for child care and housework, for example, have an interest in the existence of a low-wage informal labor market, while women who work as maids and nannies share the opposite interest in the formalization of, and higher wages for, domestic work (Ehrenreich and Hochschild 2003). The comparisons between students and faculty affirm that social and occupational status – in this case, whether one is a student or a faculty member – is a more consistent and robust predictor of diversity preferences than is race/ethnicity, gender, or class.

To be sure, students and faculty differ on more than social and occupational status. They also differ by age, education level, political beliefs, and generational cohort. Some faculty are old enough to remember the civil rights movement the emergence of Second Wave feminism, protests against the Vietnam War, and other major historical events that pushed values of gender and racial/ethnic diversity into public prominence. Students, by contrast, came of age in the post-9/11 era, when diversity discourse ran into the challenges posed by perceived threats of religious fundamentalism, terrorism, immigration, and globalization.[7] What is more, although young people in general tend to have more liberal views than older people, faculty are less politically diverse than students. Recent studies confirm that conservative views are rare among faculty members (Abrams 2016a; Gross 2013; Shields and Dunn Sr. 2016). The evidence presented throughout this book shows strong student support for campus diversity. Yet the experiments in this chapter demonstrate that faculty support is stronger still.

There is also another potential interpretation of our results that warrants further exploration. Large public research universities, many of which face significant budget constraints, tend to rely more heavily on PhD students, adjunct instructors, and lecturers on contract than do private universities. This reliance on instruction by non–tenure-track faculty is often most pronounced in the largest courses, whereas more specialized courses are more likely to be taught by tenure-track faculty. As a result, there may be a disjuncture between the faculty that most students interact with on a daily basis and the tenure-track faculty that are the main targets of diversity hiring initiatives.

Across the natural sciences and engineering, as well as most of the social sciences, the presence of women and minorities tends to be greater among these *teaching* faculty – including contract and part-time instructors, as well as graduate students – than it is among *tenure-track* faculty (Bettinger and Long 2005; Flaherty 2016a; Harper et al. 2001; Ginther and Kahn 2012; Trower and Chait 2002; West and Curtis 2006). As a result, the "faculty" that undergraduates get to know in their classes may be more diverse than the ranks of tenure-track faculty. If so, students may regard the underrepresentation of women, nonbinary, and

---

7 In addition, recent studies find that the millennial generation has a different understanding of the concepts of "diversity" and "inclusion" than baby boomers and Gen Xers. They are less inclined to think of the diversity of visible social groups and more inclined to think of ideas, unique personal identities, and experiences (Smith and Turner 2015).

nonwhite faculty as less pronounced than do the faculty themselves, which could translate into the less emphatic preferences for candidates who are women and minorities among students than among faculty that we observe in our conjoint experiments at UNM and UNR. At the same time, however, we note that the extent to which faculty influence students' conceptions of race and diversity is unclear (Morning 2011), which makes it difficult to determine whether faculty rank plays an important role.

In sum, our student-versus-faculty comparison is amenable to two distinct interpretations. First, to the extent that we are comparing "likes" with "likes," meaning that students and faculty conceptualize diversity in faculty hiring in the same way, a combination of education, socialization, generational age, and political liberalism likely accounts for the gap between student and faculty preferences on diversity. An alternative interpretation rests on the idea that students and faculty have different conceptions of faculty diversity, based on the composition of the faculty with whom they interact the most. The latter suggests a testable proposition: at colleges and universities where teaching is done primarily by a nondiverse tenure-track faculty, the differences between student and faculty preferences should be less pronounced than at larger public universities where the tenure-track ranks may be just as homogeneous, but the teaching ranks of adjuncts, contract lecturers, and graduate students are more diverse.

These two interpretations are not mutually exclusive. Both could account for parts of the difference between student and faculty preferences for diversity. For now, a main takeaway is that, when it comes to preferences for diversity in faculty hiring, differences between students and faculty are more prominent than those across racial/ethnic, gender, or class groups. The gap in student versus faculty preferences reflects differences in experiences and socialization, and possibly in an understanding of what diversity is. This divergence, moreover, could affect campus consensus on policies related to diversity. Faculty recruitment, for example, is a slow, labor-intensive, and highly deliberative process, particularly in the tenured and tenure-track ranks where universities weigh lifetime commitments. Assembling faculties that excel in scholarship, teaching, and mentoring is one of the biggest challenges universities confront. Understanding how faculty value diversity – and how the faculty's core constituency, students, do – is essential to determining how universities should approach that challenge.

9

Evidence from Other Cases

This book's core results demonstrate that students at selected US universities prioritize diversity in undergraduate admissions and in faculty recruitment. The scale of those priorities, as measured in our experiments, varies somewhat across groups – whether defined by race/ethnicity, gender, socioeconomic background, or political beliefs – but even across these divides we find far more consensus than conflict in preferences for diversity. The universities at which we conducted experiments are diverse on a number of counts. Most are public institutions, but Dartmouth is private. Some are highly selective, but others have more open admissions. The institutions span geographical regions and their student populations have widely different demographics. Yet as Chapter 4 shows, student attitudes are remarkably consistent across schools. This chapter pushes inquiry along those lines further, examining student preferences at two schools that differ from those examined so far still more fundamentally. We report on results from conjoint experiments conducted at the United States Naval Academy (Naval Academy, or USNA)[1] and at the London School of Economics and Political Science (LSE).[2]

---

[1] Our studies at the Naval Academy were conducted in collaboration with Professor John Polga-Hecimovich, as was the analysis of the results from that institution presented in this chapter. We invited all matriculated students currently enrolled, and collected data from January 30 to February 10, 2018. A total of 1,154 midshipmen completed the exercise (582 for admissions, 572 for faculty recruitment) for a combined response rate of 26 percent. The results of our USNA experiments are initially published as: Polga-Hecimovich, John, John Carey, and Yusaku Horiuchi. 2019. "Student Attitudes Toward Campus Diversity at the United States Naval Academy: Evidence from Conjoint Survey Experiments." *Armed Forces & Society*, forthcoming.

[2] Our studies at the LSE were conducted in collaboration with Professor Simon Hix, as was the analysis of the results from that institution presented in this chapter. We invited 2,393

The conjoint experiments used in each of these studies differed modestly in design from those we used at Dartmouth, UCSD, UNC, and UNR. At the Naval Academy, particularities of both the student body and the faculty warranted modifications to some of the attributes and levels used in our other experiments. Similarly, at the LSE, we adapted the sets of attributes and levels in each experiment to reflect British demographics and the British university system. These university-specific differences prevent us from pooling responses with those from the other US institutions and including them in a universal analysis. That said, the differences are pragmatic rather than conceptual, and the broad design of the conjoint experiments is consistent across all the studies. In this chapter, therefore, we present the results from the Naval Academy and from the LSE individually, and we compare them with those discussed in previous chapters.

At the risk of ruining any suspense, student preferences in favor of diversity are largely consistent, even in these quite different contexts. One prominent exception to that pattern involves attitudes on gender at the Naval Academy, where preferences *against* nonbinary applicants and candidates are strong. At the LSE, we see preferences in favor of underrepresented minority applicants, but the relative weight on demographic characteristics is less and that on socioeconomic background is more than at the American institutions.

9.1 UNITED STATES NAVAL ACADEMY

The Naval School was established in 1845, with a class of fifty students and seven professors, and changed its name to the Naval Academy in 1850.[3] Students – male and female – are referred to as midshipmen, and are naval officers-in-training. Their academic curriculum consists of required and elective courses similar to those offered at civilian colleges, as well as professional military education. Midshipmen agree to a minimum five-year active duty service obligation in exchange for their tuition,

and 2,392 LSE undergraduate students, respectively, receiving 494 and 384 complete responses for a combined response rate of 18 percent, between January 25 and February 9, 2017. The results of our LSE experiments were initially published as: Carey, John, Katie Clayton, Simon Hix, and Yusaku Horiuchi. "LSE Students' Views on Diversity on Campus." *LSE Equality, Diversity and Inclusion blog*, June 20, 2017.

[3] Other United States military service academies are the United States Military Academy (West Point), the United States Air Force Academy, the United States Coast Guard Academy, and the United States Merchant Marine Academy.

TABLE 9.1 *USNA student and faculty demographics*

	USNA faculty	Midshipmen
Race/ethnicity		
White	84.7%	64.1%
Asian	8.0%	7.2%
Black	3.2%	6.8%
Hispanic	3.8%	12.0%
Native American	0.3%	0.6%
Multiple		9.2%
Gender		
Men	68.5%	73.1%
Women	31.5%	26.9%
N	314	4,458

Note: The number of midshipmen excludes 52 international students and 53 students that declined to respond. Data provided by the institution.

and upon graduation, most are commissioned as ensigns in the Navy or second lieutenants in the Marine Corps.

The Naval Academy faculty is historically composed of roughly equal numbers of officers and civilians, and currently about half of the approximately 600 professors are civilians. The bulk of military professors are rotational officers who possess at least a master's degree and usually spend three years as faculty, while a small number of officers possess doctoral degrees and remain at the Academy until their statutory retirement. All career civilian faculty members possess PhD's and either enjoy tenure or the possibility of tenured appointment.[4]

All US service academies, including the Naval Academy, seek diverse student bodies. This means encouraging applications from women and underrepresented minority racial and ethnic groups, and also encompasses geographic diversity. Women midshipmen were first admitted in 1976, and their share of the student body has grown to about one-quarter of the student population in every entering class.

Racial strife within military units during the Vietnam War led the Department of Defense to identify as a goal for the officer corps to resemble the military, and the civilian population, as a whole. Subsequently, increasing racial and ethnic diversity became an operational priority at the Naval Academy (Dobson 2015). Reflecting this, the share of

---

[4] This contractual right distinguishes the Naval Academy from the US Military Academy and US Air Force Academy, which do not offer tenure, and the Air War College, which has only sporadically offered it.

students from underrepresented minorities groups on campus has risen, with racial or ethnic minorities making up 32 percent of midshipmen by 2017. The breakdown by ethnic groups, however, is not representative of the broader population, with overrepresentation of Hispanics and underrepresentation of African-Americans and Asian-Americans (Polga-Hecimovich, Carey, and Horiuchi 2019).

The faculty at the Naval Academy is even less diverse in terms of race/ethnicity and gender than the student body and is not reflective of the broader population. In 2017, women made up 32 percent of faculty and nonwhites just 15 percent, of whom 8 percent were Asian, 3 percent black, 4 percent Hispanic, and less than half a percent Native American (see Table 9.1).

The Debate over Diversity in the Military

The Juvenal period of life, when friendships are formed, and habits established that will stick by one; the Youth, or young men from different parts of the United States would be assembled together, and would by degrees discover that there was not that cause for those jealousies and prejudices which one part of the Union had imbibed against another part ... What, but the mixing of people from different parts of the United States during the War rubbed off these impressions? A century in the ordinary intercourse, would not have accomplished what the Seven years association in Arms did. – Letter from President George Washington to Alexander Hamilton

In his letter to Hamilton, George Washington was preoccupied with regional divides rather than racial/ethnic or gender ones, but his logic with regard to the benefits of diversity within the military still resonates.[5] Campus diversity considerations are, arguably, even more salient within the US military service academies than at other universities. The academies are the principal educational institutions for the military officer corps, and the diversity of the officer corps is regarded as essential to the mission-readiness of the military as a whole.

The US military remained racially segregated until President Truman's Executive Order 9981 of July 26, 1948. Desegregation of units followed and, by the time of the Vietnam War, the enlisted ranks were racially integrated, but the officer corps remained overwhelmingly white. The absence of minority officers contributed to racial tension throughout the armed forces that was widely regarded as presenting a threat to morale

[5] The date of this letter was September 1, 1796. Source: Ellis (2000).

and military capacity (Nalty 1986). By the 1970s, the military implemented policies to prioritize the recruitment and training of minority
officers at the military service academies and through ROTC programs,
setting goals for the numbers of minority officers. As a result, the share
of minority officers has grown substantially, although the proportions
of black, Hispanic, and Native American officers remain lower than
those groups' corresponding shares in both the enlisted ranks and the
population at large (Becton 2003, 2013).[6]

By 2003, Supreme Court Justice Sandra Day O'Connor, writing for
the majority in *Grutter* v. *Bollinger*, pointed to diversity in the military
academies as evidence of a compelling *national* interest. In short, the
diversity of the military service academies has been a linchpin in arguments that campus diversity serves broader societal goals. For this reason,
attitudes toward diversity considerations among students at the service
academies are of particular interest.

Some, however, are resistant to the idea that diversity in the military
improves organizational performance or is a desirable goal. A predominant counterargument is the so-called "unit cohesion rationale," the
notion that unit cohesion, performance, readiness, and morale would
decline if certain minority groups were allowed to serve. This argument is
based largely on the opposition of rank-and-file military personnel to the
inclusion of some identity groups into military units. The current focus
has shifted from race and ethnicity to sex and gender, with opposition to
women, gays, and most recently, transgender individuals. Notably, Belkin
(2001) challenges the unit cohesion rationale on the basis of studies from
the fields of organizational and military theory that show that whether
group members like each other has no bearing on how well organizations
perform.

A related argument against the integration of certain groups in the
military is the supposed medical risk they pose to group effectiveness.
Until a 2016 policy change, being transgender was considered a form
of mental illness making the individual unfit to serve (Department of
Defense Instruction No. 6130.03 2010). Still another line of argument
points to the values of serving military personnel as a reason to oppose
service by traditionally excluded groups. The Department of Defense's
Military Working Group, for example, cites soldiers' "values and

---

[6] As of 2010, the officer corps was 3.9 percent Asian, which is marginally higher than the
Asian share among enlisted personnel (3.7 percent) but lower than the general population
share.

beliefs ... strongly held and not amenable to change" in opposition to President Clinton's proposal for open service of gays in 1993 (Office of the Secretary of Defense 1993, p. 2).

Opposition along these lines may be prevalent at service academies, too. Like service members at large, academy students are more likely to be men and more likely to be conservative than their counterparts at civilian institutions – traits that tend to correlate with less acceptance of gay or trans rights (Kellermann 2014). The unique context of the Naval Academy thus prompted our investigation of midshipmen's preferences for applicants and faculty candidates with diverse backgrounds.

Preferences among All Midshipmen

As at the other schools at which we conducted our experiments, we split our sample of midshipmen between conjoint experiments on undergraduate admissions and faculty recruitment, followed by a series of questions on the participants' characteristics and attitudes.[7]

Figure 9.1 illustrates the estimated preferences across all attribute levels (relative to the baseline level for each attribute) for all midshipmen participants in the admissions experiment. Across all participants, relative to a white applicant, a black applicant is 5 percentage points and a Native American applicant is 3 percentage points more likely to be selected, with both estimates statistically significant at the 0.05 level. The likelihood of selection for an Asian or Hispanic applicant is statistically indiscernible from that of a white applicant.

With respect to gender, the likelihood of selection for a woman applicant is indistinguishable from that of a man, but for a gender nonbinary applicant, the likelihood plummets by fully 20 percentage points – a huge negative effect.

Socioeconomic status also weighs heavily in midshipmen participants' preferences in admissions, with an applicant whose family income is above the median (at the top 20th, 10th, or 1st percentile) 7–12 percentage points less likely to be selected than one at the median (baseline). Preferences for an applicant from a family with a below-median income

---

[7] As mentioned at the beginning of this chapter, the instruments for the conjoint experiments and the questions about respondents asked at the end of each survey differed slightly from those used at other institutions. See Polga-Hecimovich, Carey, and Horiuchi (2019) for the Naval Academy's instruments.

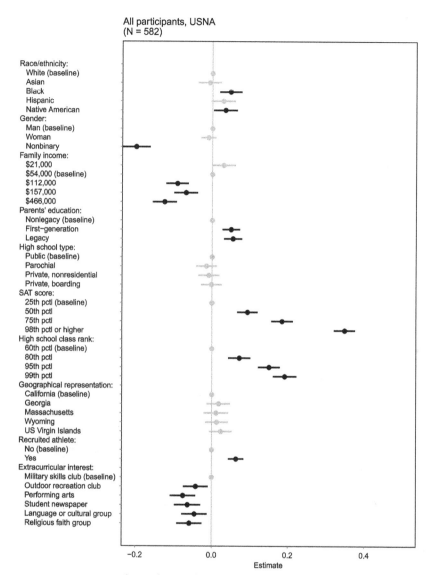

All participants, USNA
(N = 582)

FIGURE 9.1 Undergraduate admissions preferences among all student
participants at USNA

are larger compared to the baseline, but the effect is just shy of statistical
significance.

Midshipmen also favor first-generation applicants by 5 percentage
points relative to applicants whose parents had attended universities

other than the Naval Academy, and they favor legacy applicants by the same 5-percentage-point margin. Applicants' high school type does not factor systematically into preferences.

As in the results from our main analysis presented in Chapter 4, the attributes with the strongest influence on midshipmen's choices (excluding gender nonbinary status) are the direct markers of academic achievement, SAT score and high school class rank. Shifting an applicant from the Academy's 25th percentile to its 98th percentile for SAT score increases likelihood of selection by 35 percentage points, and moving class rank from the 60th percentile to the 99th percentile by 19 percentage points.

The midshipmen are, in the aggregate, indifferent to geographical region. They give admissions preference to recruited varsity athletes (6 percentage points) and prefer applicants with military skills club backgrounds over all other extracurricular interests by between 4 and 8 percentage points (statistically significant in all cases).

Figure 9.2 displays the corresponding set of estimated preferences from the faculty recruitment experiment. The results largely mirror those from the admissions experiment. With regard to race/ethnicity, we find moderate positive preferences (3 to 4 percentage points) for black, Hispanic, and Native American candidates relative to whites, and a slight positive preference (2 percentage points, but not statistically significant) for Asian faculty candidates.

For faculty slots, women candidates are preferred to men. The magnitude of the effect is small, at 2 percentage points, but it surpasses conventional statistical significance levels. More interestingly, in the faculty recruitment experiment again, we see strong negative preference toward gender nonbinary candidates, who are 12 percentage points less likely to be selected than men.

In recruitment, as in admissions, the attributes with the strongest overall effects are those that reflect scholarly achievement – research quality and, especially, teaching quality. Moving from a fair to an excellent researcher increases a candidate's likelihood of selection by 17 percentage points, other things equal, and improving from a fair to an excellent teacher boosts prospects by a whopping 44 percentage points. Among the midshipmen, quality teaching is clearly the top priority.

Other academic *bona fides* matter to a faculty candidate's prospects as well, although on a smaller magnitude. Candidates who received their doctorates from Yale (baseline) are slightly more likely (by 2 to 3 percentage points) to be selected than candidates from the state universities

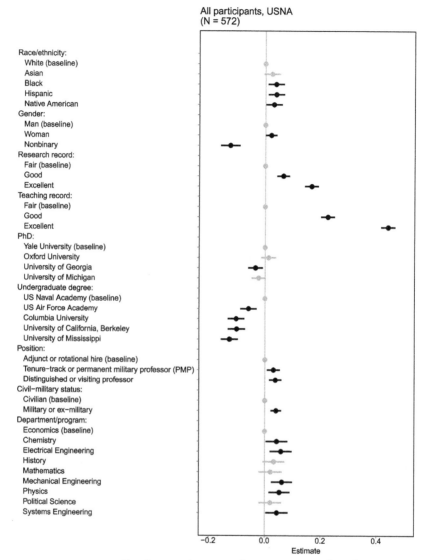

FIGURE 9.2 Faculty recruitment preferences among all student
participants at USNA

of Michigan or Georgia, and only the difference between Yale and
Georgia is statistically significant. The difference between the two elite
universities, Yale and Oxford, is not significant. Midshipmen also prefer
undergraduate alumni of their own *alma mater* over those who earned
their bachelor's degree at West Point (a rival institution, by 6 percentage

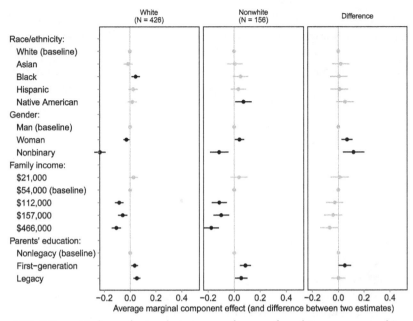

FIGURE 9.3 Undergraduate admissions preferences for white versus nonwhite student participants at USNA

points), at Columbia or Berkeley (by 10 percentage points), or at the University of Mississippi (by 13 percentage points). On the margin, they favor candidates who would be hired at higher faculty ranks over adjunct or rotational hires. And they prefer military or ex-military candidates by 4 percentage points over civilians. Finally, they exhibit overall preferences in favor of hiring faculty in the science and engineering disciplines relative to the baseline category (economics).

Preferences across Groups

By Race/Ethnicity

Figure 9.3 breaks out the estimated preferences among white versus nonwhite midshipmen. For the most part, preferences are similar across the groups. Both show moderate (but often insignificant) positive preferences for black, Hispanic, and Native American applicants relative to the baseline (white). The differences in the estimated attitudes toward applicants from minority racial/ethnic groups are never statistically distinguishable between white and nonwhite participants.

By contrast, we do find measurable preference differences between whites and nonwhites on gender. White participants *dis*favor women applicants relative to men (the baseline) by 3 percentage points whereas nonwhite participants *favor* women by 4 percentage points. Both estimates are, themselves, statistically significant, as is the 7-percentage-point difference between them. We find differences between whites and nonwhites with regard to gender nonbinary applicants as well. Whites are fully 23 percentage points less likely to select a gender nonbinary applicant relative to a man. Nonwhites disfavor nonbinary applicants less severely, by 11 percentage points, and the difference between groups is statistically significant.

With regard to socioeconomic class status of applicants, we find similar preferences across these groups. Both whites and nonwhites slightly favor applicants from low-income families, while both groups more strongly disfavoring those from the top income brackets. The effects of the latter are statistically significant, but there is no statistically discernible difference between whites and nonwhites. On parents' education, both favor first-generation applicants but also legacy applicants, relative to applicants whose parents attended universities other than the Naval Academy. With respect to first-generation applicants, the preference among nonwhites (9 percentage points) is sufficiently stronger than that among whites (4 percentage points) such that the difference is statistically significant.

The analogous figure from the faculty recruitment experiment (results included in our replication package) suggests that white and nonwhite participants both favor faculty candidates from every nonwhite racial/ethnic group relative to white candidates. The point estimates are larger among nonwhites than among whites (and the preferences among whites are not statistically discernible from zero), but the differences between groups are never statistically significant. The same applies with regard to gender. Here, both whites and nonwhites slightly favor women for faculty slots relative to men, and both also disfavor gender nonbinary candidates relative to men. Overall, white and nonwhite preferences are not statistically distinguishable on any attribute or level.

On the whole, then, we find mostly similar attitudes between white and nonwhite midshipmen toward our diversity-related attributes. We find no measurable differences in preferences toward any nonwhite racial/ethnic category. On gender, nonwhites favor women more and disfavor nonbinary applicants less in the admissions experiment. Nonwhites also favor first-generation applicants more strongly than do whites, although both groups' preferences runs in the same direction.

We also undertake analyses breaking out racial/ethnic groups separately – for example, whites versus blacks, whites versus Hispanics, and so on (results included in our replication package). For the most part, preferences are similar across groups. As at other institutions, we observe some pronounced in-group affect. For example, comparing whites versus blacks in the admissions experiment, black midshipmen are more than 30 percentage points more likely to select a black applicant than a white one, whereas white midshipmen are 5 percentage points more likely to select the black applicant, and that between-group difference is statistically significant. We observe no measurable differences between whites and blacks with respect to any other race/ethnicity category, however. In the faculty recruitment experiment, the respective figures are 15 percentage points and 2 percentage points, but the difference between groups falls just short of conventional statistical significance, which is in part due to the small number of black participants ($n = 26$).

By Gender

Figure 9.4 contrasts the preferences of men versus women in the admissions experiment. Both groups favor black, Hispanic, and Native American applicants relative to white applicants – by statistically significant margins for black and Native American applicants among women but only for black applicants among men. The differences between men's and women's preferences are never statistically discernible with regard to race/ethnicity. Nor are they distinguishable with regard to applicants' family income, nor first-generation status. Both men and women favor low-income over high-income applicants and first-generation students over those whose parents attended colleges other than the Naval Academy. Both men and women favor legacy applicants, and that preference is stronger among women (10 percentage points) than men (4 percentage points).

The more pronounced difference in attitudes, however, is with respect to gender. Women favor applicants who are women relative to those who are men by 3 percentage points, whereas men *dis*favor women relative to men by the same margin. And for gender nonbinary applicants, whom participants of both genders disfavor, the gap is even larger, with men 25 percentage points less likely to select a nonbinary applicant than a man, whereas women are 10 percentage points less likely.

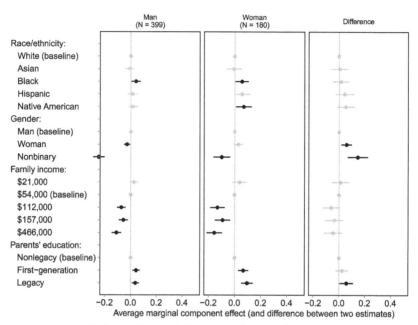

FIGURE 9.4 Undergraduate admissions preferences for woman versus man student participants at USNA

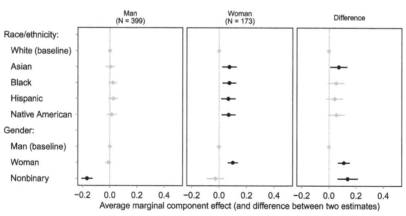

FIGURE 9.5 Faculty recruitment preferences for woman versus man student participants at USNA

Figure 9.5 compares men's versus women's preferences from the faculty recruitment experiment. As above, differences are limited with respect to race/ethnicity, with women favoring candidates from all nonwhite groups more than men do, and with a significant difference for Asians only. But again we see large differences with respect to gender. Men are, on the whole, statistically indifferent toward women faculty candidates. Women midshipmen, by contrast, are 10 percentage points more likely to select a woman than a man candidate. And men are 17 percentage points less likely to select a gender nonbinary candidate than a man, whereas women are almost indifferent toward nonbinary candidates. That animus toward nonbinary candidates is less pronounced, among both men and women, in the faculty recruitment experiment than in the admissions experiment suggests that midshipmen may regard gender nonconformity to be more objectionable among peers than among their classroom instructors.

By Socioeconomic Background

We also break midshipmen out by socioeconomic status, comparing preferences among those from families with incomes below versus above the national median. The results (included in our replication package) suggest that preferences differ little between these groups. There are no measurable differences, on either experiment, on race/ethnicity. Nor are there statistically discernible differences, in the admissions experiment, based on applicant family income. The preference among lower-income participants in favor of first-generation applicants is measurably stronger (at 17 percentage points) than that among higher-income participants (4 percentage points). Lower-income participants also favor women applicants over men whereas higher-income participants do not. On the whole, however, preference differences by socioeconomic status are limited.

By Partisanship

Finally, we break midshipmen out by political partisanship. On admissions (results included in our replication package), we find no statistically discernible differences with regard to preferences on race/ethnicity. Democrats are slightly more likely than Republicans to select applicants from each nonwhite group, but the differences do not reach statistical significance in any case. With regard to gender, Democrats lean slightly toward women applicants over men, and Republicans angle in the other direction, but the difference between groups again falls short of statistical significance. We do, once again, however, find a difference in attitudes toward gender nonbinary applicants, the now-familiar objects of intense preferences among midshipmen. As in other breakdowns, both groups disfavor gender nonbinary applicants, but Republicans (−25 percentage

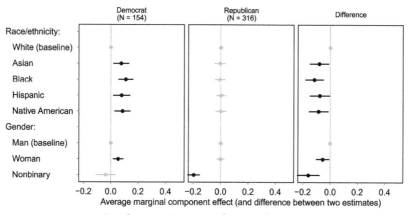

FIGURE 9.6 Faculty recruitment preferences for Democrats versus Republicans at USNA

points) do so with greater fervor than Democrats (−11 percentage points). On socioeconomic diversity, Democrats disfavor applicants from the highest family income brackets more strongly than do Republicans, and they more strongly favor first-generation applicants, compared to Republicans.

Figure 9.6 shows striking and consistent differences in preferences by partisanship in the faculty recruitment experiment. Republican midshipmen are, statistically, almost completely indifferent to the race/ethnicity of faculty candidates, and also with respect to women as opposed to men. Democratic midshipmen, by contrast, strongly favor faculty candidates from every nonwhite group (by 7 to 11 percentage points) and women (by 5 percentage points). Democrats' slight preference against gender nonbinary candidates is not statistically discernible from zero, whereas Republicans are strongly negative on nonbinary faculty (20 percentage points). On faculty recruitment, Republican and Democratic preferences are statistically distinguishable from each other on every diversity-related characteristic.

Midshipmen's Comments on Gender Nonconformity

On most counts, preferences among midshipmen line up with those of students at other universities. The most notable exception is on gender nonbinary applicants and faculty candidates. Across institutions, we find overall preferences in favor of undergraduate applicants and faculty candidates underrepresented in university communities, and generally consistent preferences across groups of participants broken out by demographics or by socioeconomic status. The preferences among midshipmen are consistent on these counts, but midshipmen's attitudes toward gender nonbinary applicants and faculty candidates, in particular, are strikingly negative. These attitudes are of particular interest because debates over gender in the military are persistent, ranging from "don't ask, don't tell" (DADT, the former official US policy on the service of gays in the military) and the openness of the armed services to gays, to the integration of women into combat units, to the eligibility of transgender individuals to serve at all. The narrative comments from participants in our survey experiments offer a potential source of more textured information on attitudes toward gender, and especially toward gender nonconformity.[8]

To recall, our survey experiments included an opportunity for participants to provide open-ended written feedback at the end of the questionnaire. Few participants wrote comments that were overtly negative toward gender nonbinary applicants or faculty candidates. Three explicitly opposed admissions – for example, "I firmly believe that USNA should never hire anyone who claims to be so-called 'Non-Binary' in gender." A handful more rejected the category of gender nonbinary altogether – for example: "There's only two genders. Thinking otherwise is a mental disorder." But this set amounted to less than one percent of all participants. Another half percent indicated confusion with regard to the concept of nonbinary gender. Some of these, however, suggest that the ambiguity was driven by institutional context rather than by individual incomprehension – for example: "If a potential applicant's gender is nonbinary, how can s/he be recruited? I.e., how can s/he be on a men or women's team if they do not identify with one gender."

In comments that referred to gender, by far the most common theme was to indicate that gender (and often race/ethnicity and family socioeconomic background) should not matter to admissions or faculty recruitment decisions. Contrary to these comments, which profess a commitment to gender-blindness, but consistent with the proposition that conjoint analysis is effective in eliciting honest opinions, our conjoint experiments reveal midshipmen's strong *dis*favor toward gender nonbinary applicants and candidates.

---

[8] See Polga-Hecimovich, Carey, and Horiuchi (2019) for a more extensive exploration of the narrative responses.

Midshipmen's Attitudes in Broader Context

Ex-Secretary of the Navy Ray Mabus (2009–2017) said that, "a more diverse force is a stronger force" (NPR 2015). This opinion is not unanimous, but the results of our conjoint experiments suggest that midshipmen, overall, support admissions and recruitment aimed at fostering diversity at the Naval Academy. Nevertheless, our findings also suggest that midshipmen's attitudes toward diversity vary across attributes. In particular, the story is more mixed with respect to gender, and runs in the other direction on gender nonconformity. Specifically, there is no overall preference for women in admissions, which perhaps reflects the debate over the full integration of women into the armed services and in combat positions (Miller and Williams 2001; Thomas and Thomas 1996). This debate is ongoing. In December 2015, then-Secretary of Defense Ash Carter announced the opening of all US military combat positions – including infantry, armor, reconnaissance, and some special operations units – to qualified women (Bradner 2015). However, on the basis of a Marine Corps study that concluded that male-only units tend to exhibit higher combat effectiveness than gender-integrated units, Marine General Joseph Dunford, the chairman of the Joint Chiefs of Staff, and Marine Corps Commandant General James Amos opposed full integration (US Marine Corps 2015).[9] In light of the mixed institutional messages coming from Department of Defense, Navy, and Marine Corps leadership regarding the combat role of women, it is not entirely surprising that midshipmen express contradictory preferences toward women undergraduate applicants versus women faculty members.

There is little uncertainty, though, regarding midshipmen attitudes toward gender nonconformity. With respect to gender nonbinary applicants and faculty candidates, nearly every group for which we estimate attitudes has negative preferences that are statistically discernible from zero. This is distinct from attitudes at other selective universities and out of line with attitudes toward other underrepresented groups.[10] But the

---

[9] The study finds that the male-only infantry units shoot more accurately, can carry more weight, and move more quickly through specific tactical exercises. It also concludes that women have higher injury rates than men, including stress fractures that likely result from carrying heavy loads.

[10] Midshipmen's negative attitudes toward gender nonbinary applicants and faculty candidates are also out of line with public positions on gender nonconformity taken by many military leaders, including at the level of branch commanders (Lamothe 2017; Luna 2018; Vanden Brook 2017) and by six former Surgeons General (Eisenla 2018),

midshipmen attitudes on this issue that we capture are consistent with the arguments that, with regard to unit cohesion, gender, and gender noncon-formity are different from race/ethnicity. Arguments for gender diversity in the military are far more recent than arguments for racial integra-tion. And to an even greater degree than the role of women in combat positions, transgender service is at the center of an active and ongoing policy debate in the United States (Department of Defense Instruction No. 6130.03 2010).[11] It also bears mention that the concept of gender nonbinary is relatively new. As such, it is possible that preferences will change relatively quickly in the years ahead, as service members' attitudes toward "don't ask, don't tell" and gays and lesbians in the military have transformed since the 1990s (Estrada and Weiss 1999; Sinclair 2009).

9.2   LONDON SCHOOL OF ECONOMICS

At the Naval Academy we examine attitudes toward diversity among a population of students on a distinctive educational and career path. The second case in this chapter examines attitudes in an environment outside the United States, with attendant differences in historical and demographic context.

The London School of Economics (LSE; officially, the London School of Economics and Political Science) was founded in 1895 by four promi-nent members of the Fabian Society, a British socialist organization formed in the late 1800s whose purpose was to promote democratic reform. It is one of eighteen constituent colleges of the University of London, a federal research university and the largest university in the United Kingdom. The LSE student body is composed of over 10,000 undergraduate and graduate students, and it has the highest percentage of international students among all universities in Great Britain at 70 percent.

Like those of most other highly selective institutions in Great Britain, the LSE's undergraduate admissions policy prioritizes decisions that are made on the grounds of "academic merit and potential" (London School of Economics 2018). The LSE, however, has also made diversity one of

---

   although not with attitudes expressed at the top of the chain of command, including by President Trump (Cooper and Gibbons-Neff 2018).

[11] Despite the formal ban, a 2016 study by the Rand Corporation estimates that there are between 1,320 and 6,630 active transgender service members in the US military (Schaefer et al. 2016).

the main objectives of its admissions decisions. After the LSE instituted a "contextualized admissions" program in 2012 that considers students' backgrounds and circumstances holistically in admissions decisions, the proportion of students coming from disadvantaged backgrounds (those living in areas with low higher education participation rates) increased by 1 percentage point from 2012 to 2016 (Sundorph, Vasilev, and Coiffait 2017). According to an admissions report from 2017 to 2018, the LSE plans to continue pursuing this policy (London School of Economics 2018).

Demographics and Diversity at the LSE

Table 9.2 shows the gender and racial/ethnic breakdown of students and faculty at the LSE in the 2017–2018 academic year.[12] Just over half of the LSE undergraduate student population is white (51 percent). Among nonwhites, 27 percent are Asian, followed by 10 percent mixed or "other," 5 percent Chinese, and 5 percent black. On gender, 57 percent of undergraduates are male, while 43 percent are female.[13]

The LSE faculty are less diverse than the student body in terms of race/ethnicity – 68 percent of instructors are white, with higher proportions among the permanent faculty, including 71 percent of assistant professors, 80 percent of associate professors, and 82 percent of full professors.[14] Just over half of all LSE faculty are female, but again, most professors in the higher ranks (full professors and associate professors) are male, a trend that mirrors many universities in the United States. There have been modest increases in the representation of underrepresented minority groups among the faculty in recent years. The gender ratio has been within one point of 50:50 every year since 2012, although it flipped from slightly more men prior to 2015 to slightly more women since. The percentage of whites dropped from 72 percent to 68

---

[12] The racial/ethnic categories that the LSE reports – in particular, the way it breaks up categories among Asian participants – is different from how we organized our survey. The LSE distinguishes "Asian" from "Chinese." We distinguished "South Asian" from "East Asian" when we asked for participants' own race. We think our categories better correspond to how ethnic identities relate to contemporary British society and to the country's colonial history.

[13] Like most US institutions, the LSE relies only on a male–female binary to report information on student and faculty sex.

[14] All data we refer to in this paragraph, but not shown in Table 9.2, are provided by the LSE.

TABLE 9.2 *LSE student and faculty demographics*

	Undergraduate		Faculty	
	N	%	N	%
Female	989	43.3	1,710	51.04
Male	1,294	56.7	1,640	48.96
White	1,165	51.0	2,286	68.24
Asian	618	27.0	305	9.10
Black	114	5.0	169	5.04
Chinese	120	5.0	139	4.15
Mixed			120	3.58
Not known	38	2.0	258	7.70
Other	231	10.0	73	2.18
Total	2,286	100.0	3,350	100.00

Note: "Other" for undergraduate students includes "Mixed." Data provided by the institution.

percent over this time period, with corresponding small increases in the percentages of various nonwhite groups.

As with many social phenomena in the past century, the US debates about diversity on university campuses have started to cross the Atlantic to the UK. Perhaps the most high-profile example of this was the argument in 2015–2016 about whether Oriel College at Oxford University should remove the statue of Cecil Rhodes, who for many students was a symbol of Britain's colonial and racist past (Castle 2016; Khomami 2015). Another example is the growing recognition of the lack of students and faculty from black and minority ethnic backgrounds at Britain's top universities (Adams and Barr 2018; Adams 2017; Turner 2017). And, in a reflection of the salience of social class in Britain, top universities are increasingly scrutinized for their proportions of students from lower-income or working class backgrounds. For example, the Sutton Trust estimates that pupils from private secondary schools are more than twice as likely to attend top universities as pupils from state schools (Gurney-Read 2015). Similarly, British students eligible for free school meals are less than half as likely to attend university as students who are not (Sundorph, Vasilev, and Coiffait 2017). In response to concerns among faculty and students, the LSE set up an Equity, Diversity and Inclusion (EDI) Taskforce in September 2015, the primary aim of which is "[t]o provide a forum in which those with operational responsibilities for equity and diversity in the School are held accountable for and supported in the delivery of their responsibilities" (EDI Taskforce 2017).

Preferences across All LSE Students

To determine what LSE students think about these issues, whether they want more diversity in undergraduate admissions and faculty recruitment, what attributes and characteristics should be prioritized, and whether there is agreement across groups, we invited all undergraduates at the LSE to participate in one of two conjoint survey experiments, on undergraduate admissions or faculty recruitment. Substantively, the experiments mirror those we conducted at US universities, but the instruments necessarily were modified to fit the British context.[15]

Figure 9.7 illustrates the results across the full set of participants on undergraduate admissions. As at the US schools, academic achievement weighs heavily on the preferences of LSE participants. A-level exam results are the strongest predictor of which applicant is selected from each pair, with a shift from the lowest level (AAB) to the highest (A*A*A*) increasing the likelihood of selection by 48 percentage points.

With respect to diversity considerations, LSE students are selectively supportive of more diversity on race/ethnicity and gender, and strongly supportive on socioeconomic grounds. They are 5 percentage points more likely to prefer a black applicant for admission over a white British one, but statistically indifferent between East, South Asian, white non-British, and white British (baseline) applicants. With respect to gender, LSE students lean toward women applicants over men by 3 percentage points. The estimate for gender non-binary applicants is similarly positive, but falls short of statistical significance.

LSE participants demonstrate strong preferences in favor of applicants from disadvantaged socioeconomic backgrounds. On family income, they disfavor each higher bracket, and favor the lower bracket, relative to the baseline (the median income), and a move from the highest to the median bracket increases the likelihood of selection by 15 percentage points. LSE participants also favor first-generation applicants over those whose parents attended university by 8 percentage points.

---

[15] For the undergraduate admissions experiment, the attributes are: race/ethnicity, gender, home/overseas residence, annual family income, secondary school type, parents' education, A-Level/IB (or equivalent) grades, and extracurricular interests. For the faculty recruitment experiment, the attributes are: race/ethnicity, gender, home/overseas residence, teaching record, research record, PhD institution, undergraduate institution, LSE academic department, the level of the faculty position, and the candidate's spouse/partner's faculty status. The complete lists of attributes and levels, along with the questions we asked after the conjoint experiments, are available in our replication package.

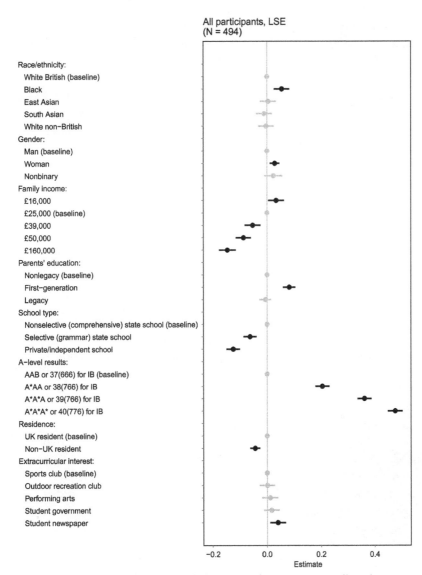

All participants, LSE
(N = 494)

FIGURE 9.7 Undergraduate admissions preferences among all student
participants at LSE

In a couple of departures from the American results, LSE students do
not favor legacy applicants. If an applicant's parents attended university,
whether it was LSE or not has no impact on choices. But LSE participants do take into account the type of high school an applicant attended,

favoring those from nonselective state schools relative to those from private schools or selective state schools. All these preferences – by family income, by parents' education, and by high school type – are consistent with preferences in favor of socioeconomically disadvantaged applicants.

Finally, for the most part, an applicant's extracurricular interests do not systematically matter, although student journalists are preferred, on the whole, to sports club athletes. LSE participants also indicate a preference for UK residents over foreign applicants.

Figure 9.8 shows remarkably similar results with regard to faculty appointments. LSE students are 6 percentage points more likely to select a black faculty candidate over a white British candidate, but the differences between a white British candidate and an East Asian, South Asian, or white non-British candidate are minuscule and statistically insignificant. Also on par with the admissions experiment, participants are 5 percentage points more likely to select a woman than a man, and the point estimate for a gender nonbinary faculty candidate is positive but not significant.

As with the admissions experiment, the strongest preferences are for indicators of scholarly achievement. Shifting from a fair research record to an excellent one increases the likelihood of selection by 24 percentage points, and the same jump on teaching reputation boosts selection prospects by over 40 percentage points. LSE students also prefer academics with degrees (PhD or undergraduate) from the most prestigious universities – Oxford, Cambridge, Yale, and of course the LSE itself – over those from other institutions. Finally, participants favor the recruitment of more permanent faculty over temporary appointments, and recruitment in mainstream academic departments/programs, such as economics or political science over those in development studies (−6 percentage points) and gender studies (−8 percentage points).[16]

Comparing Preferences across Groups

Breaking the LSE participants into different groups, we find now-familiar levels of agreement on a number of counts (results included in our replication package). For example, when we divide responses between white and all nonwhite participants in the admissions experiment, we observe no measurable differences on any preferences related to race/ethnicity or

---

[16] But the graduate-oriented curricula of these specialized programs at the LSE might have limited their resonance with the undergraduate participants in our experiments.

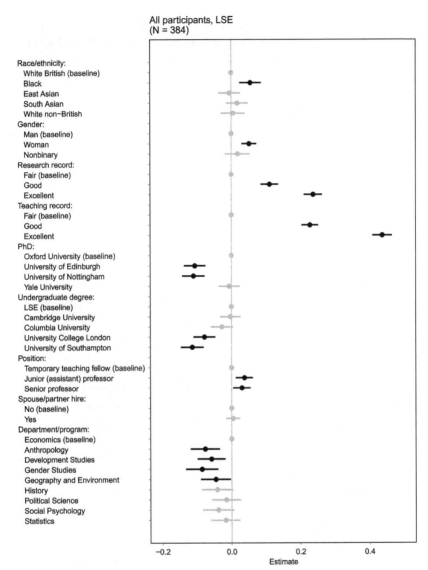

FIGURE 9.8 Faculty recruitment preferences among all student participants at LSE

gender, or on any measure of applicants' socioeconomic class. Both white and nonwhite participants are more likely to select a black applicant over the baseline white British applicant, with nonwhites leaning more heavily toward the black applicant (7 versus 3 percentage points), but the effect is insignificant among white participants. And the difference in preferences between the groups is not statistically significant. The same applies with respect to other nonwhite groups, as well as to gender. White and non-white participants alike lean toward both women and gender nonbinary applicants over men. Both groups favor applicants from lower-income families over wealthier families, and first-generation applicants over others – and all at degrees that are statistically indiscernible.

In the faculty recruitment experiment, the results are the same with respect to race/ethnicity – measurable preferences in favor of black candidates among both whites and nonwhite, and no cross-group preference differences toward any racial/ethnic category. On gender, we do find measurably stronger preferences in favor of women and nonbinary candidates among white participants than among nonwhites. There is no polarization on gender preferences, but nonwhites are, effectively, indifferent to the gender of faculty candidates.

Breaking students out by gender produces a handful of differences (results included in our replication package). In the admissions experiment, women lean toward East Asian and South Asian applicants whereas men lean against them. The differences between men and women are statistically significant, but do not reach our benchmark for preference polarization. Similarly, women participants demonstrate measurable preferences in favor of women and nonbinary applicants relative to applicants who are men, whereas participants who are men are indifferent with regard to gender. In the faculty recruitment experiment, men are indifferent with regard to both the gender and the race/ethnicity of applicants, whereas women prefer black and South Asian candidates compared to a white British ones, and women as compared to men. The difference between groups is, however, only significant for South Asian faculty candidates.

When we break LSE students out by political party identification, we find some greater differences in preferences, as we do at US universities, although these are limited to the admissions experiment (Figure 9.9).[17] In the faculty recruitment experiment (results included in our replication package), Conservative (Tory) and Labour supporters are statistically

---

[17] These comparisons warrant careful qualification. First, the British party system is more fragmented than the American system. We compare participants who identify with the two largest parties, Conservative and Labour, but this amounts to just below half of all participants. Second, our data on participants do not distinguish British from international students, so our Conservative and Labour identifiers include some non-British students. Therefore, we interpret our partisan breakouts with caution.

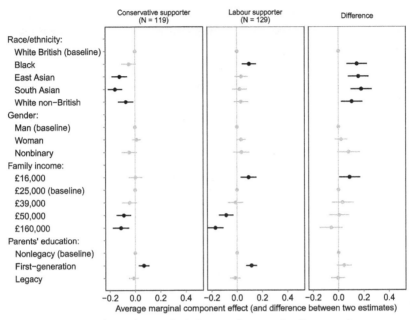

FIGURE 9.9 Undergraduate admissions preferences for Conservative versus Labour supporters at LSE

indistinguishable with respect to preferences on race/ethnicity, with both partisans favoring black candidates over the white British baseline, and indifferent with respect to other race/ethnicity categories. On admissions (Figure 9.9), however, Tories and Labour partisans separate. Labour supporters favor black applicants relative to the white British baseline; Tories lean negative with regard to black applicants (not quite statistically significant), and the difference between partisans is statistically significant. Moreover, Tories are measurably *negative* toward East Asian and South Asian applicants, as well as toward white non-British applicants, relative to the white British baseline. On each of these categories, the difference between Tories and Labour supporters is statistically discernible.

Finally, as in the United States, we asked our participants whether, in principle, they favor the consideration of race in university admissions and faculty appointments, or believe these decisions should be based entirely on academic merit. We then compared the results between those who support merit-based admissions and those who support race-conscious admissions (included in our replication package). Large majorities – 72 percent in the admissions experiment, 84 percent in the faculty appointments experiment – favor merit only. Consistent with that position, those participants display almost no statistically discernible preferences for or against applicants or candidates of any particular race/ethnicity relative to whites in either experiment. One exception is a weak but statistically distinguishable preference *for* black candidates, as compared to white British ones. Those who support the consideration of race favor black and East Asian applicants (and, curiously, non-British white applicants) in admissions, and black faculty candidates, relative to the white British baseline. For these categories, there are significant differences between the two groups.

Understanding British Attitudes toward Campus Diversity

In many ways, LSE students' attitudes toward diversity in admissions and recruitment line up with those of students in the United States. Yet we observe some notable differences. To begin, while students at the American universities we surveyed consistently prefer admissions applicants and faculty candidates from multiple different underrepresented groups including blacks, Hispanics, Native Americans, and, to an extent, Asians, LSE students express preferences in favor of black applicants and candidates only. They are consistently indifferent toward both South Asian and East Asian applicants and candidates, relative to whites.

These results may reflect the broader nature of the diversity debate in the UK as compared to the United States. In the UK, South Asians (particularly Indians) and East Asians (particularly Chinese) are widely known to excel academically in high schools, grammar schools (selective entry secondary schools), and universities. Black students, conversely, are regarded as under-performing relative to South and East Asians and to whites, and their underrepresentation at top schools has attracted criticism in recent years (Adams and Barr 2018). In a related vein, then Prime Minister David Cameron announced in 2015 that he would make ending discrimination against blacks in the workplace one of his party's greatest priorities (Cameron 2015). Absent from Cameron's initiative was reference to any other racial/ethnic group, suggesting a perception in the UK that blacks face unique obstacles and widespread, systematic underrepresentation.

LSE students also show greater positive preferences for students from more disadvantaged socioeconomic backgrounds than for students from any racial/ethnic group. Beyond the very real concerns about black representation on university campuses in the UK, broader British debates about campus diversity in university admissions have traditionally centered around class status rather than race and ethnicity. Despite the establishment of the Office of Fair Access in 2004 to monitor institutional progress at increasing the representation of socioeconomically disadvantaged students, a 2017 report produced by the nonpartisan think tank, Reform, highlights extreme gaps in access to top universities based on class and income (Sundorph, Vasilev, and Coiffait 2017). In her first speech as Prime Minister, Theresa May noted, "If you're a white, working-class boy, you're less likely than anybody else in Britain to go to university" (May 2016). She has since promised to institute sweeping reforms to address this problem, but the underrepresentation and "injustices" that individuals from lower socioeconomic backgrounds face in university admissions continues to be widely criticized in contemporary media accounts of British campus diversity (Swinford 2017; Wigmore 2016).

The preferences of LSE students, as measured in our experiments, reflect this priority for increasing the representation of students from more disadvantaged socioeconomic backgrounds. Indifference toward applicants and candidates from most racial/ethnic groups, with the exception of blacks, may reflect a diversity debate that is driven more by class than by race.

9.3 STUDENT PREFERENCES ACROSS ENVIRONMENTS

Most of this book focuses on attitudes toward diversity among students at a group of universities in the United States: Dartmouth College; the University of California, San Diego; the University of North Carolina at Chapel Hill; the University of Nevada, Reno; and the University of New Mexico. This is a diverse group of schools in terms of size, region, selectivity, student demographics, and public/private status, yet the congruence of student preferences with respect to diversity across the institutions is remarkable. This chapter extends our analysis to still more distinctive campus environments – a premier US military service academy and at an elite university in the UK. These institutions are of particular interest for a few reasons. First, debates around the value of campus diversity in the United States are especially salient at the military service academies. Moreover, these debates are not limited to the

US context. They are growing increasingly salient in a range of countries with unequal patterns of access to higher education, including Australia (Oishi 2017), Brazil (dos Santos and Anya 2006; Francis and Tannuri-Pianto 2012; Valente and Berry 2017), Germany (Braun et al. 2014), India (Bertrand, Hanna, and Mullainathan 2010), and Malaysia (Guan 2005).

The predominant conclusion from our experiments at the Naval Academy and the LSE is that student preferences in favor of diversity, and the balance between these preferences and other priorities, are consistent with those at the larger set of US civilian institutions. At both the Naval Academy and the LSE, as at other schools, the largest drivers of preferences in the conjoint experiments are metrics of scholarly achievement – grades and test scores for admissions applicants, and teaching and research records for faculty candidates. At both institutions, we also find statistically significant preferences in favor of underrepresented minority racial/ethnic groups in both admissions and faculty recruitment, and we find strong support at both schools for applicants from socioeconomically disadvantaged backgrounds. Also on par with the results from our main comparison set, when we break participants in our experiments out by their own demographic characteristics, we find broad preference consensus (either strong or mild) across groups. At neither school do preferences differ systematically by the race/ethnicity of the student.

Beneath these overarching patterns, we find some differences as well. Midshipmen at the Naval Academy, for example, do not favor (nor disfavor) women applicants for admission, despite the fact that women are outnumbered by men among midshipmen by nearly three to one. For faculty appointments, by contrast, midshipmen do favor women candidates over men, although just barely. More clearly and more distinctly from other student populations, midshipmen strongly *dis*favor gender nonbinary applicants and faculty candidates. This effect is powerful – rivaling that of academic achievement – and it applies across all groups of midshipmen, by race/ethnicity, gender, socioeconomic status, and even partisanship. Midshipmen preferences for diversity mirror debates within the US armed forces. Midshipmen appear to assimilate preferences that reflect "resolved policy disputes" (e.g., on underrepresented racial and ethnic minorities) within the broader military, but with respect to identities that are currently controversial within the military, they appear to be either more circumspect (e.g., on women in combat roles) or negatively disposed (e.g., with respect to gender nonbinary). If this is the case, then midshipmen preferences may not be static. If or when military leadership sends an unambiguous policy signal, future generations of midshipmen may be inclined to "get on board" as they have in the past.

At the LSE, students express preferences for black applicants and faculty candidates over whites at levels on par with those at American schools. Preferences for underrepresented minority groups at the LSE, however, are limited to blacks. In both the admissions and faculty recruitment experiments, preferences toward South Asians and East Asians are indistinguishable from those toward whites. On the whole, the relative weight of preferences toward underrepresented minority groups among LSE participants leans more toward socioeconomic class factors – family income, first-generation status, and high school type – than toward demographics. Notably as well, LSE students on the whole are indifferent toward legacy applicants. Across US student populations, favoritism toward legacies is the only consistent preference pushing *against* the increased inclusion of underrepresented minority groups. We can likely attribute these preferences to the nature of the campus diversity debate in the UK, which is more built on objections to class-based inequality than race-based divides.

Notwithstanding the school-specific differences, the broad picture from the Naval Academy and the LSE shows preferences in favor of increasing diversity of campus populations through the admissions and faculty recruitment processes. Despite heated debates over diversity in the press, in the courts, and sometimes on campuses themselves, these preferences are pervasive across institutions, and they are often shared across groups within each institution that are defined by demographics and socioeconomic background. In the final chapter, we turn our attention to what the preferences we discern from our experiments mean and how they might inform current debates about campus diversity.

10

What Do the Results Mean?

We begin this chapter with a summary of the results from our experiments. We highlight the main findings both in terms of the preferences estimated for our student (and faculty) participants overall, and how those preferences compare when we separate participants into different demographic and attitudinal groups and estimate preferences by groups. The strongest through-line, as reflected in the book's title, is the degree of consensus supporting demographic diversity in undergraduate admissions and faculty recruitment at colleges and universities.

With that inventory of results, we then take stock of how campus diversity, and policies aimed at promoting it, affect universities. We distinguish between effects of diversity that redound to the broader campus community versus those that impact students (and faculty) who are direct assignees of efforts to promote diversity. We note that there is ample evidence for community-level benefits, and broad recognition of them both among scholars and jurists, whereas the effects at the individual level are more contentious. We also highlight the ways our estimates of student and faculty attitudes toward diversity intersect with the evidence about diversity's effects from other sources.

The final section of the chapter turns our attention to some challenges on the near horizon for campus diversity and efforts to sustain or expand it. Legal challenges to race-conscious college and university admissions face the challenge of shifting the focus of debate from community-level effects, where diversity advocates are on stronger ground, to individual-level effects on *non*members of university communities – those denied admission to begin with. We note some reasons that the pending legal challenge from Asian applicants may make that shift more readily than did prior complaints from white plaintiffs. We then consider extensions of the motivating ideal behind campus diversity beyond how the campus community is constructed (admissions and recruitment) to how it operates in practice. We review, in particular, efforts by Harvard to discourage students from organizing their social lives around sameness rather than diversity. Finally, we note arguments that contemporary campuses suffer more from deficits in the diversity of *viewpoints* than of *identities*.

10.1   WHAT DO STUDENTS WANT? A SUMMARY OF OUR RESULTS

Scholarly achievement is the biggest factor driving student preferences in both undergraduate admissions and faculty recruitment.

- In our experiments, SAT scores and high school class rank are the two most powerful factors driving preferences on undergraduate admissions.
- Teaching record and research record are the two most powerful factors driving preferences on faculty appointments.

Students favor applicants and candidates from traditionally underrepresented groups over those from traditionally overrepresented groups.

- Our participants favor student applicants and faculty candidates from all nonwhite groups over whites.
- They prefer women and nonbinary applicants and faculty candidates over men.
- They prefer applicants from lower family income brackets over those from higher family income brackets.
- They prefer first-generation applicants over those whose parents attended college.
- They prefer applicants who attended public high schools over those who attended private schools.

Preferences for legacy applicants and recruited varsity athletes are partially inconsistent with this overall pattern in favor of campus diversity.

- Students at all of our US universities favor legacy applicants, despite evidence that legacy preferences benefit applicants from traditionally advantaged backgrounds (Hurwitz 2011; Kahlenberg 2010).

- Students at all our US universities favor recruited athletes. Although the NCAA extols college athletics as a pathway to higher education for students from disadvantaged backgrounds, research suggests that admissions preferences for varsity athletes, on net, also favor traditionally advantaged applicants (Bowen and Levin 2003).

Preferences with regard to student admissions and faculty recruitment are similar across universities and across student cohorts.

- Student preferences across the core set of universities at which we conducted experiments – Dartmouth College; the University of California, San Diego; the University of North Carolina at Chapel Hill; and the University of Nevada, Reno – are remarkably similar despite differences across the schools in region, student demographics, size, and selectivity.
- Student preferences differ little from their first year on campus to their senior year, which runs contrary to expectations that socialization on campus systematically changes attitudes toward diversity (Mendelberg, McCabe, and Thal 2017; Sidanius et al. 2008).
- Student preferences are largely similar even in university contexts different from our core set. At the University of New Mexico and at the US Naval Academy, preferences toward race/ethnicity and toward socioeconomic background are consistent with those at other US schools. At the London School of Economics, preferences are consistent in favor of blacks (the only underrepresented racial/ethnic minority category that matches the categories used in the US experiments), in favor of women, and in favor of applicants from disadvantaged socioeconomic classes.

We find broad consensus on pro-diversity preferences with regard to race/ethnicity and socioeconomic background.

- When we break participants in our experiments out by their own race/ethnicity, every group favors nonwhite applicants relative to whites in both undergraduate admissions and in faculty recruitment.
- When we break participants out by their own socioeconomic background, we find preferences across the board in favor of applicants from disadvantaged socioeconomic backgrounds relative to those from more advantaged backgrounds.

- We also find consistent preferences for underrepresented minority racial/ethnic groups and socioeconomically disadvantaged groups when we break participants out by gender.
- Even when we break participants out by whether they support or oppose taking race into consideration in college admissions and faculty appointments, we find mild consensus. In our experiments, participants on *both* sides of this divide prefer applicants and candidates from underrepresented minority racial/ethnic groups over whites.

We find no evidence of polarization of preferences on race/ethnicity and socioeconomic background.

- When we break participants in our experiments out by their own race/ethnicity, we do not find preferences in any group *against* any underrepresented minority racial/ethnic group.
- When we break participants out by partisanship, we do not find polarization on race/ethnicity or socioeconomic background. Participants who identify as Democrats prefer members of all nonwhite groups to whites in both experiments, whereas Republicans are indifferent to the race/ethnicity of undergraduate applicants and faculty candidates.
- Even when we break participants out by their level of racial resentment, we do not find polarization on race/ethnicity (or socioeconomic background). Participants who score low on the racial resentment index prefer members of all nonwhite groups to whites in both experiments. Participants who score high on the racial resentment index are indifferent to the race/ethnicity of undergraduate applicants and faculty candidates.

We find consensus preferences in favor of women but polarized preferences with regard to gender nonbinary applicants and faculty candidates.

- When we break participants out by gender, both men and women favor women over men in both undergraduate admissions and faculty recruitment. Given women's continuing underrepresentation among university faculty, the latter is consistent with most universities' efforts to increase gender diversity. But with women now in the majority among US college and university students, the consensus preference for women applicants is more puzzling.

- The only instance of preference polarization we find at any US university is with regard to gender nonconformity. When we break student participants out by their own gender, by their partisanship, or by their level of racial resentment, we find preferences on nonbinary applicants and candidates running in opposite directions. Men, Republicans, and high-racial-resentment participants *dis*favor gender nonbinary faculty candidates relative to men. Women, Democrats, and low-resentment participants favor nonbinary candidates.
- The pattern of differences across participant groups, by gender and by party, is the same at the Naval Academy as at other schools, but the overall preferences toward nonbinary applicants and candidates *among all participants* there shift strongly negative. Gender nonconformity is regarded with far greater disapproval at the service academy than on civilian campuses.

We find no differences in the rates of return to academic achievement across groups.[1]

- We find no evidence that some groups are rewarded more, or less, generously for academic achievement than others. To put it differently, in both admissions and in faculty recruitment, members of all racial/ethnic groups are increasingly likely to be selected as their levels of academic achievement rise – *and the rates of increases are indistinguishable across groups.*
- The same is true for men, women, and nonbinary applicants and faculty candidates.
- On the whole, then, some groups are preferred over others (for the most part, underrepresented minority groups over traditionally advantaged ones), but the rates at which achievement improves the prospects of selection for any applicant or candidate are the same.

---

[1] We describe many of our results as "all else equal" to denote that our estimates of preferences with respect to any particular attribute (e.g., gender, or race/ethnicity) are derived from our statistical analysis that does *not* consider interactions of multiple attributes. We recognize that, in real decisions, "all else" is seldom equal. For example, some types of applicants might have higher or lower levels of academic achievement than others. Our experiments allow us to estimate how preferences toward applicants or faculty candidates change at varying levels of academic achievement.

Faculty have stronger pro-diversity preferences than students do.

- At two universities, the University of Nevada, Reno and the University of New Mexico, we were able to include faculty as well as students in our experiments on faculty recruitment. At both schools, preferences in favor of faculty candidates from all nonwhite groups, and in favor of women and nonbinary candidates, are stronger among the faculty than among the students.
- The preference differences between faculty and students with respect to diversity characteristics are larger than cross-group differences by race/ethnicity, gender, or socioeconomic background.

All of these results indicate an overall consensus in support of diversity among the core members of university communities at the center of our study: students and faculty. Given that so much of the discussion around campus diversity emphasizes conflict, and considering the divisive debates over policies aimed at maintaining and advancing campus diversity, it is important to underscore the breadth and depth of this consensus. In navigating the world, we tend to confront decisions about abstract policies infrequently and decisions about multifaceted, complex individuals all the time. The results from our experiments and surveys suggest that opposition to affirmative action as an abstract policy does not necessarily indicate opposition to taking race/ethnicity and gender into consideration in practice. The campus communities in which we conducted our experiments are varied and far flung, yet we find remarkably consistent support across them all for prioritizing diversity in admissions and faculty recruitment. Since policies regarding diversity and merit are ultimately about people, we believe that our study sheds new light on the affirmative action debate.

Yet debates about diversity extend beyond the campus walls, and they have grown to include issues beyond who is admitted and recruited into university communities. Our experiments are limited in both these regards. Our participants include current students and some faculty. Actual applicants for admission or faculty jobs, those who applied but were denied admission or not hired, actual members of admissions offices and faculty recruitment committees, or members of the broader public all might well have different preferences. And although our experiments allow us to estimate preferences about admissions and recruitment among students (and faculty at two institutions), they speak only indirectly to broader issues related to university environments and goals. In the remaining sections of this chapter, we begin with the central themes from our experiments, the prioritization of diversity in admissions and recruitment and its effects. We then consider some broader diversity-related matters, how the results from our study can inform them, and some major challenges ahead related to diversity and attitudes toward it.

10.2 HOW DIVERSITY AFFECTS UNIVERSITY COMMUNITIES

Public and scholarly debate over efforts to promote diversity tends to focus either on the effects such policies have on university communities as a whole, or on how they affect individuals whose admission into the community is directly affected by those policies – those who are "in" but, in the absence of policies to promote diversity, might be "out." We address each in turn.

Community-Level Effects

The most sweeping and compelling case for diversity in universities – and, more generally, in organizations focused on cognitive tasks – is from Page (2007, 2017), who provides the theoretical foundation for the case that diversity improves group performance on predictive tasks, problem-solving tasks, and creative tasks. The diversity Page has in mind is cognitive – "differences in how we interpret, reason, and solve" (Page 2017, p. 2). He acknowledges that not all group goals are equally advanced by cognitive diversity and that identifying task-relevant cognitive diversity is critical to assembling effective groups. Furthermore, because it is the *combination* of skills and cognitive traits rather than the simple sum of raw talents that determines group effectiveness, the beneficial effects of diversity are such that no uniform standard (e.g., performance on a test) can be applied to individuals in order to assemble the most effective group (Page 2017, p. 14, p. 95, pp. 128–129).

Page's argument provides grounds for advocating holistic selection procedures in college admissions and faculty recruitment that take into consideration not only the mix of characteristics in a given applicant but also of the broader group the applicant would join. Indeed, although cognitive diversity is distinct from identity diversity, Page argues that identity diversity *contributes* to cognitive diversity by bringing together on campus a wider range of life experiences and perspectives. Page emphasizes two key considerations about the link between identity diversity and cognitive diversity. First, the categories by which we tend to demarcate identity diversity – including, prominently, race, ethnicity, and gender – tend to subsume a larger set of attributes that bear on cognitive perspectives (e.g., social status, behavioral norms, social networks, language, religion, neighborhood effects, historical knowledge). Second, the combination of attributes reflected in the group, not just its aggregate cognitive horsepower, is essential to its collective effectiveness. As he notes, "Pulling off just one attribute and drawing inferences will produce errors" (Page 2017, p. 134). This is the case for diversity as an intellectual asset in university communities.

BENEFITS OF STUDENT DIVERSITY. Other arguments for diversity as a collective good point to positive psychological, emotional, and social outcomes among the student body. These studies, mostly based on observational data, find that diversity among students correlates with greater openness and mutual understanding, increased intellectual development, positive personal and social outcomes, positive attitudes toward the college campus environment, leadership skills, interracial friendships, commitment to civic engagement, and bias reduction. It is this line of reasoning that has inspired universities like Duke to adopt random roommate assignment policies in an effort to bring people from disparate backgrounds together (Bauer-Wolf 2018).

Empirically, Hu and Kuh (2003) find that interacting with students from diverse backgrounds (racial, political, religious, geographical, etc.) has positive effects on cultural awareness and understanding, and on more general learning outcomes including intellectual skills, general education, personal and social development, proficiency in science and technology, and practical and vocational preparation. Rao (2019) finds similar effects across private schools in India that adopted policies to increase the presence of socioeconomically disadvantaged students among the wealthy. Umbach and Kuh (2006) find that students attending liberal arts colleges with greater racial diversity report higher levels of academic challenge, more opportunities for active and collaborative learning, a more supportive campus environment, and higher satisfaction with their college experience.

A consistent line of reasoning for admissions policies that seek to increase diversity holds that increasing the presence of underrepresented minorities on campus leads to more frequent interactions between minority and majority group members, which in turn promotes positive student outcomes (Park 2018). Bowman (2012) finds that racially diverse student bodies lead to the development of interracial friendships, and that these effects are highest on the most diverse campuses. Park, Denson, and Bowman (2013) find that socioeconomic diversity leads to increased class interactions, greater interracial interactions, and higher involvement in curricular and cocurricular diversity activities (class-based and racial/ethnic). Cross-class interaction is also higher among students attending more socioeconomically and racially diverse institutions (Park, Denson, and Bowman 2013).

These studies support an expert opinion delivered by Gurin at *Gratz v. Bollinger* and *Grutter v. Bollinger*:

Because students in late adolescence and early adulthood are at a critical stage of development, diversity (racial, economic, demographic, and cultural) is crucially important in enabling them to become conscious learners and critical thinkers, and in preparing them to become active participants in a democratic society. Universities are ideal institutions to foster such development (Gurin 1999).

The benefits of different types of diversity on college campuses are intertwined, but actions taken to foster a diverse campus community appear to be a starting point for positive diversity-related outcomes.

Benefits of diversity that accrue at the level of the whole campus community, moreover, are central to the legal rationale for taking racial and ethnic identity into account in college admissions.[2] From the initial recognition of a "compelling state interest" in diversity in the 1978 *Bakke* decision through its reference to the "educational interests of diversity" in the second *Fisher* case in 2016, the Supreme Court has leaned on community-level benefits as justification for race-conscious admissions for decades (*Regents of the University of California v. Bakke* 1978; *Fisher v. University of Texas at Austin et al.* 2016). Writing for the majority in the 2003 *Grutter* decision, Justice Sandra Day O'Connor extended the public goods rationale for diversity well beyond educational and social benefits to national security. Citing testimony from military leaders that a "racially diverse officer corps ... is essential to the military's ability to fulfill its principal mission to provide national security" (Becton 2003), she notes that campus diversity in the military academies, and within ROTC programs operating at universities throughout the country,

---

[2] There is not an analogous body of jurisprudence on race-consciousness in faculty recruitment.

amounts to a compelling national interest. O'Connor goes on to emphasize that, not only must the officer corps be racially diverse, but that officers must be trained "in a racially diverse setting" in order to provide all officers with valuable experience for the future command of the military's diverse enlisted ranks. She sums up, "[i]t requires only a small step from this analysis to conclude that our country's other most selective institutions must remain both diverse and selective" (*Grutter* v. *Bollinger* 2003). O'Connor's reasoning mirrors that of Page (2007, 2017), with the provision of national security as the task, team diversity as an essential resource, and university communities as the vehicle.

Widespread recognition of community-level benefits from diversity among students is consistent with the results from our experiments. Among our most surprising results was the degree to which preferences for prioritizing diversity in admissions and faculty recruitment are shared across groups of students. Students from traditionally dominant groups appear to recognize an educational benefit from campus diversity. These attitudes could be, at least in part, instrumental. Warikoo (2016) suggests that students at elite schools embrace a "diversity bargain," recognizing that, alongside collective, institutional benefits, campus diversity confers advantages that accrue to individuals on the job market. She quotes a student who says,

I think race [also] should be taken into consideration for the good of the university [and] for the good of the college experience, because Harvard doesn't need to send some white guy to Wall Street who has never interacted with a black person. He's going to be a business analyst under somebody who is, you know, a black guy from Penn, so he needs to know how to interact with, or to have been around people of different cultures. (Warikoo 2016, p. 98)

Consistent with this implicit bargain, Warikoo notes that some white students object if underrepresented minority students "under-supply" integrated social engagement by self-segregating on campus, such that "interaction with peers of color is a *resource* some white students feel entitled to – or sometimes wrongly deprived of" (Warikoo 2016, p. 104). Even so, our experiments show preferences consistent with broad recognition of the community-level benefits from student diversity.

FACULTY DIVERSITY. There is also substantial evidence of community-level benefits of faculty diversity. As Chapter 2 shows, nonwhites are more starkly underrepresented among faculty than among students at American universities, and women are dramatically underrepresented among faculty as well. Extensive research suggests that increasing faculty diversity could improve educational outcomes among women and racial/ethnic minority students.

For example, a range of studies show that having a professor of the same sex or race can increase student achievement and decrease gender or racial achievement gaps, particularly in fields where women or minorities are underrepresented. A large-scale longitudinal analysis controlling for various faculty, student, and course characteristics, for example, finds that having a woman instructor has a small positive effect on the likelihood of women students pursuing a given field of study as a college major, suggesting a positive role model effect for women (Bettinger and Long 2005). Along the same lines, Hoffmann and Oreopoulos (2009) find that, on the margin, having an instructor of the same gender slightly increases the grade a student earns in a course and slightly decreases the student's likelihood of dropping a class.[3]

Related research indicates that same-race teachers positively impact student outcomes in primary and secondary school (Dee 2004, 2005; Ehrenberg and Brewer 1995; Ehrenberg, Goldhaber, and Brewer 1995; Klopfenstein 2005). At the collegiate level, Rask and Bailey (2002) draw upon data on students and professors at a small liberal arts college to show that having a minority professor strongly influences minority students' choice of major. They find similar effects for gender. Price (2010) shows that black students are more likely to select and persist in STEM fields if they are taught by a black professor in STEM courses during their first year. Fairlie, Hoffmann, and Oreopoulos (2014) find that gaps between whites and underrepresented minority students across a range of performance outcomes narrow substantially when students are taught by underrepresented minority professors. Notably, however, all of these studies find little indication of offsetting effects among men or nonminority students.

Research in this vein based on observational data might be subject to selection effects because students choose their own courses and professors. Some prominent, recent experimental research overcomes this limitation, however, increasing confidence that instructor identity can affect student achievement. Capitalizing on random assignment of students to professors and mandatory enrollment in introductory math and science courses at the Air Force Academy, Carrell, Page, and West (2010) show that professor gender has a powerful impact on female students'

---

[3] Canes and Rosen (1995), Rask and Bailey (2002), and Rothstein (1995) all show similar results.

interest, participation, and performance in the STEM fields.[4] By contrast, professor gender had little effect on outcomes for men, or on outcomes for students of either gender in the humanities. They conclude that having a female professor can mitigate the gender gap in STEM. Similarly, Kofoed and McGovney (2017) use the random assignment of officer mentors to cadets at West Point to show that a female cadet who is assigned a female mentor is significantly more likely to pick her mentor's occupational branch than is a female cadet assigned to a male officer mentor. Similarly, black cadets are significantly more likely to pick their officer's occupation when assigned to black mentors than when assigned to white mentors.[5]

A substantial body of scholarship, then, suggests that the presence of intellectual mentors with common demographic characteristics can narrow gender- and race/ethnicity-based performance gaps in academic achievement. Benefits to students from groups traditionally underrepresented among faculty do not come at any measurable costs to students from traditionally dominant groups, thus advancing the institution's overall educational mission.

Individual-Level Effects

A mostly separate line of debate and inquiry addresses effects not across the campus community, but on academic and professional outcomes for *individual* students and faculty whose admission or recruitment could be directly affected by policies to promote diversity. Here again, the scholarship with regard to effects on students is far more developed than that of the effects on faculty, probably because students' greater numbers and comparability across outcomes (e.g., grades and graduation rates) facilitate systematic analysis. Whereas the evidence on community-level effects points toward a consensus on diversity's benefits, debates over individual-level effects are more contentious.

---

[4] Similarly, Bostwick and Weinberg (2018) find that having female peers increases women's likelihood of completing PhD programs in STEM fields.
[5] Metzler and Woessmann (2012) find a related effect on learning outcomes in Peruvian elementary schools, where math test scores among boys are responsive only to their teachers' expertise, not to teacher gender, whereas for girls, student–teacher gender match matters for learning. Antecol, Eren, and Ozbeklik (2015) find further evidence of this phenomenon at elementary schools in seventeen states in the United States. Finally, Lim and Meer (2017) demonstrate the importance of teacher–student gender matches in Korean middle schools; female students perform significantly better on standardized tests when assigned to female teachers, but there are few effects for male students.

Two distinct lines of research in this area focus on the match between students' academic achievement and preparation before college and the selectivity of the college they attend. Scholarship on "*under*matching" focuses on students who attend colleges that are less than the most selective they could potentially attend based on their standardized test scores and high school grades. Scholarship on "*mis*match" focuses on whether underrepresented minority students admitted under race-conscious admissions policies underperform academically at highly selective schools.

UNDERMATCH. A number of studies establish that even highly quali-fied students from low-income backgrounds apply to selective universities at rates far below those of their peers from higher-income households (Bowen, Chingos, and McPherson 2009; Hoxby and Avery 2013; Rod-erick, Coca, and Nagaoka 2011). There are various sources of this failure to match human capital with institutional capital. Students' fam-ily income, their parents' education level, their geographical proximity to selective colleges, whether they encounter high school teachers and counselors who attended selective schools, and whether their school dis-tricts are large enough to contain a critical mass of other low-income high-achieving students, all affect rates of undermatching (Hoxby and Avery 2013; Ovink et al. 2018). The effects of race/ethnicity, net of socioeconomic class status, however, are difficult to discern. Blacks undermatch at lower rates than whites overall, but at higher rates among those who qualify for highly selective schools (Ovink et al. 2018). The effects of undermatching are also subject to debate. Obser-vational studies find that undermatched students report lower levels of college satisfaction and lower income in the early postgraduation years than those who are not undermatched (Fosnacht 2014; Ovink et al. 2018).[6] Yet undermatched students also report higher levels of faculty contact in college and more opportunities for collaborative learning (Fosnacht 2014).

---

[6] The lower earnings result appears to run counter to a more comprehensive report from the American Council on Education that finds that students who attended minority-serving institutions (MSIs) – including Historically Black Colleges and Universities (HBCUs), Predominantly Black Institutions (PBIs), Hispanic-Serving Institutions (HSIs), Tribal Colleges and Universities (TCUs), and Asian-American and Native American Pacific Islander-Serving Institutions (AANAPISIs) – show *higher* rates of economic mobil-ity after graduation than do alumni from non-MSIs, which are more likely than MSIs to be highly selective.

The scholarship on undermatching indicates that the phenomenon is widespread, particularly among students from low socioeconomic status backgrounds and underresourced high schools. The problem, however, applies primarily to students who do not apply to selective schools.

MISMATCH (OR OVERMATCH). For students who are members of underrepresented minority groups or who come from socioeconomically disadvantaged backgrounds, a more salient – and contentious – line of research is on mismatch (or overmatch), which holds that efforts to promote diversity in admissions set their intended beneficiaries up for failure. An early articulation argues that black law students, owing to lower academic preparation, learn less in law school and therefore fail bar exams at higher rates than whites (Sander 2004). Sander postulates that the effect is big enough that fewer blacks pass the bar than would be the case in the absence of affirmative action. But this approach suggests that the negative effect of being over-matched swamps any positive effect of school quality. Subsequent scholarship finds mixed evidence for mismatch effects among law students and graduates (Ho 2005; Lott, Ramseyer, and Standen 2011; Rothstein and Yoon 2008), in part owing to differences in the counterfactuals against which student outcomes under race-conscious admissions are compared (Arcidiacono and Lovenheim 2016).

Research on effects on undergraduates is similarly divided. Light and Strayer (2000) find that, for students in the lowest quartile of academic preparation for college, graduation rates decline as the quality of the university increases, which suggests the potential for mismatch. Kurlaender and Grodsky (2013) exploit a snafu in the University of California's admissions process from 2004 that initially rejected over 2,000 students, then offered them slots at elite campuses. Those students – of all racial and ethnic backgrounds – earned lower grades and accrued course credits more slowly than did students admitted to the elite campuses under the standard process. But most of the differences in outcomes are mediated by social background and choice of major, leaving the authors skeptical of remedies to mismatch that would abandon holistic admissions. In another study drawing on data from the University of California system, Arcidiacono, Aucejo, and Hotz (2016) find that underrepresented minority students intending to pursue STEM majors who matriculated at the most selective campuses are more likely than white and Asian students to switch to social science or humanities tracks. Based on student-level data on precollege preparation levels, the authors suggest that such students would more likely prevail in STEM curricula at the UC system's less prestigious campuses. This result, tightly linked to a specific counterfactual, suggests an alternative path through students' university educations conditional on race-conscious admissions.

Stepping back to less finely calibrated outcomes, Cortes (2010) compares college retention and graduation rates among minority students before and after Texas's adoption of a Top Ten Percent Rule. Abandoning race-conscious admissions diminished enrollment and graduation rates among underrepresented minority students overall. Moreover, Cortes finds no support for the mismatch proposition that those minority students who "cascaded down" to less selective schools then would graduate at higher rates. Expanding the empirical scope beyond the United States, Bagde, Epple, and Taylor (2016) draw on a large data set of engineering students in India, which employs a system of admissions quotas for women and members of marginalized ethnic groups. They show that India's affirmative action policy increases the access to high-quality institutions for women and disadvantaged groups, and after examining test performance and graduation rates, they find no evidence of mismatch among students from the targeted groups who are admitted to highly selective schools.

The debate over the effects of admissions policies that aim to promote diversity hangs on a key question. Are students who attend a college to which they would not be admitted absent such policies better off than if they had not been admitted? If we assume that people know their preferences and can make fully informed choices about their options, the answer is a straightforward yes (Tiboris 2014). The students for whom college opportunities expand to higher quality schools benefit (Park 2018). Our experimental results certainly bear this out. We find the strongest preferences for prioritizing diversity in admissions among underrepresented minorities, first-generation students, and those from lower-income families. These student participants in our experiments did not appear to be ambivalent about taking diversity considerations into account.

Mismatch theory, however, resists taking such preferences at face value, which leads to a more complicated verdict. If students are systematically misinformed about their likely experience at college – specifically, if they underestimate the obstacles to academic success at highly selective institutions – then the net effects, even for students admitted under pro-diversity policies, grow more opaque (Arcidiacono et al. 2011). A pivotal factor becomes whether schools that pursue diversity in admissions can also provide resources to help students from disadvantaged academic backgrounds succeed (Arcidiacono and Lovenheim 2016).

Most of the mismatch scholarship focuses exclusively on academic achievement. A recent book by Anthony Abraham Jack (2019), *The Privileged Poor: How Elite Colleges Are Failing Disadvantaged Students*, explores the social obstacles students from traditionally marginalized groups face on college campuses. Jack's detailed accounts of student experiences at an elite university highlight that these challenges are driven as much by class as by racial/ethnic divisions, and by the starkly different habits and expectations that students' high school experiences instill. It also illustrates the degree to which students' social capital shapes their ability to connect to academic resources, and so to achieve academic success. Jack's narratives reinforce his advocacy for elite schools to be proactive in extending socialization and networking opportunities – not just with other students but also with faculty and administrative staff – to students from disadvantaged high school backgrounds as they start college.

FACULTY DIVERSITY TO MITIGATE MISMATCH. We submit that one of the key resources universities can deliver to advance this goal is a diverse faculty. The scholarship reviewed just above, which demonstrates the potential for faculty from underrepresented minority groups to mitigate academic performance gaps, speaks to this point. Yet this effect has been insufficiently appreciated in the debate up to now over affirmative action in admissions, and over mismatch in particular. Estimates of the effects on students of *admissions* policies that promote diversity are premised on the *faculty* composition as it exists. But the racial/ethnic *and gender* composition of university faculty is skewed heavily toward non-Hispanic whites and toward men, whereas underrepresented minorities and women benefit academically from teaching and mentorship from underrepresented minority and women instructors. To the extent this is the case, the issues of diversity among students and diversity among faculty are not just complementary; they are inextricably linked.

Here again, specific results from our experiments warrant attention. Preferences for diversity in faculty recruitment are widespread across students of all racial/ethnic and socioeconomic groups, and by gender, but they are consistently and measurably stronger among nonwhites than among whites, among those from lower rather than higher socioeconomic status families, and among women (with regard to women faculty candidates, specifically) than men (Figure 5.12). Students may recognize the identity imbalances among faculty and prefer to remedy them, but students who most lack mentors and role models exhibit the strongest preferences along these lines. This is one of those findings that, in retrospect, appears unsurprising, but its clarity in our experimental results stands in contrast to the attention afforded to *faculty* diversity in debates over admissions policies to promote diversity among *students*.

Although there is substantial evidence that promoting faculty diversity can yield systematic benefits for students, there is no analogous body of scholarship on whether recruitment efforts to promote diversity affect the professional success of faculty themselves.[7] In the past decade, universities have stepped up efforts to collect data on the demographic composition of applicants for faculty positions, and to advise search committees on attracting diverse candidate pools and on evaluating candidates from a wide range of backgrounds (Ellis 2018).

Sustained attention to faculty diversity is more recent than in admissions, policies to promote faculty diversity have a shorter track record, and women and racial/ethnic minorities remain far more dramatically underrepresented among faculty than among students. Universities also tend to hold data on faculty advancement closely, and particularly on promotion and tenure outcomes, because personnel policies prioritize confidentiality. For a variety of reasons, then, assessments of individual-level effects of diversity on faculty lean toward the anecdotal and tend to focus on diversity in the breach rather than in full bloom.

INFORMAL OBSTACLES TO PROMOTE FACULTY DIVERSITY.
Recent attention to the lack of mentoring infrastructure for women and minority faculty is one example suggesting the difficulty in assessing the effects of recruitment efforts. Specifically, the overrepresentation of men and whites at the highest faculty ranks may present informal obstacles to professional opportunities and advancement for traditionally marginalized groups. Egregiously but memorably, in March 2018, Stanford University's Hoover Institution hosted a conference (cosponsored by Harvard University's Belfer Center) on "applied history" in which all thirty scheduled presenters were white men. When questioned about the

---

[7] Many studies examine the professional success of women and nonwhite academics (Ards, Brintnall, and Woodard 1997; Bucklin et al. 2014; Reid 2010; Williams and Ceci 2015; Wolfinger, Mason, and Goulden 2009), but efforts to evaluate the marginal effects of efforts to promote advancement among underrepresented minority groups are less well developed.

lineup, the conference organizer and Stanford historian, Niall Ferguson, acknowledged the imbalance but offered:

"To put together a start-up, the organizer racks his brain, asks other people, invites the people he knows who work on the right kind of material and hopes that they say yes. So there was a kind of a relatively informal process of trying to identify historians not only in the United States but also in Europe who were interested in questions of a policy-relevant nature – hence, applied history." (Kerr 2018)

The responses from other scholars on social media suggest that many regard it as quite possible to find women and minority historians, but Ferguson's candid explanation may be more telling with regard to how informal networks can act as obstacles to faculty diversity. If informal networks are homophilic, and professional advancement is network-driven, then racial/ethnic and gender imbalances among faculty will self-perpetuate unless universities make conscious efforts to open professional opportunities to scholars who are less likely to be connected to such informal networks.

Wu (2017) presents another such example based on empirical evidence. Using a machine learning approach to measure gender bias in the social environment of economics as a discipline, she finds evidence of widespread hostility toward women that could impede gender equity in faculty appointments and professional advancement. Specifically, the words most frequently used on an anonymous online economics forum in discussions about women economists were demeaning and focused mainly on the women's physical appearance and personal traits. By contrast, words most frequently used in discourse about men economists followed no systematic pattern.

Other evidence suggests that gatekeeping tools used in the faculty recruitment and retention processes may systematically disadvantage certain groups over others. In an analysis of recommendation letters for faculty positions, for example, Madera et al. (2018) find that recommenders tend to use more phrases or statements that question the applicant's credentials when writing letters for women candidates than for men. Since language that raises doubt leads to more negative employment outcomes, women may be at a disadvantage compared to men when applying for faculty positions. Similarly, in a randomized experiment, Bavishi, Madera, and Hebl (2010) find that students consider black professors to be less competent than their white and Asian counterparts, and white professors to have better interpersonal skills than black and Asian professors, even when their teaching and research credentials are held equal.

A final example connects to efforts to promote faculty diversity by *cultivating* informal networks. The paradox of women's overrepresentation among students and underrepresentation among faculty is at the heart of a controversy over scholarship and mentorship programs aimed specifically at women. These programs, concentrated in the sciences where gender imbalances remain most pronounced, provide research opportunities for women and aim to cultivate mentorship relationships with senior women scientists. In May 2018, responding to a complaint by a graduate student at the University of Southern California (USC) who held that such initiatives "feel unfair" given that women outnumber men among university students, the US Department of Education opened investigations into whether the programs unlawfully discriminate against men (Korn 2018). The future of such programs might hang on whether access to same-gender mentorship is regarded as a key element of educational equality and should therefore be protected under Title IX.

Effects of Pro-Diversity Initiatives on Campus

What *do* we know about the effects of programs intended to increase diversity on campus communities? Evaluating the impact of diversity initiatives on college campuses is a new and developing research agenda, and the evidence so far is mixed. Reports sponsored by universities tend to emphasize positive effects, as does some refereed research, but other studies indicate that diversity programs can backfire.

Studies that point to the positive effects of diversity programs tend to examine whether participation in formal diversity experiences on campus correlates with diversity-related beliefs and attitudes. Spanierman et al. (2008) find that freshmen who participate in campus diversity programming develop more equitable and tolerant racial beliefs than students who do not participate. Burke and Banks (2012) find that formal diversity programs can lead students to become more conscious of racial inequalities and institutional privilege, and less resistant to learning more about issues of race and diversity.

Universities themselves also tout the benefits of diversity programs they have put in place. Several elite institutions including Brown University, Harvard University, Yale University, and Dartmouth College have published progress reports and updates that describe the steps they have taken to achieving their goals (Delalue 2018; Hanlon et al. 2016; Harvard University 2018; Polak and Bribiescas 2018). These reports include data on the growing number of underrepresented minority students and faculty on campus, as well as descriptions of specific diversity-related programs and events, resources that have been made available to under-represented minorities on campus, and changes to oversight processes and academic curricula to be more conscious of diversity considerations, among other developments. But despite this progress, there is little information available that reveals how campus communities actually *perceive* these initiatives, making it difficult to determine whether they are actually changing the climate for diversity on campus.

Some campus policies related to diversity have also attracted criticism. One of the few empirical analyses of programs intended to increase faculty diversity found no significant increases in representation for underrepresented minority groups among faculty after the hiring of a Chief Diversity Officer (Bradley et al. 2018). The authors of this study argue that universities may hire a CDO so that they appear to be committed to diversity, but do not always follow through with concrete institutional change.

Other critics suggest that policies aimed to promote consensus on diversity could foster polarization. Jeffrey Flier, the former dean of the Harvard Medical School, criticized UCLA's requirement that faculty appointment and promotion dossiers include equity, diversity, and inclusion statements, on the grounds that the meanings of those terms are, themselves, contested and have come to be associated with policy frameworks that are not politically neutral. Flier maintains that the degree of skepticism on campus about diversity-related mandates is hidden and that, in the current campus environment, "honest dialogue about the goals and consequences of these initiatives is uncommon, and overt criticism is virtually taboo. Skepticism tends to be voiced privately or in small groups rather than in public forums. Self-censorship is the rule" (Flier 2019).

Recent scholarship delivers evidence against the effectiveness of some initiatives. Focusing on diversity in the workplace, Dobbin and Kalev (2016) analyze data from 805 work establishments spanning over thirty years and find that mandatory diversity training breeds bias, racial hostility, and a general resistance to further efforts to promote diversity. Similarly, Dobbin, Schrage, and Kalev (2015) show that while some workplace diversity initiatives achieve their stated goals, successful programs are rare. Finally, Htun et al. (2018) find troubling mixed effects of mandatory sexual assault training on college students' attitudes toward women, gender roles, myths about rape and sexual assault, and willingness to report violence. Although the training has positive effects on students' awareness and understanding of sexual misconduct, it also provokes an increased willingness to express traditional gender stereotypes, more hostile sexist attitudes among white men, and an unwillingness to report cases of sexual assault among women. The authors raise the question of whether universities and organizations should even allocate money and time to sexual assault training programs when there is evidence that they could make things worse.

While none of these studies evaluates diversity initiatives that pertain to the increased representation and protection of minorities on college campuses, they underscore the need to be cautious about interpreting these programs' effects on student attitudes without clear metrics to gauge their consequences. Here, too, our study bears mention. Conjoint experiments like ours, if repeated, could help administrations more reliably assess whether the programs they have enacted are affecting how student and faculty priorities evolve and change over time, thus illuminating one potentially important effect of diversity initiatives. This would, in turn, help universities decide whether the intended benefits of the specific programs they have created are being realized among the populations they are designed to serve.

Summing Up

There is a wide range of evidence for beneficial effects at the community level of diversity, and of efforts to promote it on college campuses. Consensus on that point has provided a central pillar for jurisprudence supporting university policies to promote diversity. That consensus was also shared by participants in our survey experiments. With regard to individual-level effects, scholarly opinion about the impact of admissions policies aimed at promoting student diversity is somewhat more divided. We would suggest, however, that this debate needs to take better account of the existing gender, racial, and ethnic imbalances among faculty, and of how increasing *faculty* diversity could impact the *student* outcomes at the center of these debates. Here again, results from our experiments show that the underrepresented minority and women students for whom role models and mentors are most lacking among faculty have the strongest preferences for prioritizing diversity in faculty recruitment.

Yet we have focused here on effects on students and faculty who are *in* university communities. And of course, our survey experiments are limited to these populations. Among the biggest challenges facing campus diversity is whether and how to take into account the interests of those who remain outside university communities *because* of efforts to promote diversity. We turn attention to that topic, as well as to other challenges we regard as most prominent on the horizon for campus diversity, in the next, and final, section.

10.3   THE NEXT CHALLENGES FOR CAMPUS DIVERSITY

We close with a discussion of three issues we understand as central to debates over campus diversity moving forward. These are, in turn, (i) accounting for the effects of diversity-promotion policies on students *not* admitted,[8] (ii) universities' regulation of diversity-related *behavior* beyond the construction of the community itself, and (iii) the promotion of diversity in the ideas expressed within the community rather than just in the characteristics of its members. Each of these issues is complex and manifests itself across campuses in various ways. Nevertheless, because our survey experiments included only current students and faculty, and addressed only preferences about composition of the campus population, our results to date cannot directly address these issues. So we examine each briefly through the lens of one specific case – a lawsuit, a campus controversy, and an organization – and note the boundaries of our research and opportunities to build on it going forward.

The Asian Challenge to Race-Conscious Admissions

Applicants denied admission have long been at the center of legal challenges to affirmative action, from *Bakke* to *Hopwood* to *Grutter* and *Gratz* to *Fisher*. Since *Bakke*, the courts have weighed the claims of these plaintiffs against a collective interest (whether the state's or the university's) in diversity and generally have found that interest sufficient to permit race-conscious admissions. Note, however, that the plaintiffs in these cases were white, making them members of the demographic group that is not only the largest, but also the one with the least claim to having experienced discrimination or marginalization in other contexts. Both of those characteristics change with the next wave of legal challenges to affirmative action in college admissions.

---

[8] Impact on faculty not recruited would be analogous, but we are not aware of any political or legal mobilization on this front.

Students for Fair Admissions (SFFA), representing an Asian applicant (denied admission), potential future applicants, and parents of potential future applicants, filed suit against Harvard University in 2014.[9] They claim that Harvard's admissions practices discriminated against its members in a manner that violates Title VI of the Civil Rights Act, which prohibits any institution receiving federal funding from excluding persons on the ground of race, color, or national origin (United States Code 1964).

The case was argued in the First Federal District Court in October and November 2018, and closing arguments were revisited in February 2019. At the time this book went to press, the court had not issued its decision. Nevertheless, documents filed by SFFA and by Harvard lay out the evidence each side regards as essential to its case.

At the heart of the SFFA case are claims that Harvard discriminates against Asian applicants, that race/ethnicity is the predominant factor in its consideration of many applicants, and that its admissions practices pursue a predetermined mix of racial and ethnic characteristics among students. Harvard rates applicants with indices on academic achievement, extracurricular activities, athletics, personal qualities, and overall. SFFA's statistical analyses indicate that the number of Asian applicants admitted would be far higher if admissions decisions were based only academic achievement, or on academics plus extracurriculars – and SFFA presents evidence that studies conducted by Harvard's own Office of Institutional Research reached similar conclusions, but that those results were not made public (Arcidiacono 2018; Mortara et al. 2018).

Harvard disputes SFFA's interpretation of the data, precisely on grounds that holistic evaluation of its applicants, which considers information not included in SFFA's analyses, produces quite different outcomes (Card 2017). The divergent conclusions hang on how one treats Harvard's ratings in the most subjective domains of the admissions process. According to documents from the case, Harvard staff have scored Asian applicants relatively low on personal qualities (including "likability ... helpfulness, courage, kindness," and whether the applicant is a "good person," and has good "human qualities") (Mortara et al. 2018,

---

[9] SFFA is also representing a white plaintiff in a suit filed against the University of North Carolina at Chapel Hill, on grounds similar to those claimed by white plaintiffs in previous court challenges, who contend that the university relied on race as a dominant factor in evaluating minority applicants whose admission then displaced the white applicant with a stronger record of academic achievement (Hoover 2019a).

pp. 9–10), as well as on the overall index, which itself is a separate, subjective evaluation by admissions officers rather than a simple composite of other indices (Arcidiacono 2018, p. 5). SFFA's strategy hangs on persuading the court that those low scores on personal qualities and overall merit indicate systematic discrimination against Asian applicants and cause harm to its plaintiffs that outweighs any interest advanced by Harvard's current admissions policies.

Previous claims along these lines, from white plaintiffs, have been viewed skeptically at least in part because, as members of the largest demographic group, with the largest numbers of college applicants (both accepted and denied admission), the likelihood of any given white applicant to have been supplanted by a minority applicant was limited (Fryer and Loury 2005; Kane 1998). White applicants also cannot easily claim to have experienced adversity because of their race or ethnicity in areas *outside* college admissions. On both counts, the claims of Asian litigants are stronger. Asians make up a smaller share of the US population than either Hispanics or blacks, and a smaller share of college students in most universities, but SFFA's complaint makes clear that they are overrepresented among academic high-achievers in Harvard's applicant pool (Mortara et al. 2018), placing more favorable arithmetic behind the claim of an Asian plaintiff than a white one that he or she would have been admitted in the absence of affirmative action. What is more, Asian historical claims to have experienced overt discrimination have face value, which may fuel skepticism with respect to Harvard's treatment of Asian applicants' personal qualities.

Here again, our experimental results bear mention. Although Asians are not underrepresented among university students relative to their population share, as are blacks, Hispanics, and Native Americans, our participants favor Asian applicants – and faculty candidates – over whites. These pro-Asian preferences are generally not as large as those for members of underrepresented minority groups, but they are consistently positive and often statistically significant. Within the holistic choice exercises of the conjoint experiments, then, our participants regarded Asian applicants and faculty candidates sympathetically. Although not dispositive, this is at least consistent with the idea that Asians confront greater adversity than whites on dimensions not captured by our conjoint profiles, and that members of *current* university communities may evaluate Asian applicants with this in mind.

University Policies to Shape Where Students Should Eat, Play, Dance, and Sing

Another Harvard-based controversy illustrates a separate challenge facing university efforts to cultivate campus diversity and reap its benefits. In 1984, Harvard issued an ultimatum to its then all-male social clubs (called "final clubs" in Harvard parlance) that they must admit women or lose recognition and official affiliation with the university (Sanger 1984). Those that opted to remain single-gender were de-recognized in 1985 (The New York Times 1987). In the years since, other single-gender clubs, including women-only sororities, flourished among Harvard students despite lack of formal affiliation.

In February 2016, Harvard's Faculty of Arts and Sciences ratified a report holding that student body diversity is essential to the mission of the university (Clark and Khurana 2016). But the Harvard faculty's conception of diversity extends beyond the *identities* of the students to encompass *how they interact*. In the words of a report from Harvard's Committee on Unrecognized Single-Gender Social Organizations (SGSOs):

We want our students to engage with each other not only in their classes but where they eat, play, dance, sing, act, debate, write, throw, catch, relax, and, of course, study. We seek to achieve this goal through very deliberate choices in the way in which the College is structured. (Clark and Khurana 2016)

Former Harvard President Drew Faust followed this report in May 2016 with her announcement of a policy aimed at discouraging students from joining SGSOs such as final clubs, sororities, and fraternities. Faust did not ban the organizations outright, but stated unambiguously that the administration regarded their effect on the institution as negative and reaffirmed the policy of withholding from any member of an SGSO an array of recognitions and benefits Harvard can confer – for example, leadership positions in campus organizations, team captaincies, and institutional endorsements for prestigious fellowships (Faust 2016). Faust's move attracted opposition among faculty, a group of whom advanced a motion to roll back the anti-SGSO policy by preventing Harvard from punishing students in any way for "joining, or affiliating with, any lawful organization, political party, or social, political, or other affinity group" (Natanson and Xiao 2017). The motion was defeated in a vote of the Arts and Sciences faculty with 90 in favor and 130 opposed, in November 2017 (Florence and Karr 2017).

On December 5, 2017, Faust and Harvard Corporation Senior Fellow William F. Lee reaffirmed the existing policy with a statement that lays out in the strongest terms Harvard's belief in diversity as an institutional good:

We self-consciously seek to admit a class that is diverse on many dimensions, including on gender, race, and socioeconomic status ... [T]hat diversity is central to our mission, as well as to our understanding of an effective educational environment in which students learn from exploring their differences. (Faust and Lee 2017)

The statement goes on to describe SGSOs as "a product of another era, a time when Harvard's student body was all male, culturally homogeneous, and overwhelmingly white and affluent" (Faust and Lee 2017). It holds that, even when unrecognized, the clubs "stand in the way of our ability to provide a fully challenging and inclusive educational experience to the diverse students currently on our campus," and that "it cannot be seriously disputed that the overall impact is negative." By May 2018, Harvard's Dean of Students Office had published rules for student organizations to gain (or regain) institutional recognition. These involved publishing data on the gender breakdown of members, publicly affirming gender inclusivity in membership and recruitment policies, and documented training for board members on prevention of sexual assault and hazing (Bolotnikova 2018).

Harvard's new rules sought to level the status of campus organizations traditionally dominated by men, but the initial effects were ambiguous, with membership in sororities dropping precipitously whereas membership in all-men SGSOs remained stable (Brown 2019). In December 2018, a group of fraternities, sororities, and three students filed lawsuits against Harvard in both state and federal court, alleging that the university's policies discriminate against members on the basis of sex by punishing students who join single-sex groups (Field 2018). The university responded with motions to dismiss the suits, contending that its policies are gender- and sex-neutral, that students who chose to matriculate at Harvard do so understanding the rules, and that SGSOs have no right to impose *their* culture on Harvard, which chooses to dedicate resources "to students whose decisions reflect the college's aspirations for inclusivity" (Hurtado 2019). When this book went to press, the lawsuit was unresolved.

Harvard's ideal sets a far higher bar than simply recruiting a diverse student population. It uses the currency of institutional resources –

leadership positions and endorsements for honors and fellowships – to restructure students' incentives on whom to associate with, and how. If the gains from diversity can only be fully realized when students "eat, play, dance, sing, etc." together, then reaping diversity's benefits may require universities to regulate campus social life in ways that extend well beyond the considerations in admissions and faculty recruitment at the center of this study.

Diversity of Ideas

Finally, recent years have witnessed a drumbeat of media and scholarly attention to perceived ideological and intellectual intolerance on college campuses. Protests against guest speakers attract widespread coverage, probably because such one-off events focus around a specific incident. The controversial ideas might be connected to issues of identity, as with the disruption of a lecture by sociologist Charles Murray at Middlebury College in 2017, whose arguments about the roots of racial inequality attracted opposition (Kean 2017), but not necessarily, as with the protests at Smith College leading to the "disinvitation" of International Monetary Fund Director Christine Lagarde as commencement speaker in 2014 (Pérez-Peña 2014). And below the level of high-profile invitees, there is a current of criticism holding that campus life more generally, inside classrooms and out, is constrained by orthodoxy of thought, particularly around ideas related to identity, inequality, and marginalization (Al-Gharbi 2017; Langbert 2018).

To our knowledge, the most expansive effort to confront intellectual orthodoxy on campuses is Heterodox Academy, an organization of university faculty and graduate students with over 2,500 members (circa 2019), who subscribe to the following statement:

I believe that university life requires that people with diverse viewpoints and perspectives encounter each other in an environment where they feel free to speak up and challenge each other. I am concerned that many academic fields and universities currently lack sufficient viewpoint diversity – particularly political diversity. I will support viewpoint diversity in my academic field, my university, my department, and my classroom. (Al-Gharbi N.d.)

Heterodox Academy members tend to perceive a bigger threat to viewpoint diversity from the political left than from the political right (Heying 2017; Lee 2017). The organization's survey data suggest that, among students themselves, political conservatives perceive more pressure not to express their views on gender, race, and politics than do political liberals (Stevens 2017).

Heterodox Academy publishes a blog and a podcast, and makes available web-based tools promoting viewpoint diversity. Conceptually, viewpoint diversity appears to be tethered even more closely to cognitive diversity (Page 2007, 2017) than is identity diversity. To the extent that cognitive diversity yields intellectual benefits to university communities, it is a short leap to value viewpoint diversity as well. But that leap leaves open the question of whether and how universities can craft policies to promote viewpoint diversity on campus. Opposition to limits on expression, such as campus speech codes, might be one rallying point, but proactive policies to *encourage* viewpoint diversity raise a raft of questions. How would inadmissible levels of viewpoint homogeneity be identified, and by whom? Are there some domains or disciplines in which viewpoint diversity should be valued more than in others? What are the viable remedies to excessive viewpoint homogeneity and how should they be applied?

Prominent advocates of viewpoint diversity contend that the forces suppressing diversity and enforcing orthodoxy are largely informal and socially constructed (Kuran 1995). But the design of formal, institutional measures to reshape behaviors driven by social norms is notoriously difficult (Bicchieri 2016; Helmke and Levitsky 2004). The University of Chicago has attempted to make some headway in this regard, publishing a set of guiding principles expressing its commitment to freedom of speech and freedom of expression, which affirm that:

it is not the proper role of the University to attempt to shield individuals from ideas and opinions they find unwelcome, disagreeable, or even deeply offensive. Although the University greatly values civility, and although all members of the University community share in the responsibility for maintaining a climate of mutual respect, concerns about civility and mutual respect can never be used as a justification for closing off discussion of ideas, however offensive or disagreeable those ideas may be to some members of our community. (Stone et al. 2015)

As of early in 2019, nearly sixty colleges and universities around the country had adopted or endorsed the Chicago principles, or had issued similar statements affirming their commitment to the diversity of ideas on their campuses (Foundation for Individual Rights in Education 2019). Then, on March 1, 2019, President Trump announced his intention to sign an executive order to cut off federal research funding to universities that fail to support free speech (Mangan 2019). As this book went to press, it was not clear how such a failure would be defined or how such policy might be enforced. Moving forward, the Chicago principles might become a focal point for campus policies on viewpoint diversity, or perhaps federal government intervention will scramble the signals, but this debate is at an early stage relative to that over diversity of identity.

* * *

We have argued here that there is a hidden consensus on campus diversity. In our experiments, involving thousands of students and faculty from seven universities, large and small, private and public, throughout the United States and outside it, we find consistent support for prioritizing diversity interests in admissions and faculty recruitment. Those preferences are shared more broadly than we had expected, perhaps because we were conditioned by campus debates and attendant media coverage that emphasize the depth of divisions on campus over diversity. That we find less division than we anticipated is encouraging, but we do not mean to diminish the challenges ahead. The students and faculty we examined from *inside* the campus walls prioritize diversity, but other participants in this debate have other priorities, and powerful arguments. We hope, with this book, to have shed new light on how campus communities think about some key elements in the diversity debates, but debates over how we construct those communities and how we govern them are not going away.

Bibliography

Abrams, Sam. 2016*a*. "Professors Moved Left Since 1990s, Rest of Country Did Not." January 9. https://heterodoxacademy.org/2016/ 01/09/professors-moved-left-but-country-did-not/. Heterodox Academy. (Last Accessed: June 3, 2017).

Abrams, Sam. 2016*b*. "There Are Conservative Professors. Just Not in These States." July 1. https://nyti.ms/2rfW7wd. *New York Times*. (Last Accessed: June 3, 2017).

Adams, Richard. 2017. "British Universities Employ No Black Academics in Top Roles, Figures Show." January 19. www.theguardian.com/education/2017/jan/ 19/british-universities-employ-no-black-academics-in-top-roles-figures-show. *Guardian*. (Last Accessed: May 10, 2018).

Adams, Richard, and Caelainn Barr. 2018. "Oxford Faces Anger over Failure to Improve Diversity among Students." May 22. www.theguardian.com/ education/2018/may/23/oxford-faces-anger-over-failure-to-improve-diversity-among-students. *Guardian*. (Last Accessed: May 24, 2018).

Agan, Amanda, and Sonja Starr. 2018. "Ban the Box, Criminal Records, and Racial Discrimination: A Field Experiment." *Quarterly Journal of Economics* 133(1): 191–235.

Agarwal, James, Wayne S. DeSarbo, Naresh K. Malhotra, and Vithala R. Rao. 2015. "An Interdisciplinary Review of Research in Conjoint Analysis: Recent Developments and Directions for Future Research." *Customer Needs and Solutions* 2(1): 19–40.

Ahmed, Sara. 2012. *On Being Included: Racism and Diversity in Institutional Life*. Durham, NC: Duke University Press.

Al-Gharbi, Musa. 2017. "A Lack of Ideological Diversity Is Killing Social Research." April 6. https://philarchive.org/archive/MUSALO. *Times Higher Education*. (Last Accessed: June 25, 2018).

Al-Gharbi, Musa. N.d. "HeterodoxAcademy.org." https://heterodoxacademy .org/. Heterodox Academy. (Last Accessed: August 29, 2017).

American Association of University Professors. 1993. "The Status of Non-Tenure-Track Faculty." Report available at: www.aaup.org/report/status-non-tenure-track-faculty.

Angrist, Joshua D., and Jorn-Steffen Pischke. 2009. *Mostly Harmless Economet-rics*. Princeton, NJ: Princeton University Press.

Antecol, Heather, Ozkan Eren, and Serkan Ozbeklik. 2015. "The Effect of Teacher Gender on Student Achievement in Primary School: Evidence from a Randomized Experiment." *Journal of Labor Economics* 33(1): 63–89.

Arcidiacono, Peter, and Michael Lovenheim. 2016. "Affirmative Action and the Quality-Fit Tradeoff." *Journal of Economic Literature* 54(1): 3–51.

Arcidiacono, Peter, Esteban Aucejo, Patrick Coate, and V. Joseph Hotz. 2014. "Affirmative Action and University Fit: Evidence from Proposition 209." *IZA Journal of Labor Economics* 3(7): 1–42.

Arcidiacono, Peter, Esteban M. Aucejo, and Joseph Hotz. 2016. "University Differences in the Graduation of Minorities in STEM Fields: Evidence from California." *American Economic Review* 106(3): 525–562.

Arcidiacono, Peter, Esteban M. Aucejo, and Ken Spenner. 2012. "What Happens after Enrollment? An Analysis of the Time Path of Racial Differences in GPA and Major Choice." *IZA Journal of Labor Economics* 1(1): 5.

Arcidiacono, Peter, Esteban M. Aucejo, Hanming Fang, and Kenneth I. Spen-ner. 2011. "Does Affirmative Action Lead to Mismatch? A New Test and Evidence." *Quantitative Economics* 2(3): 303–333.

Arcidiacono, Peter S. 2018. "Expert Report of Peter S. Arcidiacono, Students for Fair Admissions, Inc. v. Harvard." June 15. http://samv91khoyt2i553a2t1s05i-wpengine.netdna-ssl.com/wp-content/uploads/2018/06/Doc-415-1-Arcidiacono-Expert-Report.pdf. Document 415-1. United States District Court for the District of Massachusetts.

Arditi, Lynn. 2015. "Brown, PC Students Protest Racial Discrimination on Campus." November 13. www.providencejournal.com/article/20151113/NEWS/151119682. *Providence Journal*. (Last Accessed: September 1, 2017).

Ards, Sheila, Michael Brintnall, and Maurice Woodard. 1997. "The Road to Tenure and Beyond for African American Political Scientists." *Journal of Negro Education* 66(2): 159.

Ashenkas, Jeremy, Haeyoun Park, and Adam Pearce. 2017. "Even With Affirma-tive Action, Blacks and Hispanics Are More Underrepresented at Top Colleges Than 35 Years Ago." August 24. https://nyti.ms/2woapTC. *New York Times*. (Last Accessed: August 26, 2017).

Associated Press. 2016. "Student Group Calls University of New Mexico Seal Offensive." April 17. www.foxnews.com/us/2016/04/17/student-group-calls-university-new-mexico-seal-offensive.html. Associated Press. (Last Accessed: August 29, 2017).

Aung, Khin Mai. 2012. "Asian-American Quotas Are Imaginary; Need for Diver-sity Is Real." December 19. https://nyti.ms/2LcIrcl. *New York Times*. (Last Accessed: August 29, 2017).

Baert, Stijn. 2018. "Hiring Discrimination: An Overview of (Almost) All Cor-respondence Experiments Since 2005." In *Audit Studies: Behind the Scenes with Theory, Method, and Nuance*, ed. S. Michael Gaddis. Cham, Switzerland: Springer International Publishing, 63–77.

Bagde, Surendrakumar, Dennis Epple, and Lowell Taylor. 2016. "Does Affirma-tive Action Work? Caste, Gender, College Quality, and Academic Success in India." *American Economic Review* 106(6): 1495–1521.

Baldez, Lisa. 2002. *Why Women Protest: Women's Movements in Chile*. Cambridge, MA: Cambridge University Press.

Bansak, Kirk, Jens Hainmueller, Daniel J. Hopkins, and Teppei Yamamoto. 2018. "The Number of Choice Tasks and Survey Satisficing in Conjoint Experiments." *Political Analysis* 26(01): 112–119.

Bauer-Wolf, Jeremy. 2018. "Little Drama with Duke's Random Roommate Policy." December 19. www.insidehighered.com/news/2018/12/19/little-drama-dukes-random-roommate-policy. *Inside Higher Ed*. (Last Accessed: January 17, 2019).

Bavishi, Anish, Juan M. Madera, and Michelle R. Hebl. 2010. "The Effect of Professor Ethnicity and Gender on Student Evaluations: Judged Before Met." *Journal of Diversity in Higher Education* 3(4): 245–256.

Baynes, Terry. 2012. "Asian-American Rift over Supreme Court Affirmative Action Case." August 14. http://reut.rs/PVR6uC. Reuters. (Last Accessed: September 15, 2017).

Bechtel, Michael M., and Kenneth F. Scheve. 2013. "Mass Support for Global Climate Agreements Depends on Institutional Design." *Proceedings of the National Academy of Sciences of the United States of America* 110(34): 13763–13768.

Becton, Julius W. 2003. "Consolidated Brief of Lt. Gen. Julius W. Becton, Jr., et al." Amici Curiae at. 7-9, Grutter (No. 02-241), *Gratz v. Bollinger*, 539 U.S. 244 (2003). Available on WestLaw at 2003 WL 1787554.

Becton, Julius W. 2013. "Brief of Lt. Gen. Julius W. Becton, Jr., et al." Amici Curiae (No 11-345), *Fisher v. Texas* (2013), 570 U.S. _. Available at: www.scotusblog.com/wp-content/uploads/2016/08/11-345-respondent-amicus-becton.pdf.

Belkin, Aaron. 2001. "The Pentagon's Gay Ban Is Not Based on Military Necessity." *Journal of Homosexuality* 41(1): 103–119.

Bell, Myrtle P., David A. Harrison, and Mary E. McLaughlin. 1997. "Asian American Attitudes toward Affirmative Action in Employment." *Journal of Applied Behavioral Science* 33(3): 356–377.

Berrey, Ellen. 2015. *The Enigma of Diversity: The Language of Race and the Limits of Racial Justice*. Chicago, IL: University of Chicago Press.

Berrien, Hank. 2017. "UNM Students Protest Funding of Shapiro Speech." February 26. www.dailywire.com/news/13869/unm-students-protest-funding-shapiro-speech-hank-berrien#. *Daily Wire*. (Last Accessed: August 29, 2017).

Bertrand, Marianne, and Esther Duflo. 2016. "Field Experiments on Discrimination." In *Handbook of Field Experiments*, eds. A. Banerjee, and E. Duflo. Cambridge, MA: Abdul Latif Jameel Poverty Action Lab.

Bertrand, Marianne, and Sendhil Mullainathan. 2004. "Are Emily and Greg More Employable Than Lakisha and Jamal? A Field Experiment on Labor Market Discrimination." *American Economic Review* 94(4): 991–1013.

Bertrand, Marianne, Rema Hanna, and Sendhil Mullainathan. 2010. "Affirmative Action in Education: Evidence from Engineering College Admissions in India." *Journal of Public Economics* 94(1–2): 16–29.

Bettinger, Eric P., and Bridget Terry Long. 2005. "Do Faculty Serve as Role Models? The Impact of Instructor Gender on Female Students." *American Economic Review* 95(2): 152–157.

Bever, Lindsey. 2016. "Students Were Told to Select Gender Pronouns. One Chose 'His Majesty' to Protest 'Absurdity'." October 7. https://wapo .st/2cZAuWI?tid=ss_tw&utm_term=.dcabb7fbd900. *Washington Post*. (Last Accessed: December 18, 2017).

Bicchieri, Cristina. 2016. *Norms in the Wild: How to Diagnose, Measure, and Change Social Norms*. Oxford, UK: Oxford University Press.

Blashill, Aaron J., and Kimberly K. Powlishta. 2009. "The Impact of Sexual Orientation and Gender Role on Evaluations of Men." *Psychology of Men & Masculinity* 10(2): 160–173.

Bolotnikova, Marina N. 2018. "Social Clubs Must File Gender Breakdown." May 10. www.harvardmagazine.com/2018/05/social-clubs-must-file-gender-breakdown. *Harvard Magazine*. (Last Accessed: June 25, 2018).

Bostwick, Valerie K., and Bruce A. Weinberg. 2018. "Nevertheless She Persisted? Gender Peer Effects in Doctoral Studies Programs." NBER Working Paper 25028, available at: www.nber.org/papers/w25028.pdf.

Bowen, William G., and Derek Curtis Bok. 1998. *The Shape of the River: Long-Term Consequences of Considering Race in College and University Admissions*. Princeton, NJ: Princeton University Press.

Bowen, William G., and Sarah A. Levin. 2003. *Reclaiming the Game: College Sports and Educational Values*. Princeton, NJ: Princeton University Press.

Bowen, William G., Matthew M. Chingos, and Michael S. McPherson. 2009. *Crossing the Finish Line: Completing College at America's Public Universities*. Princeton, NJ: Princeton University Press.

Bowman, Nicholas A. 2012. "Structural Diversity and Close Interracial Relationships in College." *Educational Researcher* 41(4): 133–135.

Bowman, Nicholas A., Nida Denson, and Julie J. Park. 2016. "Racial/Cultural Awareness Workshops and Post-College Civic Engagement: A Propensity Score Matching Approach." *American Educational Research Journal* 53(6): 1556–1587.

Bradley, Steven W., James R. Garven, Wilson W. Law, and James E. West. 2018. "The Impact of Chief Diversity Officers on Diverse Faculty Hiring." NBER Working Paper No. 24969, available at: www.nber.org/papers/w24969.

Bradner, Eric. 2015. "U.S. Military Opens Combat Positions to Women." December 3. www.cnn.com/2015/12/03/politics/u-s-military-women-combat-positions/index.html. CNN. (Last Accessed: April 29, 2018).

Braun, Sebastian, Nadja Dwenger, Dorothea Kübler, and Alexander Westkamp. 2014. "Implementing Quotas in University Admissions: An Experimental Analysis." *Games and Economic Behavior* 85: 232–251.

Brown, Ann J., William Swinyard, and Jennifer Ogle. 2003. "Women in Academic Medicine: A Report of Focus Groups and Questionnaires, with Conjoint Analysis." *Journal of Women's Health* 12(10): 999–1008.

Brown, Madeline M., John M. Carey, Katherine Clayton, Yusaku Horiuchi, and Lauren K. Martin. 2017. "Are University Communities Deeply Divided over the Value of Diversity on Campus? Understanding Students' Preferences via Conjoint Analysis." Working paper, available at SSRN: https://papers.ssrn.com/sol3/papers.cfm?abstract_id=2775464.

Brown, Sarah. 2018. "Mizzou's Freshman Class Shrank by a Third over 2 Years. Here's How It's Trying to Turn That Around." June 1. www.chronicle.com/article/Mizzou-s-Freshman-Class/243570. *Chronicle of Higher Education.* (Last Accessed: March 11, 2019).

Brown, Sarah. 2019. "Harvard Cracks Down on All-Male Clubs. But It's Women's Groups That Have Vanished." January 8. www.chronicle.com/article/Harvard-Cracks-Down-on/245436. *Chronicle of Higher Education.* (Last Accessed: January 23, 2019).

Bucklin, Brenda A., Morgan Valley, Cheryl Welch, Zung Vu Tran, and Steven R. Lowenstein. 2014. "Predictors of Early Faculty Attrition at One Academic Medical Center." *BMC Medical Education* 14(27): 1–7.

Bugarin, Rod M. 2012. "Scores Aren't the Only Qualification." December 19. https://nyti.ms/2LfWm1t. *New York Times.* (Last Accessed: August 29, 2017).

Burke, Meghan A., and Kira Hudson Banks. 2012. "Sociology by Any Other Name." *Teaching Sociology* 40(1): 21–33.

Burton, Nancy W., and Leonard Ramist. 2001. "Predicting Success in College: SAT Studies of Classes Graduating Since 1980 (Research Report No. 2001-2)." The College Board. Available at: http://research.collegeboard.org/sites/default/files/publications/2012/7/researchreport-2001-2-predicting-college-success-sat-studies.pdf.

California State Legislature. 1996. "Proposition 209, Section 31(a)." California Legislature.

Cameron, David. 2015. "The Conservatives Have Become the Party of Equality." October 26. www.theguardian.com/commentisfree/2015/oct/26/david-cameron-conservatives-party-of-equality. *Guardian.* (Last Accessed: June 3, 2018).

Canes, Brandice J., and Harvey S. Rosen. 1995. "Following in Her Footsteps? Faculty Gender Composition and Women's Choices of College Majors." *ILR Review* 48(3): 486–504.

Card, David. 2017. "Report of David Card, Ph.D. Students for Fair Admissions, Inc. v. Harvard." December 20. https://projects.iq.harvard.edu/files/diverse-education/files/expert_report_as_filed_d._mass._14-cv-14176_dckt_000419_033_filed_2018-06-15.pdf. Document 419-33. United States District Court for the District of Massachusetts.

Carey, John, and Yusaku Horiuchi. 2018. "Carey and Horiuchi: Debating without Deprecating." February 6. *Dartmouth.* (Last Accessed: December 30, 2018).

Carey, John M., Kevin Carman, Katherine Clayton, Yusaku Horiuchi, Mala N. Htun, and Brittany Ortiz. 2018. "Who Wants to Hire a More Diverse Faculty? A Conjoint Analysis of Faculty and Student Preferences for Gender and Racial/Ethnic Diversity." Forthcoming at Politics, Groups, and Identities. Available at: www.tandfonline.com/doi/abs/10.1080/21565503.2018.1491866.

Carlson, Elizabeth. 2015. "Ethnic Voting and Accountability in Africa: A Choice Experiment in Uganda." *World Politics* 67(2): 353–385.

Carrell, Scott E., Marianne E. Page, and James E. West. 2010. "Sex and Science: How Professor Gender Perpetuates the Gender Gap." *Quarterly Journal of Economics* 125(3): 1101–1144.

Caruso, Eugene M., Dobromir A. Rahnev, and Mahzarin R. Banaji. 2009. "Using Conjoint Analysis to Detect Discrimination: Revealing Covert Preferences from Overt Choices." *Social Cognition* 27(1): 128–137.

Castle, Stephen. 2016. "Oxford University Will Keep Statue of Cecil Rhodes." January 29. https://nyti.ms/1KeOo6q. *New York Times*. (Last Accessed: May 10, 2018).

CBS News. 2017. "At Least 3 Arrested as Hundreds Protest on UNC Campus against Confederate Statue." August 23. www.cbsnews.com/news/arrests-protests-unc-chapel-hill-silent-sam-confederate-statue/. CBS News. (Last Accessed: August 29, 2017).

Chang, Mitchell. 1999. "Does Racial Diversity Matter? The Educational Impact of a Racially Diverse Undergraduate Population." *Journal of College Student Development* 40(4): 377–395.

Chang, Mitchell J., Alexander W. Astin, and Dongbin Kim. 2004. "Cross-Racial Interaction among Undergraduates: Some Consequences, Causes, and Patterns." *Research in Higher Education* 45(5): 529–553.

Charles, Camille Z., Mary A. Fischer, Margarita A. Mooney, and Douglas S. Massey. 2009. *Taming the River: Negotiating the Academic, Financial, and Social Currents in Selective Colleges and Universities*. Princeton, NJ: Princeton University Press.

Chemerinsky, Erwin, and Howard Gillman. 2017. *Free Speech on Campus*. New Haven, CT: Yale University Press.

Chong, Dennis, and James N. Druckman. 2007. "Framing Public Opinion in Competitive Democracies." *American Political Science Review* 101(4): 637–655.

Clark, Suzannah, and Rakesh Khurana. 2016. "Charge." www.fas.harvard.edu/committee-unrecognized-single-gender-social-organizations. Committee on Unrecognized Single-Gender Social Organizations. (Last Accessed: January 25, 2018).

Clarke, Hansen. 2012. "Protecting the Rights of Convicted Criminals: Ban the Box Act of 2012." December 20. http://wapo.st/TD4Yiv?tid=ss_tw&utm_term=.c459b9ec570c. *Washington Post*. (Last Accessed: January 14, 2018).

Clayton, Katherine, Jeremy Ferwerda, and Yuskau Horiuchi. 2019. "Exposure to Immigration and Admission Preferences: Evidence from France." Working paper, available at SSRN: https://papers.ssrn.com/sol3/papers.cfm?abstract_id=3268904.

Cooper, Helene, and Thomas Gibbons-Neff. 2018. "Trump Approves New Limits on Transgender Troops in the Military." March 24. https://nyti.ms/2uchW2K. *New York Times*. (Last Accessed: January 2, 2019).

Cortes, Kalena E. 2010. "Do Bans on Affirmative Action Hurt Minority Students? Evidence from the Texas Top 10% Plan." *Economics of Education Review* 29: 1110–1124.

Cummings, William. 2017. "States Are Starting to Recognize a Third Gender: Non-Binary." June 21. www.usatoday.com/story/news/2017/06/21/third-gender-option-non-binary/359260001/. *USA Today*. (Last Accessed: February 16, 2018).

Cunningham, Jalin P., Melissa C. Rodman, and Ignacio Sabate. 2016. "Harvard House Masters Now Called 'Faculty Deans'." February 25. www.thecrimson.com/article/2016/2/25/house-master-new-name/. *Harvard Crimson*. (Last Accessed: September 1, 2017).

Darolia, Rajeev, Cory Koedel, Paco Martorell, Katie Wilson, and Francisco Perez-Arce. 2016. "Race and Gender Effects on Employer Interest in Job Applicants: New Evidence from a Resume Field Experiment." *Applied Economics Letters* 23(12): 853–856.

Dartmouth College. 2016. "Climate Assessment for Learning, Living, and Working." Available at: www.dartmouth.edu/~oir/rankinandassociates finalreport.pdf.

Dee, Thomas S. 2004. "Teachers, Race, and Student Achievement in a Randomized Experiment." *Review of Economics and Statistics* 86(1): 195–210.

Dee, Thomas S. 2005. "A Teacher Like Me: Does Race, Ethnicity, or Gender Matter?" *American Economic Review* 95(2): 158–165.

Delalue, Shontay. 2018. "2018 DIAP Annual Report." Brown University. Available at: www.brown.edu/about/administration/institutional-diversity/sites/oidi/files/2018_DIAP_Annual_Report_Brown_University.pdf.

Deming, David J., Noam Yuchtman, Amira Abulafi, Claudia Goldin, and Lawrence F. Katz. 2016. "The Value of Postsecondary Credentials in the Labor Market: An Experimental Study." *American Economic Review* 106(3): 778–806.

Denson, N., and M. J. Chang. 2009. "Racial Diversity Matters: The Impact of Diversity-Related Student Engagement and Institutional Context." *American Educational Research Journal* 46(2): 322–353.

Department of Defense Instruction No. 6130.03. 2010. "Medical Standards for Appointment, Enlistment, or Induction in the Military Services." US Department of Defense. Available at: www.med.navy.mil/sites/nmotc/nami/arwg/Documents/WaiverGuide/DODI_6130.03_JUL12.pdf.

Dhar, Rohin. 2013. "Do Elite Colleges Discriminate against Asians?" April 24. https://priceonomics.com/post/4879428301/do-elite-colleges-discriminate-against-asians. Priceonomics. (Last Accessed: August 29, 2017).

Dixon Hall, Maria A. 2018. "Hard Questions about Diversity, Honest Answers." September 23. www.chronicle.com/article/Hard-Questions-About/244563. *Inside Higher Ed.* (Last Accessed: January 17, 2019).

Dobbin, Frank. 2009. *Inventing Equal Opportunity*. Princeton, NJ: Princeton University Press.

Dobbin, Frank, and Alexandra Kalev. 2016. "Why Diversity Programs Fail." *Harvard Business Review* 94(7).

Dobbin, Frank, Daniel Schrage, and Alexandra Kalev. 2015. "Rage against the Iron Cage: The Varied Effects of Bureaucratic Personnel Reforms on Diversity." *American Sociological Review* 80(5): 1014–1044.

Dobson, Matthew Singer. 2015. *How to Get into a Service Academy. A Step-by-Step Guide to Getting Qualified, Nominated, and Appointed.* Lanham, MD: Rowman and Littlefield.

dos Santos, Sales Augusto, and Obianuju C. Anya. 2006. "Who Is Black in Brazil? A Timely or a False Question in Brazilian Race Relations in the Era of Affirmative Action?" *Latin American Perspectives* 33(4): 30–48.

EDI Taskforce. 2017. "Progress Report on Equity, Diversity, and Inclusion Matters at LSE (2015–17)." London School of Economics and Political Science. Available at: https://info.lse.ac.uk/staff/divisions/Equity-Diversity-and-Inclusion/EDI-at-LSE/EDI-Taskforce.

Ehrenberg, Ronald, and Dominic J. Brewer. 1995. "Did Teachers' Verbal Ability and Race Matter in the 1960s? Coleman Revisited." *Economics of Education Review* 14(1): 1–21.

Ehrenberg, Ronald, Daniel Goldhaber, and Dominic Brewer. 1995. "Do Teachers' Race, Gender, and Ethnicity Matter? Evidence from the National Education Longitudinal Study of 1988." *Industrial and Labor Relations Review* 48(3): 547–561.

Ehrenreich, Barbara, and Arlie Russell Hochschild, eds. 2003. *Global Woman: Nannies, Maids, and Sex Workers in the New Economy.* New York, NY: Metropolitan Books.

Eisenla, Kristofer. 2018. "Six Former Surgeons General Rebut Pentagon Assertions about Medical Fitness of Transgender Troops." April 25. www.palmcenter.org/six-former-surgeons-general-rebut-pentagon-assertions-about-medical-fitness-of-transgender-troops/. Palm Center. (Last Accessed: January 2, 2019).

Ellis, Evelynn. 2018. "Personal Communication with Dartmouth College Vice President for Institutional Diversity."

Ellis, Joseph J. 2000. *Founding Brothers: The Revolutionary Generation.* New York, NY: Alfred A. Knopf.

Ely, Robin J. 1995. "The Power in Demography: Women's Social Constructions of Gender Identity at Work." *Academy of Management Journal* 38(3): 589–634.

Espenshade, Thomas J., and Alexandria Walton Radford. 2009. *No Longer Separate, Not Yet Equal: Race and Class in Elite College Admission and Campus Life.* Princeton, NJ: Princeton University Press.

Espenshade, Thomas J., Chang Y. Chung, and Joan L. Walling. 2004. "Admission Preferences for Minority Students, Athletes, and Legacies at Elite Universities." *Social Science Quarterly* 85(5): 1422–1446.

Estrada, Armando X., and David J. Weiss. 1999. "Attitudes of Military Personnel toward Homosexuals." *Journal of Homosexuality* 37(4): 83–97.

Fairlie, Robert W., Florian Hoffmann, and Philip Oreopoulos. 2014. "A Community College Instructor Like Me: Race and Ethnicity Interactions in the Classroom." *American Economic Review* 104(1048): 2567–2591.

Faust, Drew, and William F. Lee. 2017. "Unrecognized Single-Gender Social Organizations." December 5. www.harvard.edu/president/news/2017/unrecognized-single-gender-social-organizations. Harvard University Office of the President. (Last Accessed: January 25, 2018).

Faust, Drew Gilpin. 2016. "Letter on Single-Gender Social Organizations." May 6. www.harvard.edu/president/news/2016/letter-on-single-gender-social-organizations. Harvard University Office of the President. (Last Accessed: January 25, 2018).

Feldman, Stanley, and Leonie Huddy. 2005. "Racial Resentment and White Opposition to Race-Conscious Programs: Principles or Prejudice?" *American Journal of Political Science* 49(1): 168–183.

Field, Andy Tsubasa. 2018. "Fraternities and Sororities Sue Harvard Over Its Policy against Single-Sex Groups." December 3. www.chronicle .com/article/FraternitiesSororities/245251/. *Chronicle of Higher Education.* (Last Accessed: December 4, 2018).

Finkelstein, Martin J., Valerie Martin Conley, and Jack H. Schuster. 2016. "Taking the Measure of Faculty Diversity." TIAA Institute. Report available at: www.tiaainstitute.org/sites/default/files/presentations/2017-02/taking_the_ measure_of_faculty_diversity.pdf.

Fisher, Gabriel. 2015. "Princeton and the Fight over Woodrow Wilson's Legacy." November 25. www.newyorker.com/news/news-desk/princeton-and-the-fight-over-woodrow-wilsons-legacy. *New Yorker.* (Last Accessed: September 1, 2017).

Fisher v. *University of Texas at Austin et al.* 2013. 570, U.S.

Fisher v. *University of Texas at Austin et al.* 2016. 579, U.S.

Flaherty, Colleen. 2016a. "More Faculty Diversity, Not on Tenure Track." August 22. www.insidehighered.com/news/2016/08/22/study-finds-gains-faculty-diversity-not-tenure-track. *Inside Higher Ed.* (Last Accessed: June 22, 2017).

Flaherty, Colleen. 2016b. "Not Just 'Musical Chairs'." September 19. www .insidehighered.com/news/2016/09/19/beyond-well-funded-individual-campus-initiatives-experts-urge-collaboration. *Inside Higher Ed.* (Last Accessed: March 11, 2019).

Flaherty, Colleen. 2018a. "Closing the Pay Gap." May 18. www.insidehighered .com/news/2018/05/18/u-denver-settles-eeoc-agreeing-pay-266-million-seven-female-law-professors-who. *Inside Higher Ed.* (Last Accessed: January 17, 2019).

Flaherty, Colleen. 2018b. "Diversifying a Classic Humanities Course." April 12. www.insidehighered.com/news/2018/04/12/responding-student-criticism-its-foundational-humanities-course-too-white-reed. *Inside Higher Ed.* (Last Accessed: June 27, 2018).

Flaherty, Colleen. 2018c. "Gender, Pay, and a 'Black Box'." December 4. www.insidehighered.com/news/2018/12/04/u-arizona-being-sued-once-again-alleged-discrimination-against-women-terms-salary. *Inside Higher Ed.* (Last Accessed: January 17, 2019).

Flier, Jeffrey. 2019. "Against Diversity Statements." January 3. www.chronicle .com/article/Against-Diversity-Statements/245400?key=nbhuwAvuzuO_LrP4o ugFwHrrRyzhMLdpkTVNprA1jOBJ1on44SVF8LOtNz4eFGCCMzBrYjJFcz VpZnZJdWZBdWRnN2M2aDFSamJYUENkSE9sOHhUcGNiR2JEWQ *Chronicle of Higher Education.* (Last Accessed: January 6, 2019).

Florence, Joshua J., and Mia C. Karr. 2017. "In Victory for Administrators, Anti-Sanctions Faculty Motion Fails." November 8. www.thecrimson .com/article/2017/11/8/lewis-motion-defeated/. *Harvard Crimson*. (Last Accessed: January 25, 2018).

Flores, Stella M., and Catherine L. Horn. 2015. "Texas Top Ten Percent Plan: How It Works, What Are Its Limits, and Recommendations to Consider." Educational Testing Service. Available at: www.ets.org/Media/ Research/pdf/flores_white_paper.pdf.

Fosnacht, Kevin. 2014. "Selectivity and the College Experience: How Undermatching Shapes the College Experience among High-Achieving Students." Working paper, available at: http://cpr.indiana.edu/uploads/Fosnacht%20-%20Selectivity%20and%20the%20college%20experience%20-%20AERA14 %20v3.pdf.

Foundation for Individual Rights in Education. 2019. "Chicago Statement: University and Faculty Body Support." January 9. www.thefire.org/chicago-statement-university-and-faculty-body-support/. FIRE. (Last Accessed: January 17, 2019).

Francis, Andrew M., and Maria Tannuri-Pianto. 2012. "The Redistributive Equity of Affirmative Action: Exploring the Role of Race, Socioeconomic Status, and Gender in College Admissions." *Economics of Education Review* 31(1): 45–55.

Franco, Annie, Neil Malhotra, Gabor Simonovits, and L. J. Zigerell. 2017. "Developing Standards for Post-Hoc Weighting in Population-Based Survey Experiments." *Journal of Experimental Political Science* 4(02): 161–172.

Freedle, Roy O. 2003. "Correcting the SAT's Ethnic and Social-Class Bias: A Method for Reestimating SAT Scores." *Harvard Educational Review* 73(1): 1–43.

Friedersdorf, Conor. 2015. "The New Intolerance of Student Activism: A Fight over Halloween Costumes at Yale Has Devolved into an Effort to Censor Dissenting Views." November 9. www.theatlantic.com/politics/archive/2015/ 11/the-new-intoleranceof-student-activism-at-yale/414810/. *Atlantic*. (Last Accessed: July 3, 2017).

Fruscione, Joseph. 2014. "When Colleges Rely on Adjuncts, It's the Students Who Lose." July 25. www.pbs.org/newshour/making-sense/when-a-college-contracts-adjunctivitis-its-the-students-who-lose/. PBS. (Last Accessed: September 19, 2017).

Fryer, Roland, and Glenn Loury. 2005. "Affirmative Action and Its Mythology." NBER Working Paper No. 11464, available at: www.nber.org/papers/w11464.

Fryer, Roland G., and Steven D. Levitt. 2004. "The Causes and Consequences of Distinctively Black Names." *Quarterly Journal of Economics* 119(3): 767–805.

Fukurai, Hiroshi, and Belinda Lum. 1997. "The Ironies of Affirmative Action: Empirical Analyses of UC Students' Views on Fallacies and Problems of Affirmative Action." *California Sociologist* 17–18: 91–128.

Gaddis, S. Michael. 2015. "Discrimination in the Credential Society: An Audit Study of Race and College Selectivity in the Labor Market." *Social Forces* 93(4): 1451–1479.

Geiser, Saul. 2015. "The Growing Correlation between Race and SAT Scores: New Findings from California." Center for Studies in Higher Education. Available at: www.cshe.berkeley.edu/sites/default/files/shared/publications/docs/ROPS.CSHE_.10.15.Geiser.RaceSAT.10.26.2015.pdf.

Geiser, Saul, and Maria Veronica Santelices. 2007. "Validity of High-School Grades in Predicting Student Success beyond Freshman Year: High-School Record vs. Standardized Tests as Indicators of Four-Year College Outcomes Introduction and Policy Context." Research & Occasional Paper Series CSHE.6.0. Available at: http://files.eric.ed.gov/fulltext/ED502858.pdf.

Gilens, Martin, Paul M. Sniderman, and James H. Kuklinski. 1998. "Affirmative Action and the Politics of Realignment." *British Journal of Political Science* 28: 159–183.

Ginther, Donna K., and Shulamit Kahn. 2012. "Education and Academic Career Outcomes for Women of Color in Science and Engineering." Committee on Women in Science, Engineering, and Medicine. Conference summary available at: www.nap.edu/read/18556/chapter/11.

Gladwell, Malcolm. 2005. "Getting In." October 10. www.newyorker.com/magazine/2005/10/10/getting-in. *New Yorker*. (Last Accessed: August 26, 2017).

Glick, Peter, Mariah Wilkerson, and Marshall Cuffe. 2015. "Masculine Identity, Ambivalent Sexism, and Attitudes toward Gender Subtypes." *Social Psychology* 46(4): 210–217.

Glotfelter, Michael Ann, and Veanne N. Anderson. 2017. "Relationships between Gender Self-esteem, Sexual Prejudice, and Trans Prejudice in Cisgender Heterosexual College Students." *International Journal of Transgenderism* 18(2): 182–198.

Goldin, Claudia, and Lawrence F. Katz. 2010. "Putting the Co in Education: Timing, Reasons, and Consequences of College Coeducation from 1835 to the Present." NBER Working Paper No. 16281, available at: www.nber.org/papers/w16281.pdf.

Graf, Nikki. 2019. "73% of Americans Say Race, Ethnicity Should Not Factor into College Admissions." February 25. www.pewresearch.org/fact-tank/2019/02/25/most-americans-say-colleges-should-not-consider-race-or-ethnicity-in-admissions/. Pew Research Center. (Last Accessed: March 6, 2019).

Graham, David. 2015. "Black Tape over Black Faculty Portraits at Harvard Law School." November 19. www.theatlantic.com/politics/archive/2015/11/harvard-law-faculty-black-tape/416877/. *Atlantic*. (Last Accessed: September 1, 2017).

Gratz v. Bollinger. 2003. 539 U.S. 244.

Green, Erica L. 2018. "Sex Assault Rules under DeVos Bolster Defendants' Rights and Ease College Liability." November 16. https://nyti.ms/2zfrBFY. *New York Times*. (Last Accessed: January 17, 2019).

Green, Paul E., and V. Srinivasan. 1978. "Conjoint Analysis in Consumer Research: Issues and Outlook." *Journal of Consumer Research* 5(2): 103–123.

Griffin, Bryan W. 2004. "Grading Leniency, Grade Discrepancy, and Student Ratings of Instruction." *Contemporary Educational Psychology* 29(4): 410–425.

Gross, Neil. 2013. *Why Are Professors Liberal and Why Do Conservatives Care?* Cambridge, MA: Harvard University Press.

Grutter v. Bollinger. 2003. 539 U.S. 306.

Guan, Lee Hock. 2005. "Affirmative Action in Malaysia." *Southeast Asian Affairs* 2005: 211–228.

Gurin, Patricia. 1999. "Expert Report of Patricia Gurin." In *The Compelling Need for Diversity in Higher Education, Gratz et al. v. Bollinger et al. No. 97-75237 and Grutter et al. v. Bollinger et al. No. 97-75928.* Ann Arbor, MI: University of Michigan.

Gurney-Read, Josie. 2015. "Independent School Pupils 'Twice as Likely to Attend Elite Universities'." January 27. www.suttontrust.com/newsarchive/independent-school-pupils-twice-as-likely-to-attend-elite-universities/. The Sutton Trust. (Last Accessed: May 10, 2018).

Hainmueller, Jens. 2012. "Entropy Balancing for Causal Effects: A Multivariate Reweighting Method to Produce Balanced Samples in Observational Studies." *Political Analysis* 20(1): 25–46.

Hainmueller, Jens, and Daniel J. Hopkins. 2015. "The Hidden American Immigration Consensus: A Conjoint Analysis of Attitudes toward Immigrants." *American Journal of Political Science* 59(3): 529–548.

Hainmueller, Jens, Daniel J. Hopkins, and Teppei Yamamoto. 2014. "Causal Inference in Conjoint Analysis: Understanding Multidimensional Choices via Stated Preference Experiments." *Political Analysis* 22(1): 1–30.

Hainmueller, Jens, Dominik Hangartner, and Teppei Yamamoto. 2015. "Validating Vignette and Conjoint Survey Experiments against Real-World Behavior." *Proceedings of the National Academy of Sciences of the United States of America* 112(8): 2395–400.

Hancock, Ange-Marie. 2016. *Intersectionality: An Intellectual History.* New York, NY: Oxford University Press.

Hanlon, Phil, Carolyn Dever, Evelynn Ellis, and Rick Mills. 2016. "Action Plan for Inclusive Excellence." Dartmouth College. Report available at: https://inclusive.dartmouth.edu/sites/ie.dev/files/ie/wysiwyg/2016-05-action-plan_0.pdf.

Harper, Elizabeth P., Roger G. Baldwin, Bruce G. Gansneder, and Jay L. Chronister. 2001. "Full-Time Women Faculty off the Tenure Track: Profile and Practice." *Review of Higher Education* 24(3): 237–257.

Harris, Emma, and Elana Jaffe. 2015. "DPS Officer Accused of Assaulting Latinx Conference Delegate." November 15. www.browndailyherald.com/2015/11/15/dps-officer-accused-of-assaulting-latinx-conference-delegate-2/. *Brown Daily Herald.* (Last Accessed: September 1, 2017).

Hartocollis, Anemona. 2015. "Yale Lecturer Resigns after Email on Halloween Costumes." December 7. https://nyti.ms/1NGWFv5. *New York Times.* (Last Accessed: August 29, 2017).

Hartocollis, Anemona. 2018. "Asian-Americans Suing Harvard Say Admissions Files Show Discrimination." April 4. https://nyti.ms/2EkFFgS. *New York Times.* (Last Accessed: April 7, 2018).

Harvard University. 2018. "Pursuing Excellence on a Foundation of Inclusion." Harvard University Presidential Task Force on Inclusion and Belonging.

Report available at: https://inclusionandbelongingtaskforce.harvard.edu/files/inclusion/files/harvard_inclusion_belonging_task_force_final_report_full_web_180327.pdf.

Harvard University Archives. 1922*a*. "Minutes of the Committee Appointed by the President of the University to Consider and Report to the Governing Boards Principles and Methods for More Effective Sifting of Candidates for Admission to the University." Meeting of June 21, 1922.

Harvard University Archives. 1922*b*. "Statistical Report of the Statisticians to the Subcommittee Appointed to Collect Statistics: Dean Chester N. Greenough, Chairman, Dean Wallace B. Donham, Dean Henry W. Holmes." Abbot Lawrence Lowell Papers #387 Admission to Harvard College.

Harvard University Archives. 1923. "Letter from the Committee on Methods of Sifting Candidates for Admission to Lowell." Abbot Lawrence Lowell Papers #387 Admission to Harvard College.

Harvard University Archives. 1925. "Report of the Special Committee Appointed to Consider the Limitation of Numbers." Abbot Lawrence Lowell Papers #184 Limitation of Numbers.

Harvard University Archives. 1928. "Recommendations from the Committee on Admission and the Committee on Instruction adopted by the Faculty of the Arts and Sciences." Abbot Lawrence Lowell Papers #111 Committee on Admissions.

Harvard University Archives. 1933. "Distribution of Probable Freshman Applicants for Houses According to Rank List, Race, Type of School Represented." Dean of Harvard College Correspondence File 1933–1957.

Harvard University Working Group on Diversity and Inclusion. 2015. "Report of the Harvard College Working Group on Diversity and Inclusion." Harvard University. Report available at: http://diversity.college.harvard.edu/files/collegediversity/files/diversity_and_inclusion_working_group_final_report_2.pdf?m=1447857004.

Heller, Nathan. 2016. "The Big Uneasy: What's Roiling the Liberal-Arts Campus?" May 30. www.newyorker.com/magazine/2016/05/30/the-new-activism-of-liberal-arts-colleges. *New Yorker*. (Last Accessed: July 3, 2017).

Helmke, Gretchen, and Steven Levitsky. 2004. "Informal Institutions and Comparative Politics: A Research Agenda." *Perspectives on Politics* 2(4): 725–740.

Herek, Gregory M. 2002. "Gender Gaps in Public Opinion about Lesbians and Gay Men." *Public Opinion Quarterly* 66(1): 40–66.

Heying, Heather. 2017. "First, They Came for the Biologists." October 2. www.wsj.com/articles/first-they-came-for-the-biologists-1506984033. *Wall Street Journal*. (Last Accessed: June 25, 2018).

Ho, Daniel E. 2005. "Affirmative Action's Affirmative Actions: A Reply to Sander." *The Yale Law Journal* 114(8): 2011–2016.

Hoffmann, Florian, and Philip Oreopoulos. 2009. "A Professor Like Me: The Influence of Instructor Gender on College Achievement." *Journal of Human Resources* 44(2): 479–494.

Holbrook, Allyson L., and Jon A. Krosnick. 2010. "Social Desirability Bias in Voter Turnout Reports: Tests Using the Item Count Technique." *Public Opinion Quarterly* 74(1): 37–67.

Holland, Paul W. 1986. "Statistics and Causal Inference." *Journal of the American Statistical Association* 81(396): 945–960.

Holland, Paul W. 2003. "Causation and Race." Educational Testing Service. Report available at: https://onlinelibrary.wiley.com/doi/epdf/10.1002/j.2333-8504.2003.tb01895.x.

Hoover, Eric. 2019a. "That Other Affirmative-Action Case: The Battle Over UNC's Admissions Policies Heats Up." January 18. www.chronicle.com/article/That-Other-Affirmative-Action/245519. *Chronicle of Higher Education.* (Last Accessed: January 23, 2019).

Hoover, Eric. 2019b. "What Do Americans Think about Affirmative Action? It Depends on How You Ask." February 27. www.chronicle.com/article/What–Do-Americans-Think-About/245779. *Chronicle of Higher Education.* (Last Accessed: March 6, 2019).

Hopwood v. *Texas.* 1996. 78 F.3d 932.

Horiuchi, Yusaku, Daniel M. Smith, and Teppei Yamamoto. 2018a. "Measuring Voters' Multidimensional Policy Preferences with Conjoint Analysis: Application to Japan's 2014 Election." *Political Analysis* 26(2): 190–209.

Horiuchi, Yusaku, Daniel Smith, and Teppei Yamamoto. 2018b. "Identifying Voter Preferences for Politicians' Personal Attributes: A Conjoint Experiment in Japan." Forthcoming, Political Science Research and Methods. Available at: www.cambridge.org/core/journals/political-science-research-and-methods/article/identifying-voter-preferences-for-politicians-personal-attributes-a-conjoint-experiment-in-japan/95AD.

Horiuchi, Yusaku, Zachary Markovich, and Teppei Yamamoto. 2019. "Does Conjoint Analysis Mitigate Social Desirability Bias?" Working paper, available at: www.cambridge.org/core/membership/services/aop-file-manager/file/5c2e26148d275163 18ae9203/APMM-2019-Teppei-Yamamoto.pdf.

Horn, Catherine, and Stella Flores. 2003. "Percent Plans in College Admissions: A Comparative Analysis of Three States' Experiences." The Civil Rights Project at Harvard University. Report available at: www.civilrightsproject.ucla.edu/research/college-access/admissions/percent-plans-in-college-admissions-a-comparative-analysis-of-three-states2019-experiences/horn-percent-plans-2.

Horowitz, Juliana Menasce, and Gretchen Livingston. 2016. "How Americans View the Black Lives Matter Movement." July 8. www.pewresearch.org/fact-tank/2016/07/08/how-americans-view-the-black-lives-matter-movement/. Pew Research Center. (Last Accessed: January 17, 2018).

Hoxby, Caroline, and Christopher Avery. 2013. "The Missing 'One-Offs': The Hidden Supply of High-Achieving, Low-Income Students." *Brookings Papers on Economic Activity* 2013(1): 1–65.

Htun, Mala. 2016. *Inclusion without Representation in Latin America: Gender Quotas and Ethnic Reservations.* New York, NY: Cambridge University Press.

Htun, Mala, and Juan Pablo Ossa. 2013. "Political Inclusion of Marginalized Groups: Indigenous Reservations and Gender Parity in Bolivia." *Politics, Groups and Identities* 1(1): 4–25.

Htun, Mala, Carlos Contreras, Melanie Sayuri Dominguez, Francesca R. Jensenius, and Justine Tinkler. 2018. "Implementing the Rights Revolution?

Effects of Sexual Misconduct Training on University Campuses." Working paper, available at: https://malahtun.files.wordpress.com/2018/11/htun_etal_greyarea_20181.pdf.

Hu, Shouping, and George D. Kuh. 2003. "Diversity Experiences and College Student Learning and Personal Development." *Journal of College Student Development* 44(3): 320–334.

Huddy, Leonie, and Stanley Feldman. 2009. "On Assessing the Political Effects of Racial Prejudice." *Annual Review of Political Science* 12: 423–47.

Hurtado, Patricia. 2019. "Harvard Fires Back in Legal Battle over Single-Sex Greek Clubs." February 9. www.bloomberg.com/news/articles/2019-02-09/harvard-fires-back-in-legal-battle-over-single-sex-greek-clubs. Bloomberg. (Last Accessed: February 12, 2019).

Hurwitz, Michael. 2011. "The Impact of Legacy Status on Undergraduate Admissions at Elite Colleges and Universities." *Economics of Education Review* 30: 480–492.

Iyengar, Sheena. 2011. *The Art of Choosing*. New York, NY: Twelve.

Ithacan. 2015. "Open Letter: The Case against Tom Rochon." November 7. https://theithacan.org/opinion/open-letter-the-case-against-tom-rochon/. *Ithacan*. (Last Accessed: September 1, 2017).

Jack, Anthony Abraham. 2019. *The Privileged Poor: How Elite Colleges Are Failing Disadvantaged Students*. Cambridge, MA: Harvard University Press.

Jacobs, Peter. 2017. "The Ivy League's History of Discriminating against Jews." December 4. www.businessinsider.com/the-ivy-leagues-history-of-discriminating-against-jews-2014-12. *Business Insider*. (Last Accessed: August 29, 2017).

Jaschik, Scott. 2015. "SAT Scores Drop and Racial Gaps Remain Large." September 3. www.insidehighered.com/news/2015/09/03/sat-scores-drop-and-racial-gaps-remain-large. *Inside Higher Education*. (Last Accessed: September 15, 2017).

Jaschik, Scott. 2016. "Michigan State Sets Off Debate by Eliminating a Women's Lounge in Student Union." August 8. www.insidehighered.com/news/2016/08/08/michigan-state-sets-debate-eliminating-womens-lounge-student-union. *Inside Higher Ed*. (Last Accessed: January 9, 2019).

Jaschik, Scott. 2018a. "Sit-In at Wells over Diversity Issues." May 10. www.insidehighered.com/quicktakes/2018/05/10/sit-wells-over-diversity-issues. *Inside Higher Ed*. (Last Accessed: June 27, 2018).

Jaschik, Scott. 2018b. "Sit-In over Diversity Issues at College of Wooster." January 26. www.insidehighered.com/quicktakes/2018/01/26/sit-over-diversity-issues-college-wooster. *Inside Higher Ed*. (Last Accessed: June 27, 2018).

Jaschik, Scott. 2019. "Tulane Agreement with OCR Leads to Debate over Gender Bias." January 14. www.insidehighered.com/news/2019/01/14/tulane-agreement-ocr-leads-debate-over-gender-bias. *Inside Higher Ed*. (Last Accessed: January 17, 2019).

Jencks, Christopher, and Meredith Phillips. 2011. *The Black-White Test Score Gap*. Washington, DC: Brookings Institution Press.

Jiang, Junyan, and Dali L. Yang. 2016. "Lying or Believing? Measuring Preference Falsification from a Political Purge in China." *Comparative Political Studies* 49(5): 600–634.

Johnson v. Board of Regents of the University System of Georgia. 2000. 106 F. Supp. 2d 1362.

Jones, Eric R. 2018. "In Solidarity with Ryan Spector." February 7. *Dartmouth Review.* (Last Accessed: December 30, 2018).

Kahlenberg, Richard D. 2010. *Affirmative Action for the Rich: Legacy Preferences in College Admissions.* New York, NY: Century Foundation Press.

Kain, John F., Daniel M. O'Brien, and Paul A. Jargowsky. 2005. "Hopwood and the Top 10 Percent Law: How They Have Affected the College Enrollment Decisions of Texas High School Graduates." Manuscript prepared for the Texas Schools Project at the University of Texas at Dallas. Available at: www.utdallas.edu/research/tsp-erc/pdf/wp_kain_2005_hopwood_top_10_percent.pdf.

Kam, Cindy D., and Camille D. Burge. 2018. "Uncovering Reactions to the Racial Resentment Scale across the Racial Divide." *Journal of Politics* 80(1): 314–320.

Kane, Thomas. 1998. "Racial and Ethnic Preferences in College Admissions." In *The Black-White Test Score Gap*, eds. Christopher Jencks, and Meredith Phillips. Washington, DC: Brookings Institution Press, 431–456.

Karabel, Jerome. 2005. *The Chosen: The Hidden History of Admission and Exclusion at Harvard, Yale, and Princeton.* New York, NY: Houghton Mifflin.

Katznelson, Ira. 2005. *When Affirmative Action Was White: An Untold History of Racial Inequality in Twentieth-Century America.* New York, NY: W. W. Norton.

Kean, Danuta. 2017. "Bell Curve Author Charles Murray Speaks Out after Speech Cut Short by Protests." March 6. www.theguardian.com/books/2017/mar/06/bell-curve-author-charles-murray-speaks-out-after-speech-cut-short-by-protests. *Guardian.* (Last Accessed: June 25, 2018).

Kellermann, Michael. 2014. "Self-Selection and Opposition to Gay Rights among Military Career-Seekers." *Politics, Groups, and Identities* 2(3): 443–458.

Kerr, Emma. 2018. "Multiple Steves and Pauls: A History Panel Sets Off a Diversity Firestorm." March 15. www.chronicle.com/article/Multiple-Steves-and/242841. *Chronicle of Higher Education.* (Last Accessed: June 6, 2018).

Khomami, Nadia. 2015. "Oxford Students Step Up Campaign to Remove Cecil Rhodes Statue." December 22. www.theguardian.com/education/2015/dec/22/oxford-students-campaign-cecil-rhodes-statue-oriel-college. *Guardian.* (Last Accessed: May 10, 2018).

Kinder, Donald R., and Allison Dale-Riddle. 2012. *The End of Race? Obama, 2008, and Racial Politics in America.* New Haven, CT: Yale University Press.

Kinder, Donald R., and Lynn M. Sanders. 1990. "Mimicking Political Debate with Survey Questions: The Case of Opinion on Affirmative Action for Blacks." *Social Cognition* 8(1): 73–103.

Kinder, Donald R., and Lynn M. Sanders. 1996. *Divided by Color: Racial Politics and Democratic Ideals.* Chicago, IL: University of Chicago Press.

Kipnis, Laura. 2017. *Unwanted Advances: Sexual Paranoia Comes to Campus.* New York, NY: Harper.

Klopfenstein, Kristin. 2005. "Beyond Test Scores: The Impact of Black Teacher Role Models on Rigorous Math Taking." *Contemporary Economic Policy* 23(3): 416–428.

Kofoed, Michael S., and Elizabeth McGovney. 2017. "The Effect of Same-Gender and Same-Race Role Models on Occupation Choice: Evidence from Randomly Assigned Mentors at West Point." *Journal of Human Resources* 54(2): 0416–7838r1.

Kopicki, Allison. 2014. "Answers on Affirmative Action Depend on How You Pose the Question." April 22. https://nyti.ms/1f24CjL. *New York Times.* (Last Accessed: December 9, 2017).

Korn, Melissa. 2018. "Do Pro-Women Groups on Campus Discriminate against Men?" May 23. www.wsj.com/articles/do-pro-women-groups-on-campus-discriminate-against-men-1527067800. *Wall Street Journal.* (Last Accessed: May 24, 2018).

Kravitz, David A., Tiffany M. Bludau, and Stephen L. Klineberg. 2008. "The Impact of Anticipated Consequences, Respondent Group, and Strength of Affirmative Action Plan on Affirmative Action Attitudes." *Group & Organization Management* 33(4): 361–391.

Kreuter, F., S. Presser, and R. Tourangeau. 2008. "Social Desirability Bias in CATI, IVR, and Web Surveys: The Effects of Mode and Question Sensitivity." *Public Opinion Quarterly* 72(5): 847–865.

Krosnick, Jon A. 1999. "Survey Research." *Annual Review of Psychology* 50(1): 537–567.

Krosnick, Jon A., and Duane F. Alwin. 1987. "An Evaluation of a Cognitive Theory of Response-Order Effects in Survey Measurement." *Public Opinion Quarterly* 51(2): 201–219.

Krumpal, Ivar. 2013. "Determinants of Social Desirability Bias in Sensitive Surveys: A Literature Review." *Quality & Quantity* 47(4): 2025–2047.

Kuhn, Patrick M., and Nick Vivyan. 2018. "Reducing Turnout Misreporting in Online Surveys." *Public Opinion Quarterly* 82(2): 300–321.

Kuran, Timur. 1995. *Private Truths, Public Lies: The Social Consequences of Preference Falsification.* Cambridge, MA: Harvard University Press.

Kurlaender, Michal, and Eric Grodsky. 2013. "Mismatch and the Paternalistic Justification for Selective College Admissions." *Sociology of Education* 86(4): 294–310.

Lamothe, Dan. 2017. "Trump Wants to Ban Transgender Military Troops. His Top General Feels Differently." September 26. http://wapo.st/2xDzlRC?tid=ss_tw&utm_term=.51b8a2a615ca. *Washington Post.* (Last Accessed: January 2, 2019).

Langbert, Mitchell. 2018. "Homogeneous: The Political Affiliations of Elite Liberal Arts College Faculty." April 24. https://nas.org/articles/homogenous_political_affiliations_of_elite_liberal. National Association of Scholars. (Last Accessed: June 25, 2018).

Lannon, Paul G. 2015. "Transgender Student Admissions: The Challenge of Defining Gender in a Gender Fluid World." April 22. https://bostonbarjournal

.com/2015/04/22/transgender-student-admissions-the-challenge-of-defining-gender-in-a-gender-fluid-world/. *Boston Bar Journal.* (Last Accessed: September 19, 2017).

Lartey, James. 2015. "Harvard 'Black Tape' Vandalism Brings Law School's Controversial Past to Fore." November 21. www.theguardian.com/education/2015/nov/21/harvard-law-school-black-tape-vandalism-royall-must-fall-movement. *Guardian.* (Last Accessed: September 1, 2017).

Lavergne, Marcus. 2015. "Diversity: An Open Conversation." December 8. http://nevadasagebrush.com/blog/2015/12/08/diversity-an-open-conversation/. *Nevada Sagebrush.* (Last Accessed: August 29, 2017).

Lee, Frances. 2017. "Why I've Started to Fear My Fellow Social Justice Activists." October 13. www.yesmagazine.org/people-power/why-ive-started-to-fear-my-fellow-social-justice-activists-20171013. *YES! Magazine.* (Last Accessed: June 25, 2018).

Leeper, Thomas J., Sara B. Hobolt, and James Tilley. 2018. "Measuring Subgroup Preferences in Conjoint Experiments." Working paper, available at: https://s3.us-east-2.amazonaws.com/tjl-sharing/assets/MeasuringSubgroupPreferences.pdf.

Lemann, Nicholas. 2018. "How Affirmative Action Really Works." November 30. www.chronicle.com/article/How-Affirmative-Action-Really/245237. *Chronicle of Higher Education.* (Last Accessed: January 17, 2019).

Leon, Raul A. 2014. "The Chief Diversity Officer: An Examination of CDO Models and Strategies." *Journal of Diversity in Higher Education* 7(2): 77–91.

Leonhardt, David. 2015. "California's Upward-Mobility Machine." September 16. https://nyti.ms/1iiahEO. *New York Times.* (Last Accessed: August 26, 2017).

Leslie, Sarah-Jane, Andrei Cimpian, Meredith Meyer, and Edward Freeland. 2015. "Expectations of Brilliance Underlie Gender Distributions across Academic Disciplines." *Science* 347(6219): 262–265.

Lewis, Sophie. 2016. "Affirmative Action Bake Sale Sparks Protests at University of Texas." October 28. www.cnn.com/2016/10/28/us/university-bake-sale-trnd. CNN. (Last Accessed: April 28, 2017).

Light, Audrey, and Wayne Strayer. 2000. "Determinants of College Completion: School Quality or Student Ability?" *Journal of Human Resources* 35(2): 299–332.

Lilla, Mark. 2017. *The Once and Future Liberal: After Identity Politics.* New York, NY: Harper Press.

Lim, Jaegeum, and Jonathan Meer. 2017. "The Impact of Teacher-Student Gender Matches." *Journal of Human Resources* 52(4): 979–997.

Locks, Angela M., Sylvia Hurtado, Nicholas A. Bowman, and Leticia Oseguera. 2008. "Extending Notions of Campus Climate and Diversity to Students' Transition to College." *Review of Higher Education* 31(3): 257–285.

Loftin, R. Bowen. 2016. "Diversity and Inclusion Training." https://chancellor.missouri.edu/news/diversity-and-inclusion-training/. Office of the Chancellor at the University of Missouri. (Last Accessed: September 1, 2017).

London School of Economics. 2018. "2017/18 Undergraduate Admissions Policy." Available at: https://info.lse.ac.uk/staff/services/Policies-and-procedures/Assets/Documents/uGAdmPol.pdf.

Long, Mark C. 2004. "Race and College Admissions: An Alternative to Affirmative Action?" *Review of Economics and Statistics* 86(4): 1020–1033.

Long, Mark C. 2007. "Affirmative Action and Its Alternatives in Public Universities: What Do We Know?" *Public Administration Review* 67(2): 315–330.

Longoria, Richard T. 2009. *Meritocracy and Americans' Views on Distributive Justice*. Landham, MD: Lexington Books.

Lott, John R., J. Mark Ramseyer, and Jeffrey Standen. 2011. "Peer Effects in Affirmative Action: Evidence from Law Student Performance." *International Review of Law & Economics* 31: 1–15.

Lukainoff, Gregory, and Jonathan Haidt. 2015. "The Coddling of the American Mind." September 4. www.theatlantic.com/magazine/archive/2015/09/the-coddling-of-the-american-mind/399356/. *Atlantic*. (Last Accessed: July 3, 2017).

Lukainoff, Gregory, and Jonathan Haidt. 2018. *The Coddling of the American Mind: How Good Intentions and Bad Ideas Are Setting Up a Generation for Failure*. New York, NY: Penguin Press.

Luna, Brad. 2018. "After Two Years of Open Transgender Service, Consensus from Military Leadership That Inclusive Policy Works." June 29. www.palmcenter.org/after-two-years-of-open-transgender-service-consensus-from-military-leadership-that-inclusive-policy-works/. *Washington Post*. (Last Accessed: January 2, 2019).

MacDonald, Heather. 2017. "Those 'Snowflakes' Have Chilling Effects Even beyond the Campus." April 21. www.wsj.com/articles/those-snowflakes-have-chilling-effects-even-beyond-the-campus-1492800913 *Wall Street Journal*. (Last Accessed: September 13, 2017).

MacNell, Lillian, Adam Driscoll, and Andrea N. Hunt. 2015. "What's in a Name: Exposing Gender Bias in Student Ratings of Teaching." *Innovative Higher Education* 40(4): 291–303.

Madera, Juan M., Michelle R. Hebl, Heather Dial, Randi Martin, and Virgina Valian. 2018. "Raising Doubt in Letters of Recommendation for Academia: Gender Differences and Their Impact." Forthcoming, *Journal of Business and Psychology*.

Magann, Matthew. 2018. "Magann: An Unjust 'Solidarity'." February 8. *Dartmouth*. (Last Accessed: December 30, 2018).

Mangan, Katherine. 2019. "Trump Says He'll Sign Order Requiring Colleges to Protect Free Speech." March 2. www.chronicle.com/article/Trump-Says-He-ll-Sign-Order/245812/. *Chronicle of Higher Education*. (Last Accessed: March 2, 2019).

Marin, Patricia, and Edgar K. Lee. 2003. "Appearance and Reality in the Sunshine State: The Talented 20 Program in Florida." The Civil Rights Project at Harvard University. Report available at: www.civilrightsproject.ucla.edu/research/college-access/admissions/appearance-and-reality-in-the-sunshine-state-the-talented-20-program-in-florida/marine-appearnace-reality-sunsh.

Massachusetts Institute of Technology. 2010. "Report on the Initiative for Faculty Race and Diversity. PSB 09-11-0629." Report available at: http://web.mit.edu/provost/raceinitiative/report.pdf.

Massey, Douglas S., Camille Z. Charles, Garvey F. Lundy, and Mary J. Fischer. 2003. *The Source of the River: The Social Origins of Freshmen at America's Selective Colleges and Universities*. Princeton, NJ: Princeton University Press.

May, Theresa. 2016. "Statement from the New Prime Minister Theresa May." Speech. July 13. www.gov.uk/government/speeches/statement-from-the-new-prime-minister-theresa-may. (Last Accessed: June 3, 2018).

McCauley, Byron. 2015. "Editorial: UC Listened. Mizzou Didn't." November 13. www.cincinnati.com/story/opinion/editorials/2015/11/13/uc-listened-mizzou/75697010/. *Cincinnati Enquirer*. (Last Accessed: September 1, 2017).

McChesney, Jasper. 2018. "Representation and Pay of Women of Color in the Higher Education Workforce." CUPA-HR. Research brief available at: www.cupahr.org/wp-content/uploads/CUPA-HR-Brief-Women-Of-Color.pdf.

McWhorter, John H. 2015. "Closed Minds on Campus." November 27. www.wsj.com/articles/closed-minds-on-campus-1448634626. *Wall Street Journal*. (Last Accessed: June 27, 2018).

Mendelberg, Tali, Katherine T. McCabe, and Adam Thal. 2017. "College Socialization and the Economic Views of Affluent Americans." *American Journal of Political Science* 61(3): 606–623.

Merritt, Deborah J. 2008. "Bias, the Brain, and Student Evaluations of Teaching." *St. John's Law Review* 82(1): 235–288.

Metzler, Johannes, and Ludger Woessmann. 2012. "The Impact of Teacher Subject Knowledge on Student Achievement: Evidence from Within-Teacher Within-Student Variation." *Journal of Development Economics* 99(2): 486–496.

Miller, Laura, and John Allen Williams. 2001. "Civil Rights vs. Combat Effectiveness? Military Policies on Gender and Sexuality." In *Soldiers and Civilians: The Civil-Military Gap and American National Security*, eds. Peter D. Feaver, and Richard H. Kohn. Cambridge, MA: Massachusetts Institute of Technology Press, 361–402.

Mitchell, Carmen. 2018. "Why Colleges Should Require Faculty Diversity Statements." November 15. www.insidehighered.com/views/2018/11/15/benefits-faculty-diversity-statements-opinion. *Inside Higher Ed*. (Last Accessed: January 17, 2019).

Montgomery, Jacob M., Brendan Nyhan, and Michelle Torres. 2018. "How Conditioning on Posttreatment Variables Can Ruin Your Experiment and What to Do about It." *American Journal of Political Science* 62(3): 760–775.

Moore, David W. 2003. "Public: Only Merit Should Count in College Admissions." June 24. http://news.gallup.com/poll/8689/public-only-merit-should-count-college-admissions.aspx. Gallup. (Last Accessed: December 17, 2017).

Morning, Ann Juanita. 2011. *The Nature of Race: How Scientists Think and Teach about Human Difference*. Berkeley, CA: University of California Press.

Mortara, Adam K., John M. Hughes, Paul M. Sanford, William S. Consovoy, Thomas R. McCarthy, J. Michael Connolly, Patrick Strawbridge, and Michael H. Park. 2018. "Plaintiff's Memorandum of Reasons in Support of

Its Motion for Summary Judgment. Students for Fair Admissions v. Harvard." June 15. http://samv91khoyt2i553a2t1s05i-wpengine.netdna-ssl.com/wp-content/uploads/2018/06/Doc-413-Memo-in-Support-of-MSJ.pdf. Document 413. United States District Court for the District of Massachusetts.

Moshiri, Farrokh, and Peter W. Cardon. 2019. "Best Practices to Increase Racial Diversity in Business Schools: What Actually Works According to a Nationwide Survey of Business Schools." *Journal of Education for Business* 94(2): 113–124.

Moss-Racusin, Corinne A., John F. Dovidio, Victoria L. Brescoll, Mark J. Graham, Jo Handelsman, and Shirley Tilghman. 2012. "Science Faculty's Subtle Gender Biases Favor Male Students." *Proceedings of the National Academy of Sciences* 109(41): 16474–16479.

Mullin, Andi. 2013. "Banning the Box in Minnesota – and across the United States!" December 2. www.communitycatalyst.org/blog/banning-the-box-in-minnesota-and-across-the-united-states#.WlwQMVQ-dn4. Community Catalyst. (Last Accessed: January 14, 2018).

Murphy, Kate. 2015. "The Irate8 Stage Silent Protest at UC." November 18. www.cincinnati.com/story/news/2015/11/18/irate8-stage-silent-protest/75989138/. *Cincinnati Enquirer*. (Last Accessed: September 1, 2017).

Nalty, Bernard C. 1986. *Strength for the Fight: A History of Black Americans in the Military*. New York, NY: Free Press.

Napolitano, Janet, Nicholas B. Dirks, Linda Katehi, Michael V. Drake, Gene Block, Dorothy Leland, Kim A. Wilcox, Pradeep Khosla, Susan Desmond-Hellman, Henry T. Yang, George R. Blumenthal, Barbara Allen-Diaz, and Paul Alivisatos. 2014. "Campus Climate Study: Committed to a Healthy and Inclusive Climate." March 19. http://campusclimate.ucop.edu/results/index.html. University of California Office of the President. (Last Accessed: May 7, 2017).

Naskidashvili, Nana. 2015. "Students March through MU Student Center in Protest of Racial Injustice." October 1. www.columbiamissourian.com/news/higher_education/students-march-through-mu-student-center-in-protest-of-racial/article_4b8e3458-688b-11e5-8412-9b38a4d41eb8.html. *Columbia Missourian*. (Last Accessed: September 1, 2017).

Natanson, Hannah, and Derek G. Xiao. 2017. "For Second Time, Faculty File Motion against Social Group Sanctions." August 22. www.thecrimson.com/article/2017/8/22/new-faculty-motion-sanctions/. *Harvard Crimson*. (Last Accessed: January 25, 2018).

National Center for Education Statistics. 2016. "Digest of Education Statistics, 2016." Available at: https://nces.ed.gov/programs/digest/d16/tables/dt16_306.10.asp.

NCAA. N.d. "Title IX Frequently Asked Questions." www.ncaa.org/about/resources/inclusion/title-ix-frequently-asked-questions#how. NCAA.org. (Last Accessed: August 26, 2017).

Nederhof, Anton J. 1985. "Methods of Coping with Social Desirability Bias: A Review." *European Journal of Social Psychology* 15(3): 263–280.

Neumark, David. 2016. "Experimental Research on Labor Market Discrimination." NBER Working Paper No. 22022, available at: www.nber.org/papers/w22022.

New York Times. 1987. "Fighting All-Male Clubs at Harvard." December 27. https://nyti.ms/2mg36ld. *New York Times*. (Last Accessed: January 25, 2018).

New York Times. 2017. "Some Colleges Have More Students from the Top 1 Percent Than the Bottom 60. Find Yours." January 18. https://nyti.ms/2jRhxJH. *New York Times*. (Last Accessed: January 28, 2018).

News and Observer. 2015. "UNC-Chapel Hill Needs a Balanced Response to Student Demands." November 24. www.newsobserver.com/opinion/editorials/article46328155.html. *News and Observer*. (Last Accessed: August 29, 2017).

Norman, Jim. 2019. "Americans' Support for Affirmative Action Programs Rises." February 27. https://news.gallup.com/poll/247046/americans-support-affirmative-action-programs-rises.aspx. Gallup. (Last Accessed: March 6, 2019).

Norton, Michael I., John M. Darley, and Joseph A. Vandello. 2004. "Casuistry and Social Category Bias." *Journal of Personality and Social Psychology* 87(6): 817–831.

Norton, Michael I., Samuel R. Sommers, Joseph A. Vandello, and John M. Darley. 2006. "Mixed Motives and Racial Bias: The Impact of Legitimate and Illegitimate Criteria on Decision Making." *Psychology, Public Policy, and Law* 12(1): 36–55.

NPR. 2015. "Navy Secretary Believes Combat Positions Should Be Open to Qualified Women." September 11. https://n.pr/1Qsp5MZ. NPR. (Last Accessed: April 29, 2018).

Nunley, John M., Adam Pugh, Nicholas Romero, and Richard Alan Seals. 2014. "An Examination of Racial Discrimination in the Labor Market for Recent College Graduates: Estimates from the Field." *Berkeley Electronic Journal of Economic Analysis and Policy* 5(3): 1093–1125.

Office of Institutional Analytics, UNM. 2017. "The University of New Mexico Spring 2017 Official Enrollment Report." Report available at: http://oia.unm.edu/facts-and-figures/oer-spr-2017.pdf.

Office of the Secretary of Defense. 1993. "Summary Report of the Military Working Group." US Department of Defense.

Oh, Euna, Chun-Chung Choi, Helen A. Neville, Carolyn J. Anderson, and Joycelyn Landrum-Brown. 2010. "Beliefs about Affirmative Action: A Test of the Group Self-Interest and Racism Beliefs Models." *Journal of Diversity in Higher Education* 3(3): 163–176.

Oh, Hannah. 2015. "CMC Students Feel Marginalized, Demand Resources and Resignations." November 12. http://claremontindependent.com/cmc-students-feel-marginalized-demand-resources-and-resignations/. *Claremont Independent*. (Last Accessed: September 1, 2017).

Oishi, Nana. 2017. "Workforce Diversity in Higher Education: The Experiences of Asian Academics in Higher Educaton." Report prepared for the Asia Institute at the University of Melbourne, available at: https://arts.unimelb.edu.au/__data/assets/pdf_file/0012/2549496/AA-Report_Final-Copy_Web_5Nov.pdf.

Oppenheimer, Daniel. 2015. "Why Student Athletes Continue to Fail." April 20. http://time.com/3827196/why-student-athletes-fail/. *Time*. (Last Accessed: September 19, 2017).

Ovink, Sarah, Demetra Kalogrides, Megan Nanney, and Patrick Delaney. 2018. "College Match and Undermatch: Assessing Student Preferences, College Proximity, and Inequality in Post-College Outcomes." *Research in Higher Education* 59(5): 553–590.

Page, Scott E. 2007. *The Difference: How the Power of Diversity Creates Better Groups, Firms, Schools, and Societies*. Princeton, NJ: Princeton University Press.

Page, Scott E. 2017. *The Diversity Bonus: How Great Teams Pay Off in the Knowledge Economy*. Princeton, NJ: Princeton University Press.

Pager, Devah, and Lincoln Quillian. 2005. "Walking the Talk? What Employers Say Versus What They Do." *American Sociological Review* 70: 355–380.

Pappano, Laura. 2017. "More Diversity Means More Demands." August 4. https://nyti.ms/2huqyfo. *New York Times*. (Last Accessed: August 29, 2017).

Park, J. J., N. Denson, and N. A. Bowman. 2013. "Does Socioeconomic Diversity Make a Difference? Examining the Effects of Racial and Socioeconomic Diversity on the Campus Climate for Diversity." *American Educational Research Journal* 50(3): 466–496.

Park, Julie J. 2009. "Taking Race into Account: Charting Student Attitudes towards Affirmative Action." *Research in Higher Education* 50(7): 670–690.

Park, Julie J. 2018. *Race on Campus: Debunking Myths with Data*. Cambridge, MA: Harvard Education Press.

Park, Julie J., and Nida Denson. 2009. "Attitudes and Advocacy: Understanding Faculty Views on Racial/Ethnic Diversity." *Journal of Higher Education* 80(4): 415–438.

Paxson, Christina H. 2016. "Pathways to Diversity and Inclusion: An Action Plan for Brown University." Brown University. Report available at: https://brown.edu/web/documents/diversity/actionplan/diap-full.pdf.

Pearce, Matt. 2015. "Hunger Striker Gives Credit to Fellow Activists Fighting Racism at University of Missouri." November 10. www.latimes.com/nation/la-na-missouri-hunger-striker-20151110-story.html. *Los Angeles Times*. (Last Accessed: September 1, 2017).

Peralta, Eyder. 2016. "Following Protests, Ithaca College President Announces Retirement." January 14. https://n.pr/1OkUpNv. NPR. (Last Accessed: September 1, 2017).

Pérez-Peña, Richard. 2014. "After Protests, I.M.F. Chief Withdraws as Smith College's Commencement Speaker." May 12. https://nyti.ms/1oJOfsH. *New York Times*. (Last Accessed: June 25, 2018).

Petroni, Sarah. 2018. "Petroni: Support for the Trips Directorate." February 6. *Dartmouth*. (Last Accessed: December 30, 2018).

Pettit, Emma. 2019. "'My Merit and My Blackness Are Fused to Each Other'." January 11. www.chronicle.com/article/My-MeritMy-Blackness/245462. *Chronicle of Higher Education*. (Last Accessed: January 23, 2019).

Pew Research Center. 2016. "On Views of Race and Inequality, Blacks and Whites Are Worlds Apart." June 27. www.pewsocialtrends.org/2016/06/27/on-views-of-race-and-inequality-blacks-and-whites-are-worlds-apart/. Pew Research Center. (Last Accessed: January 17, 2018).

Piper, Julia. 2018. "When a Chief Diversity Officer Is Not Enough." September 16. www.chronicle.com/article/When-a-Chief-Diversity-Officer/244528. *Chronicle of Higher Education*. (Last Accessed: January 17, 2019).

Plaster, Madison. 2015. "Second 'Racism Lives Here' Event Calls for Administration to Act on Social Injustices." October 1. www.themaneater.com/stories/2015/10/1/second-racism-lives-here-event-calls-administratio/. *Maneater*. (Last Accessed: September 1, 2017).

Polak, Ben, and Rick Bribiescas. 2018. "Update on $50 Million Faculty Excellence and Diversity Initiative." October 3. https://news.yale.edu/2018/10/03/update-50-million-faculty-excellence-and-diversity-initiative. Yale University. (Last Accessed: January 2, 2019).

Polga-Hecimovich, John, John M. Carey, and Yusaku Horiuchi. 2019. "Student Attitudes toward Campus Diversity at the United States Naval Academy: Evidence from Conjoint Survey Experiments." Forthcoming at Armed Forces and Society. Available at: https://journals.sagepub.com/doi/pdf/10.1177/0095327X18824665.

Price, Joshua. 2010. "The Effect of Instructor Race and Gender on Student Persistence in STEM Fields." *Economics of Education Review* 29: 901–910.

Princeton University Office of Communications. 2016. "Trustees Call for Expanded Commitment to Diversity and Inclusion." April 4. www.princeton.edu/news/2016/04/04/trustees-call-expanded-commitment-diversity-and-inclusion. Princeton University Office of Communications. (Last Accessed: September 1, 2017).

Putnam, Robert D. 2015. *Our Kids: The American Dream in Crisis*. New York, NY: Simon & Schuster.

Quintana, Chris. 2018a. "What Do 'White Guys' Think about Race? This Professor Is Trying to Find Out." June 3. www.chronicle.com/article/What-Do-White-Guys-Think/243555. *Chronicle of Higher Education*. (Last Accessed: June 29, 2018).

Quintana, Chris. 2018b. "What's on the Mind of the Private-College President? 3 Insights from a New Report." September 20. www.chronicle.com/article/What-s-on-the-Mind-of-the/244578. *Chronicle of Higher Education*. (Last Accessed: January 17, 2019).

Rand, Thomas M., and Kenneth N. Wexley. 1975. "Demonstration of the Effect, 'Similar to Me,' in Simulated Employment Interviews." *Psychological Reports* 36(2): 535–544.

Rankin, Susan R., and Robert Dean Reason. 2005. "Differing Perceptions: How Students of Color and White Students Perceive Campus Climate for Underrepresented Groups." *Journal of College Student Development* 46(1): 43–61.

Rao, Gautam. 2019. "Familiarity Does Not Breed Contempt: Diversity, Discrimination and Generosity in Delhi Schools." *American Economic Review* 109(3): 774–809.

Rask, Kevin N., and Elizabeth M. Bailey. 2002. "Are Faculty Role Models? Evidence from Major Choice in an Undergraduate Institution." *Journal of Economic Education* 33(2): 99–124.

Reardon, Sean F., Rachel Baker, and Daniel Klasik. 2012. "Race, Income, and Enrollment Patterns in Highly Selective Colleges, 1982–2004." Report prepared for the Stanford University Center for Education Policy Analysis, available at: http://inequality.stanford.edu/sites/default/files/reardon-baker-klasik_race_income_select_college.pdf.

Reardon, Sean F., Rachel Baker, Matt Kasman, Daniel Klasik, and Joseph B. Townsend. 2018. "What Levels of Racial Diversity Can Be Achieved with Socioeconomic-Based Affirmative Action? Evidence from a Simulation Model." *Journal of Policy Analysis and Management* 37(3): 630–657.

Regents of the University of California v. Bakke. 1978. 438 U.S. 265.

Reid, Landon D. 2010. "The Role of Perceived Race and Gender in the Evaluation of College Teaching on RateMyProfessors.com." *Journal of Diversity in Higher Education* 3(3): 137–152.

Richman, Wendy L., Sara Kiesler, Suzanne Weisband, and Fritz Drasgow. 1999. "A Meta-Analytic Study of Social Desirability Distortion in Computer-Administered Questionnaires, Traditional Questionnaires, and Interviews." *Journal of Applied Psychology* 84(5): 754–775.

Roderick, Melissa, Vanessa Coca, and Jenny Nagaoka. 2011. "Potholes on the Road to College." *Sociology of Education* 84(3): 178–211.

Rosen, Andy. 2017. "After Sending Lord Jeff Packing, Amherst College Picks Mammoth as Mascot." April 3. www.bostonglobe.com/metro/2017/04/03/after-sending-lord-jeff-packing-amherst-college-picks-mammoth-mascot/2pT6Etr7n1jrjCwFRANK8M/story.html. *Boston Globe*. (Last Accessed: August 29, 2017).

Rosenbaum, Paul R. 1984. "The Consequences of Adjustment for a Concomitant Variable That Has Been Affected by the Treatment." *Journal of the Royal Statistical Society. Series A (General)* 147(5): 656.

Rothstein, Donna S. 1995. "Do Female Faculty Influence Female Students' Educational and Labor Market Attainments?" *ILR Review* 48(3): 515–530.

Rothstein, Jesse, and Albert H. Yoon. 2008. "Affirmative Action in Law School Admissions: What Do Racial Preferences Do?" NBER Working Paper 14276, available at: www.nber.org/papers/w14276.pdf.

Rubin, Donald B. 1974. "Estimating Causal Effects of Treatments in Randomized and Nonrandomized Studies." *Journal of Educational Psychology* 66(5): 688–701.

Rubin, Donald B. 2005. "Causal Inference Using Potential Outcomes." *Journal of the American Statistical Association* 100(469): 322–331.

Salovey, Peter. 2015. "Statement from President Salovey: Toward a Better Yale." November 17. https://news.yale.edu/2015/11/17/statement-president-salovey-toward-better-yale. YaleNews. (Last Accessed: September 1, 2017).

Samson, Frank L. 2009. *Race and the Limits of American Meritocracy*. Doctoral Dissertation, Stanford University.

San Diego Union Tribune. 2010. "New UCSD Racial Incident Sparks Rage, Confrontation." February 20. www.sandiegouniontribune.com/sdut-new-ucsd-racial-incident-sparks-rage-confrontation-2010feb20-htmlstory.html. *San Die-go Union Tribune*. (Last Accessed: August 29, 2017).

Sander, Richard, and Stuart Taylor. 2012. *Mismatch: How Affirmative Action Hurts Students It's Intended to Help, and Why Universities Won't Admit It*. New York, NY: Basic Books.

Sander, Richard H. 2004. "A Systemic Analysis of Affirmative Action in American Law Schools." *Stanford Law Review* 57(11): 367–483.

Sanger, David E. 1984. "Harvard Is Battling All-Male Clubs." November 24. https://nyti.ms/2mg0ZgU. *New York Times*. (Last Accessed: January 25, 2018).

Santelices, Maria Veronica, and Mark Wilson. 2015. "The Revised SAT Score and Its Potential Benefits for the Admission of Minority Students to Higher Education." *Education Policy Analysis Archives* 23: 113.

Saul, Stephanie. 2016. "Public Colleges Chase Out-of-State Students, and Tuition." July 7. https://nyti.ms/29CAv30. *New York Times*. (Last Accessed: September 19, 2017).

Sax, Linda J., and Marisol Arredondo. 1999. "Student Attitudes toward Affirmative Action in College Admissions." *Research in Higher Education* 40(4): 439–459.

Schaefer, Agnes, Radha Iyengar, Srikanth Kadiyala, Jennifer Kavanagh, Charles Engel, Kayla Williams, and Amii Kress. 2016. *Assessing the Implications of Allowing Transgender Personnel to Serve Openly*. Washington, DC: RAND Corporation.

Sears, Greg J., and Patricia M. Rowe. 2003. "A Personality-Based Similar-to-Me Effect in the Employment Interview: Conscientiousness, Affect- Versus Competence-Mediated Interpretations, and the Role of Job Relevance." *Canadian Journal of Behavioural Science* 35(1): 13–24.

Shenk, Joshua. 1991. "Harvard Admissions off the Hook (But What about Those Legacies?)." June 6. www.thecrimson.com/article/1991/6/6/harvard-admissions-off-the-hook-but/. *Harvard Crimson*. (Last Accessed: August 29, 2017).

Shields, Jon A., and Joshua M. Dunn Sr. 2016. *Passing on the Right: Conservative Professors in the Progressive University*. New York, NY: Oxford University Press.

Sidanius, James, Shana Levin, Colette van Laar, and David O. Sears. 2008. *The Diversity Challenge: Social Identity and Intergroup Relations on the College Campus*. New York, NY: Russell Sage Foundation.

Sinclair, G. Dean. 2009. "Homosexuality and the Military: A Review of the Literature." *Journal of Homosexuality* 56(6): 701–718.

Skrentny, John D. 2002. *The Minority Rights Revolution*. Cambridge, MA: Belknap Press of Harvard University Press.

Smith, Christie, and Stephanie Turner. 2015. "The Radical Transformation of Diversity and Inclusion: The Millennial Influence." Deloitte University Leadership Center for Inclusion. Report available at: http://deloi.tt/2c9OfnX.

Smith, William A. 1998. "Gender and Racial/Ethnic Differences in the Affirmative Action Attitudes of U.S. College Students." *Journal of Negro Education* 67(2): 127.

Sniderman, Paul M., and Thomas Leonard Piazza. 1993. *The Scar of Race.* Cambridge, MA: Belknap Press of Harvard University Press.

Snyder, Thomas D. 1993. "120 Years of American Education: A Statistical Portrait Center for Education Statistics." National Center for Education Statistics. Report available at: https://nces.ed.gov/pubs93/93442.pdf.

Snyder, Thomas D., Cristobal de Brey, and Sally A. Dillow. 2016. "Digest of Education Statistics 2015." National Center for Education Statistics. Report available at: https://nces.ed.gov/programs/digest/d15/tables/dt15_315.20.asp?current=yes.

Sohn, So Young, and Yong Han Ju. 2010. "Conjoint Analysis for Recruiting High Quality Students for College Education." *Expert Systems with Applications* 37(5): 3777–3783.

Southern Coalition for Social Justice. 2017. "Our Actions." www.southern coalition.org/program-areas/. Southern Coalition for Social Justice. (Last Accessed: January 14, 2018).

Spanierman, Lisa B., Helen A. Neville, Hsin-Ya Liao, Joseph H. Hammer, and Ying-Fen Wang. 2008. "Participation in Formal and Informal Campus Diversity Experiences: Effects on Students' Racial Democratic Beliefs." *Journal of Diversity in Higher Education* 1(2): 108–125.

Splawa-Neyman, Jerzy. 1990. "On the Application of Probability Theory to Agricultural Experiments. Essay on Principles. Section 9 (translated in 1990)." *Statistical Science* 5(4): 465–480.

Stacey, Kevin. 2016. "Brown Releases Final Action Plan to Create a Diverse and Inclusive Campus." February 1. https://news.brown.edu/articles/2016/02/diap. *News from Brown.* (Last Accessed: September 1, 2017).

Stark, Philip, Kellie Ottoboni, and Anne Boring. 2016. "Student Evaluations of Teaching (Mostly) Do Not Measure Teaching Effectiveness." Available at ScienceOpen Research: www.scienceopen.com/document?id=25ff22be-8a1b-4c97-9d88-084c8d98187a.

Steeh, Charlotte, and Maria Krysan. 1996. "Trends: Affirmative Action and the Public, 1970–1995." *Public Opinion Quarterly* 60(1): 128–158.

Stevens, Sean. 2017. "The Campus Expression Survey: Summary of New Data." December 20. https://heterodoxacademy.org/the-campus-expression-survey-summary-of-new-data/. Heterodox Academy. (Last Accessed: June 25, 2018).

Stewart, Abigail, and Virginia Valian. 2018. *An Inclusive Academy: Achieving Diversity and Excellence.* Cambridge, MA: Massachusetts Institute of Technology Press.

Stinebrickner, Todd, and Ralph Stinebrickner. 2011. "Math or Science? Using Longitudinal Expectations Data to Examine the Process of Choosing a College Major." NBER Working Paper No. 16869, available at: http://economics .uwo.ca/people/stinebrickner_docs/mathorscience.pdf.

Stolberg, Sheryl Gay. 2016. "University of Cincinnati to Pay $4.85 Million to Family of Man Killed by Officer." January 18. https://nyti.ms/1V2abi3. *New York Times.* (Last Accessed: September 1, 2017).

Stone, Geoffrey R., Marianne Bertrand, Angela Olinto, Mark Siegler, David A. Strauss, Kenneth W. Warren, and Amanda Woodward. 2015. "Report of the Committee on Freedom of Expression." University of Chicago Committee

on Freedom of Expression. Report available at: https://provost.uchicago
.edu/sites/default/files/documents/reports/FOECommitteeReport.pdf.

Strezhnev, Anton, Elissa Berwick, Jens Hainmueller, Daniel Hopkins, and Teppei
Yamamoto. 2017. "cjoint: AMCE Estimator for Conjoint Experiments."
Version 2.0.6, https://cran.r-project.org/web/packages/cjoint/index.html.

Students for Fair Admissions. 2014. "Students for Fair Admissions, Inc., vs. President and Fellows of Harvard College (Harvard Corporation); and the Hon-
orable and Reverend the Board of Directors." Available at: http://studentsfor
fairadmissions.org/wp-content/uploads/2014/11/SFFA-v.-Harvard-Complaint
.pdf.

Students for Fair Admissions. 2017. "Students for Fair Admissions, Inc., v. University of Texas at Austin." June 27. https://studentsforfairadmissions.org/.
Travis County District Court. (Last Accessed: September 14, 2017).

Sundorph, Emilie, Danail Vasilev, and Louis Coiffait. 2017. "Joining the
Elite: How Top Universities Can Enhance Social Mobility." Reform, available at: www.reform.uk/wp-content/uploads/2017/09/Joining-The-Elite-how-
top-universities-can-enhance-social-mobility.pdf.

Swinford, Steven. 2017. "White Working Class Children Victims of Racial
'Injustices', Theresa May-Backed Review Finds." October 3. www.telegraph
.co.uk/news/2017/10/03/white-working-class-children-victims-racial-injustices-
theresa/. *Telegraph*. (Last Accessed: June 3, 2018).

Synnott, Maria Graham. 1974. "A Social History of Admissions Policies at
Harvard, Yale, and Princeton, 1900–1930." PhD Dissertation, University of
Massachusetts.

Tabs, E. D. 2002. "The Gender and Racial/Ethnic Composition of Postsecondary
Instructional Faculty and Staff, 1992–98." National Center for Education
Statistics. Report available at: https://nces.ed.gov/pubs2002/2002160.pdf.

Tadlock, Barry L., Andrew R. Flores, Donald P. Haider-Markel, Daniel C.
Lewis, Patrick R. Miller, and Jami K. Taylor. 2017. "Testing Contact Theory and Attitudes on Transgender Rights." *Public Opinion Quarterly* 81(4):
956–972.

Tang, Briana. 2015. "Students Stage a Protest in Solidarity with Missouri
and Yale, Drawing Both Support and Controversy." November 12. www
.thedartmouth.com/article/2015/11/students-stage-a-protest-in-solidarity-with-
missouri-and-yale-drawing-both-support-and-controversy. *Dartmouth*. (Last
Accessed: June 28, 2018).

Teele, Dawn Langan, Joshua Kalla, and Frances Rosenbluth. 2018. "The Ties
That Double Bind: Social Roles and Women's Underrepresentation in Politics."
American Political Science Review 112(3): 525–541.

Terenzini, Patrick T., Ernest T. Pascarella, Leonard Springer, Amaury Nora, and
Betsy Palmer. 1996. "Attitudes toward Campus Diversity: Participation in a
Racial or Cultural Awareness Workshop." *The Review of Higher Education*
20(1): 53–68.

Tesler, Michael, and David O. Sears. 2010. *Obama's Race: The 2008 Election
and the Dream of a Post-Racial America*. Chicago, IL: University of Chicago
Press.

Thomas, Patricia J., and Marie D. Thomas. 1996. "Integration of Women in the Military: Parallels to the Progress of Homosexuals?" In *Out of Force: Sexual Orientation and the Military*, eds. Gregory M. Herek, Jared B. Jobe, and Ralph M. Carney. Chicago, IL: University of Chicago Press, 65–85.

Tiboris, Michael. 2014. "What's Wrong with Undermatching?" *Journal of Philosophy of Education* 48(4): 646–664.

Torche, Florencia. 2015. "Analyses of Intergenerational Mobility." *Annals of the American Academy of Political and Social Science* 657(1): 37–62.

Tourangeau, Roger, and Ting Yan. 2007. "Sensitive Questions in Surveys." *Psychological Bulletin* 133(5): 859–883.

Trachtenberg, Ben. 2018. "The 2015 University of Missouri Protests and Their Lessons for Higher Education Policy and Administration." *Kentucky Law Journal* 107(1): 61–121.

Trower, Cathy A., and Richard P. Chait. 2002. "Faculty Diversity." March-April. https://harvardmagazine.com/2002/03/faculty-diversity.html. *Harvard Magazine*. (Last Accessed: March 13, 2019).

Tuch, Steven A., and Ronald Weitzer. 1997. "Trends: Racial Differences in Attitudes toward the Police." *Public Opinion Quarterly* 61(4): 642–663.

Tugend, Alina. 2018. "How Serious Are You about Diversity Hiring?" June 17. www.chronicle.com/article/How-Serious-Are-You-About/243684. *Chronicle of Higher Education*. (Last Accessed: January 17, 2019).

Turner, Camilla. 2017. "'Don't Blame Cambridge University for Lack of Black Students,' Says Students' Society." May 3. www.telegraph.co.uk/news/2017/05/03/dont-blame-cambridge-lack-black-students-saysleading-students/. *Telegraph*. (Last Accessed: May 10, 2018).

Turner, Caroline Sotello Viernes, Juan Carlos González, and J. Luke Wood. 2008. "Faculty of Color in Academe: What 20 Years of Literature Tells Us." *Journal of Diversity in Higher Education* 1(3): 139–168.

Tuvel, Rebecca. 2017. "In Defense of Transracialism." *Hypatia* 32(2): 263–278.

Umbach, Paul D., and George D. Kuh. 2006. "Student Experiences with Diversity at Liberal Arts Colleges: Another Claim for Distinctiveness." *Journal of Higher Education* 77(1): 169–192.

United States Census Bureau. 2010. "Overview of Race and Hispanic Origin: 2010." C2010BR-02. Report available at: www.census.gov/prod/cen2010/briefs/c2010br-02.pdf.

United States Census Bureau. 2011. "The White Population: 2010." C2010BR-05. Report available at: www.census.gov/prod/cen2010/briefs/c2010br-05.pdf.

United States Code. 1964. "Civil Rights Act of 1964 § 7, 42 U.S.C. § 2000e et seq (1964)." Available at: www.gpo.gov/fdsys/pkg/USCODE-2008-title42/html/USCODE-2008-title42-chap21-subchapV.htm.

Unz, Ron. 2012. "The Myth of American Meritocracy." November 28. www.unz.com/runz/the-myth-of-american-meritocracy/. *American Conservative*. (Last Accessed: August 29, 2017).

US Marine Corps. 2015. "Marine Corps Force Integration Plan: Executive Summary." Memorandum. Available at: www.documentcloud.org/documents/2394531-marine-corps-force-integration-plan-summary.html.

Valente, Rubia R., and Brian J. L. Berry. 2017. "Performance of Students Admitted through Affirmative Action in Brazil." *Latin American Research Review* 52(1): 18–34.

Valls, Andrew. 1999. "The Libertarian Case for Affirmative Action." *Social Theory and Practice* 25(2): 299–323.

Vance, J. D. 2016. *Hillbilly Elegy: A Memoir of a Family and Culture in Crisis.* New York, NY: Harper.

Vanden Brook, Tom. 2017. "Accept, Treat Transgender Troops, Adm. Mike Mullen Tells Congress." July 25. *USA Today.* https://usat.ly/2vXLo8R. (Last Accessed: January 2, 2019).

Vedder, Richard. 2015. "Athletics: The Good, the Bad and the Ugly." August 18. *Forbes.* www.forbes.com/sites/ccap/2015/08/18/athletics-the-good-the-bad-and-the-ugly/2/#13c74f1860e7. (Last Accessed: September 19, 2017).

Victor, John, Monica Wang, and Victor Wang. 2015. "More Than 1,000 Gather in Solidarity." November 10. http://yaledailynews.com/blog/2015/11/10/more-than-1000-gather-in-solidarity/. *Yale Daily News.* (Last Accessed: September 1, 2017).

Wall Street Journal. 2015. "Yale's Little Robespierres: Students Berate Faculty Who Try to Defend Free Speech." November 9. www.wsj.com/articles/yales-little-robespierres-1447115476. *Wall Street Journal.* (Last Accessed: April 28, 2017).

Wang, Ming-Hung, Kenneth R. Thomas, Chan Fong, and Gladys Cheing. 2003. "A Conjoint Analysis of Factors Influencing American and Taiwanese College Students' Preferences for People with Disabilities." *Rehabilitation Psychology* 48(3): 195–201.

Warikoo, Natasha Kumar. 2016. *The Diversity Bargain: And Other Dilemmas of Race, Admissions, and Meritocracy at Elite Universities.* Chicago, IL: University of Chicago Press.

Watanabe, Teresa, and Larry Gordon. 2015. "Claremont McKenna College Students Embrace a Lesson in Activism." November 13. www.latimes.com/local/lanow/la-me-ln-students-claremont-mckenna-react-racial-tensions-20151113-story.html. *Los Angeles Times.* (Last Accessed: September 1, 2017).

Watkins, Matthew. 2015. "If UT Loses Supreme Court Case, It Could Face Another Top 10 Percent 'Crisis'." December 11. www.texastribune.org/2015/12/11/if-ut-loses-supreme-court-case-it-could-face-anoth/. *Texas Tribune.* (Last Accessed: August 29, 2017).

Waugh, Scott L. 2018. "New EDI Statement Requirement for Regular Rank Faculty Searches." Available at: https://equity.ucla.edu/news-and-events/new-edi-statement-requirement-for-regular-rank-faculty-searches/.

Weldon, S. Laurel. 2008. "Intersectionality." In *Politics, Gender, and Concepts: Theory and Methodology,* eds. Gary Goertz, and Amy G. Mazur. Cambridge, MA: Cambridge University Press, 193–218.

Weldon, S. Laurel. 2011. *When Protest Makes Policy: How Social Movements Represent Disadvantaged Groups.* Ann Arbor, MI: University of Michigan Press.

West, Martha S., and John W. Curtis. 2006. "Organizing around Gender Equity." July 20. www.aaup.org/NR/rdonlyres/63396944-44BE-4ABA-9815-

5792D93856F1/0/AAUPGenderEquityIndicators2006.pdf. American Association of University Professors. (Last Accessed: July 13, 2018).

Whitford, Emma. 2018*a*. "Seton Hall Students Occupied Administration Building in Quest for Institutional Change." November 6. www.insidehighered.com/news/2018/11/06/seton-hall-students-occupied-administration-building-quest-institutional-change. *Inside Higher Ed.* (Last Accessed: January 17, 2019).

Whitford, Emma. 2018*b*. "Several Colleges Are Responding to Requests to Remove Gender from Scholarship Eligibility Requirements." November 5. www.insidehighered.com/news/2018/11/05/several-colleges-are-responding-requests-remove-gender-scholarship-eligibility. *Inside Higher Ed.* (Last Accessed: January 17, 2019).

Whitford, Emma. 2018*c*. "UCLA's Mobile App Aims to Replace Campus Climate Surveys." June 22. www.insidehighered.com/news/2018/06/22/uclas-mobile-app-aims-replace-campus-climate-surveys. *Inside Higher Ed.* (Last Accessed: January 17, 2019).

Whitla, Dean K., Gary Orfield, William Silen, Carole Teperow, Carolyn Howard, and Joan Reede. 2003. "Educational Benefits of Diversity in Medical School: A Survey of Students." *Academic Medicine* 78(5): 460–6.

Wigmore, Tim. 2016. "The Lost Boys: How the White Working Class Got Left Behind." October 20. www.newstatesman.com/politics/education/2016/09/lost-boys-how-white-working-class-got-left-behind. New Statesman. (Last Accessed: June 3, 2018).

Williams, Wendy M., and Stephen J. Ceci. 2015. "National Hiring Experiments Reveal 2:1 Faculty Preference for Women on STEM Tenure Track." *Proceedings of the National Academy of Sciences of the United States of America* 112(17): 5360–5.

Wolfinger, Nicholas H., Mary Ann Mason, and Marc Goulden. 2009. "Stay in the Game: Gender, Family Formation and Alternative Trajectories in the Academic Life Course." *Social Forces* 87(3): 1591–1621.

Wong, Alia, and Adrienne Green. 2016. "Campus Politics: A Cheat Sheet." April 4. www.theatlantic.com/education/archive/2016/04/campus-protest-roundup/417570/. *Atlantic.* (Last Accessed: August 29, 2017).

Worthington, Roger L., Rachel L. Navarro, Michael Loewy, and Jeni Hart. 2008. "Color-Blind Racial Attitudes, Social Dominance Orientation, Racial-Ethnic Group Membership and College Students' Perceptions of Campus Climate." *Journal of Diversity in Higher Education* 1(1): 8–19.

Wu, Alice. 2017. "Gender Stereotyping in Academia: Evidence from Economic Job Market Rumors Forum." Working paper, available at: http://calwomenofecon.weebly.com/uploads/9/6/1/0/96100906/wu_ejmr_paper.pdf.

Yale University. 2016. "Report on Faculty Diversity and Inclusivity in the Faculty of Arts and Sciences." May 19. http://fassenate.yale.edu/reports-and-surveys. Yale University. (Last Accessed: July 13, 2018).

Yale University Office of the President. 2015. "An Excellent Faculty Is a Diverse Faculty." November 3. http://president.yale.edu/excellent-faculty-diverse-faculty. Yale University. (Last Accessed: July 13, 2018).

Young, Iris Marion, and Danielle S. Allen. 2011. *Justice and the Politics of Difference*. Princeton, NJ: Princeton University Press.

Zhang, Jingwen. 2015. "Students Protest Racial Discrimination at Sit-In." November 13. amherststudent.amherst.edu/?q=article/2015/11/13/students-protest-racial-discrimination-sit *Amherst Student*. (Last Accessed: September 1, 2017).

Zwick, Rebecca. 2013. "Disentangling the Role of High School Grades, SAT Scores, and SES (Research Report ETS RR-113-09)." Educational Testing Service. Report available at: www.ets.org/Media/Research/pdf/RR-13-09.pdf.

Index